BECOMING MIRACLE WORKERS

SOCIAL PROBLEMS AND SOCIAL ISSUES

An Aldine de Gruyter Series of Texts and Monographs

SERIES EDITOR

Joel Best

Southern Illinois University at Carbondale

BECOMING MIRACLE WORKERS

Language and Meaning in Brief Therapy

GALE MILLER

ALDINE DE GRUYTER

New York

ABOUT THE AUTHOR

Gale Miller is Professor of Sociology in the Department of Social and Cultural Sciences at Marquette University. He has published over twenty books and numerous journal articles. Much of his research has focused on social problems theory and how social policies are implemented within contemporary human service institutions.

Dr. Miller's most recent interests include cross-cultural research on brief therapy and related constructivist approaches to human troubles and social problems.

ALDINE DE GRUYTER
A division of Walter de Gruyter, Inc.
200 Saw Mill River Road
Hawthorne, New York 10532

This publication is printed on acid free paper ∞

Library of Congress Cataloging-in-Publication Data
Miller, Gale.
    Becoming miracle workers : language and meaning in brief therapy /
Gale Miller.
        p.   cm. — (Social problems and social issues)
    Includes bibliographical references and index.
    ISBN 0-202-30570-8 (cloth : alk. paper). — ISBN 0-202-30571-6
(pbk. : alk. paper)
        1. Brief psychotherapy.   2. Psychotherapy patients—Language.
3. Psychotherapists—Language.   I. Title.   II. Series.
RC480.55.M48   1997
616.89'14—dc21   97-3300
                                                                              CIP

Manufactured in the United States of America

10 9 8 7 6 5 4 3 2 1

To My Constructivist Friends in
Sociology and Brief Therapy

CONTENTS

PART III   IMPLICATIONS OF BRIEF THERAPY

PREFACE

One of the reasons why I remember the purchase of my first new car is because of an event that occurred during the final negotiations. I was a graduate student in sociology at the time. When the manager of the automobile agency heard this bit of information, he began to tell me about a noted psychologist at the local university who had recently purchased a similar car from the same agency. His logic, I surmise, was that I too could be a local luminary if I purchased the car in question. The salesman, who had up to that point successfully persuaded me that this was the best car in the whole world for me, immediately interceded in the interaction. He warned the agency manager, saying something like, "No, no, don't say that, it won't work with him. Sociologists and psychologists can't stand each other." I smiled, and nodded in agreement. The agency manager said, "Oh," and immediately shifted to a new sales strategy.

While the salesman's advice and my assent are accurate in many cases, it does not apply to this project. This book is an example of how a sociologist can get along with psychologists, social workers, psychiatrists, and other human service professionals with whom we are sometimes said to compete. Our "getting along" is possible because each of us—in our own time and ways—have developed complementary approaches to language, meaning, and human troubles. Brief therapists have developed an approach to solving personal troubles that draws from, and applies, ideas that have also shaped constructivist sociology, a perspective that has greatly influenced my work, at least, since leaving graduate school. Brief therapists and constructivist sociologists are different, but able to learn from one another.

Indeed, the significant differences discussed in this book do not involve sociologists and brief therapists. The differences are between brief therapists, on the one hand, and practitioners of psychotherapy and family therapy, on the other hand. While many of these differences are discussed at length later in the book, one indicator of them is brief therapists' description of the people who seek their services as *clients*. This terminology may be contrasted with the language of *patients* used by many other therapists. At the very least, this difference suggests how brief therapy departs from therapy approaches that are based on the medical model. It is also suggestive of other distinctive aspects of brief therapists' orientations to therapist-client relationships, and to the solving of clients' troubles. Brief therapists are radicals within the therapy profession. They challenge other therapists to rethink their conventional assumptions and practices, and they have developed alternative techniques and strategies for doing unconventional therapy.

This book might be understood as a report on the lessons that I have learned from brief therapists. I hope that it is useful to therapists engaged in diverse practices, particularly to those who are involved in—or simply curious about—brief therapy. I have also written the book with the concerns of academically oriented audiences in mind. I am particularly mindful of the concerns of sociologists, but I believe the book also speaks to issues of interest to psychologists, social workers, social psychologists, and family studies scholars. This study is an example of how sociology may be used to analyze clinical practices and settings.

More precisely, it is a contribution to the sociology of the clinic, a field that is concerned with the organization and implications of clinical practices for clinicians, their clients and patients, and society. The sociology of the clinic is not designed to compete with clinicians by offering alternative services to clients, but to "work with" clinicians by closely studying how clinical settings are organized and how clinical work is done. While sociologists of the clinic may sometimes raise issues that trouble clinicians and others, their studies also display skills and knowledge that are often unrecognized or taken for granted by members of clinical settings.

This study, for example, emphasizes the interactional and interpretive skills of brief therapists and their clients. I treat the therapists and clients as artful conversationalists who use language to achieve diverse practical ends. Other recent studies in the sociology of the clinic that merit special notice are Gubrium's (1992) comparative study of two family therapy clinics, and Peräkylä's (1995) and Silverman's (1997) analyses of HIV counseling as conversations. While they are concerned with different therapy approaches than this study, these sociological analyses also highlight aspects of the artful processes through which clinical work is done, and clinical relationships are built.

One of the many choices that I have made in writing this book involves terminology. The choice turned on whether to describe my own approach and that of brief therapists as constructionist or constructivist. The former term is widely used in sociology, but others (particularly therapists, social workers, and psychologists) often use the term *constructivist*. To avoid confusion, I have chosen to use the language of constructivism. I mention this because some readers may assign great significance to my choice, but I see it as a practical solution to a practical problem. It is nothing more than that. Readers interested in the debates and nuances sometimes associated with these terms would do well to consult Franklin's (1995) and Franklin and Nurius's (1996) recent writings.

I must, of course, mention and thank the many brief therapists and clients who have allowed me to observe their activities. In order to keep their identities confidential, I will not mention their names. I have also been aided in this project by several people who have read and commented on the manuscript: Insoo Kim Berg, Steve de Shazer, Jim Holstein, Wally Gingerich, Diane Miller, Jeff Sachse, and Bob Emerson, who provided me with particularly helpful comments. Insoo, Steve, and Jim have graciously allowed me to "bend their ears" about this project from time to time. Diane Miller—being my wife—has contributed to this project in diverse ways, including adjusting to my evening visits to the clinic, and listening to my worries about where the project might go, and about whether it would ever get done. I must also mention Richard Koffler's (executive editor, Aldine de Gruyter) contribution to this project. I especially appreciate his willingness to take on a book that does not easily fit in the typical marketing categories of most contemporary publishers. The name for this book emerged from a telephone conversation with Courtney Marlaire, a colleague at Marquette University. Surely, this collaboration also makes her responsible for half of whatever errors you may find in this text.

CHAPTER 1

OPENING MOVES

I grew up on a farm in southern Iowa during the 1950s and 1960s. My childhood and teen years were quite unremarkable. I attended the local public schools where I proved to be a lazy and mediocre—but not always uninterested—student. While I participated in several school sports from grammar school through high school, I still successfully managed to avoid distinguishing myself at any of them. I occupied the last chair in the coronet section of the band for over two years. Eventually I noticed that even the beginners were outperforming me, and decided that musical achievement was not in my future. Not only was I not elected to an office in student government, my name was never raised as a possibility. And I used not a minute of my eighteen years on the farm to develop an appreciation for the beauty and joys of the bucolic life.

None of this is to say, however, that I was inept at, or uninterested in, everything. Indeed, I was highly skilled at getting in trouble with adults, particularly with my family, teachers, and those who defined themselves as protectors of the local morality. These and other adults in my life regularly complained about me and expressed their worries about how I might turn out, even though few of my offenses were serious. Only a minority of my adventures would have justified arrest or expulsion from school had I been caught. The words that might have been used to characterize me during this time are underachiever, disobedient, incorrigible, disruptive, know-it-all, undependable, and smart ass. These were the sorts of words that the superintendent of my high school used to describe me during a private meeting on my graduation night. He seemed happy to see me gone.

Now, from my perspective, all of this was much ado about very little. My troublemaking was not malicious, and might even be described as a side effect of my other—quite sensible—activities. My troubles usually emerged from having fun with my friends (several of whom were also adept at upsetting adults), misunderstandings with others, standing up for my rights, youthful curiosity and experimentation, and simply trying to deal with the

1

circumstances of life. Nor was I a full-time troublemaker. While I sometimes went through extended periods of being continuously in trouble, I also experienced stretches of trouble-free life. Most of the time, however, my troublemaking involved isolated and episodic events. I would make a teacher mad one week, upset a family member the next, irritate a church official, police officer, or merchant two weeks later, and so on.

I tell you this story because, when I think back on this period in my life, I am struck by what is absent from the story. Despite my chronic troublemaking, I was never referred to a psychologist, social worker, psychiatrist, or other therapist for counseling. I only remember this possibility being discussed a few times. Of course, who knows what was said in my absence? It seems that while I was a problem to the adults in my life, they treated me as *their* problem. They reacted by warning me, scolding me, threatening me, giving me "one last chance," and punishing me. They also conveyed to me the lessons that they had learned from their—more mature—life experiences, described my inevitable descent into serious criminal activity if I did not change my ways, praised me when I acted like a "good boy," and initiated projects intended to get me interested in positive activities. Their problem literally went away when I left home to start a new life on my own.

It is unlikely that I would be treated similarly today. The period since my childhood has seen the professionalization of counseling and the spread of therapy services throughout American and many other societies. Even small, relatively isolated schools—like the ones that I attended—provide counseling services today. Further, courts routinely refer offenders to therapists, and members of the clergy make similar referrals, if they do not offer their own counseling services to their congregations. Families often voluntarily enter therapy in order to better understand and deal with children and teenagers who act as I did. Or parents might call one of the many counselors who dispense advice via television and the radio.

But this does not exhaust the choices to be made in referring children and others to counseling today. There is also the matter of what kind of therapy should be used. Corsini and Welding (1989), for example, include fifteen different kinds of psychotherapy in their overview of the field, and Lynn and Garske (1985) discuss twelve psychotherapy models and methods. These listings are a bit deceiving, however, since some of the categories include more than one type of therapy. This is also true of family therapy, which Goldenberg and Goldenberg (1991) subdivide into ten categories and which Hansen and L'Abate (1982) discuss as thirteen types. And there are therapies that do not easily fit into any psychotherapy and family therapy categories, such as narrative therapy (White and Epston 1990; Freedman and Combs 1996).

The ready availability of diverse therapy services today also suggests how public attitudes about counseling have changed since my early troublemaking days. Issues that were once likely to be treated as private matters—to be handled discretely by families, the police, and school officials—are now more likely to be treated as conditions requiring the intervention of experts, including therapists (Gubrium and Holstein 1995a, 1995b). We now seek therapists' services in dealing with a wide range of personal troubles, including some that we acknowledge are less serious than others. I was recently reminded of this circumstance when I was asked, during a seminar about therapy, "So, who is your therapist?" Such a question would have been strange—maybe even offensive—in my youth, but it is quite appropriate today. After all, why wouldn't I have a therapist?

I must also admit that there are times when I wonder what would have happened to me had I been referred to a therapist. My wonderment is not about whether my behavior would have changed; who can know about that? My interest, instead, is in how my behavior and I would have been defined by the therapist, and the treatment strategies that the therapist would have used to change my behavior. We further consider these issues in the next section, where I describe three scenarios of what might have happened to me had I been referred for counseling.

Three Counseling Possibilities

One possible source of counseling for me would have been psychoanalysis. This would have involved several—maybe many—meetings with a therapist who would assume that my troublesome behavior was a symptom of a more basic problem or disorder. That is, my behavior would have been treated as a sign of poor mental health and inadequate maturation. It might also have been classified much as other "diseases" are classified by medical professionals. While the *Diagnostic and Statistical Manual of Mental Disorders* (DSM) published by the American Psychiatric Association (1994) lists several potential categories for classifying my behavior, I suspect that it would have been diagnosed as evidence of Oppositional Defiant Disorder. According to the DSM,

> Negativistic and defiant behaviors are expressed by persistent stubbornness, resistance to directions, and unwillingness to compromise, give in, or negotiate with adults or peers. Defiance may also include deliberate or persistent testing of limits, usually by ignoring orders, arguing, and failing to accept blame for misdeeds. Hostility can be directed at adults or peers and is shown by deliberately annoying others or by verbal aggression. . . . Manifestations of the disorder are almost invariably present in the home setting, but may not be evident at school or in the community. Symptoms of the disorder are typically

more evident in interactions with adults or peers whom the individual knows well, and thus may not be apparent during clinical examination. Usually individuals with this disorder do not regard themselves as oppositional or defiant, but justify their behavior as a response to unreasonable demands or circumstances. (1994:91–92)

Does that sound familiar? But diagnosing my behavior as symptomatic of Oppositional Defiant Disorder is not as simple as it might seem at first glance. This category could have only been applied to my situation if my psychoanalyst also determined that my defiant behavior was more severe than that of other people of my age, and that it had resulted in "significant impairment in social, academic, or occupational functioning" (ibid., 91). If, in my psychoanalyst's judgment, these conditions did not apply, then he or she might have considered a different psychiatric category and diagnosis. It is also possible that my psychoanalyst might have concluded that my defiant behavior was not sufficiently severe to warrant professional treatment, even if it was upsetting to others.

Had treatment been offered, a major goal of my psychoanalyst would have involved uncovering and exposing the hidden, underlying realities associated with my troublesome behavior. This would have likely included discussions about my early childhood experiences, and their significance for understanding my psychosexual development and the intrapsychic processes that lie behind my troublesome behavior. Indeed, virtually any past experience might have been considered in these discussions since psychoanalysts assume that all behavior is meaningful and potentially relevant to therapy. The therapy might also have included analysis of my dreams, and activities designed to "work through" my resistance to change. Much of the working through would have focused on my conscious and unconscious fantasies, which, from a psychoanalytic perspective, are defensive compensations for past conflicts and deprivations. Getting better would have required that I put these fantasies behind me.

If successful, my discussions with the psychoanalyst would have resulted in insight into my life, self, and troubles. I could use this new self-knowledge to take greater control over my life and to liberate myself from past—inappropriate—behaviors and choices. The behaviors would no longer be necessary since their causes would have been discovered and treated. Put differently, psychoanalytically created insight would make it possible for me to become a new person, one who is less disordered and therefore enjoys increased mental health.

A second source of counseling for me could have been behavioral therapy. While my behavioral therapist might have classified my "maladaptive" behavior within a professional category, she would have oriented to me and my troubles differently than my psychoanalyst. One of the most important differences would have been the behavioral therapist's primary focus on my present behavior. She would have shown little interest in the conflicts and deprivations of my early life, or in discovering unconscious resistances and processes. Nor would this therapist have cared about helping me develop insight and self-knowledge so that I might make better choices about my life. For a behavioral therapist, my problem would have been behavioral and learned. She would have assumed that I acted as I did because aspects of my environment reinforced the behaviors that others found to be disturbing. Indeed, my behavioral therapist might have said that, since my critics were part of my behavioral environment, it was likely that they unwittingly contributed to my ongoing troublesomeness.

Based on these assumptions, my behavioral therapist would have initiated a treatment program designed to eliminate my maladaptive behavior, and to reinforce desired behaviors. A simplistic description of the program would emphasize how my therapist rewarded (positively reinforced) me for acting in preferred ways, and perhaps punished (aversively responded to) me for continuing to make trouble. In actual practice, I think my therapist would have selected a more sophisticated response than this, although it would still have been based on these basic behavioralist assumptions and principles.

One possible response is contingency contracting. That is, my therapist and I might have developed an agreement that specified which of my behaviors should be increased and which should be reduced. The contract would have also described when and how I was to be rewarded for positive behavior and punished for negative behavior. The rewards might have included the chance to stay up late at night, use the car, or stay all night at a friend's house. Aversive treatment would have probably involved temporarily taking away something that I valued and/or being isolated from others for a time. The contract would have also included agreements about who could reward and punish my behavior, and perhaps even included a plan for eventually making me the primary dispenser of rewards and punishments. Behavioral therapists define the latter circumstance as self-control.

Behavioral therapists use these and related strategies to "teach" their clients new behaviors. Learning, for these therapists, consists of conditioned responses to environmental stimuli. They are not interested in transforming the personalities of their clients or expanding the clients' free will. These are unrealistic and unattainable goals for behavioral therapists because they define human behavior as driven by environmental factors, not our personalities or free will. Successful behavioral therapy might have made me happier, but only because I would have learned behaviors that fit better with the world in which I lived. My "adaptive" behavior would be no less responsive to environmental rewards and punishments than my previous "maladaptive" behavior.

Finally, the adults in my young life might have arranged for me to talk to an existential therapist. The focus of these meetings would have been on the unique ways in which I interpreted aspects of my life, and how the interpretations were related to the everyday decisions that I made. This focus reflects two major assumptions of existential therapists. They assume that we are all limited by social, biological, physical, and other "objective facts" that exist in the world "out there," and that each person's experiences with these facts is different because we all interpret the world in our own ways. Everyone's life and personality are, from this point of view, unique.

My existential therapist might have gone on to explain to me that my personality is a blend of facts over which I have limited control and imagined possibilities that are under my control. Our lives consist of what now exists, and what might be in the future. Much of my existential therapy would have been concerned with the development of greater awareness of the facts and possibilities of my life, and how they were shaped by my everyday decisions, particularly decisions that I made with little or no existential reflection. My therapist might have further explained that mature people, or "authentic beings," make decisions that realistically accept the facts of life, but that also enhance the future possibilities of their lives. The best decisions, he would have said, involve choosing change over repeating the past.

No doubt, the most surprising aspect of my existential therapy experience would have been the day that my therapist told me that my troublemaking behavior was not a sign of personal strength and independence, but an expression of conformism. This approach to troubles treats them as part of a passive orientation that overemphasizes people's powerlessness in dealing with the facts of their lives, and ignores the possibilities for building different future lives. My existential therapist might have further characterized my troublesome behavior as immature, inauthentic, or as part of my existential sickness. Whatever the terminology chosen, he would most certainly have assumed that the solution to my problems required that I overcome my passive orientation by taking responsibility for my life by choosing to change.

Among the likely techniques used by my existential therapist to get me to take responsibility would have been confrontation. He would have intentionally made me uncomfortable and even angry in order to get me to think about the choices that I had been making. He would have shown no interest in my theorizing about traumatic childhood experiences or how others unintentionally rewarded my troublesome ways, but would have insisted on talking about my present behaviors and decisions. It is also possible that my existential therapist would have asked me to focus. This technique involves turning one's attention to a bodily state (such as fear, anxiety, or anger), trying to fully experience it, and then finding the word that best captures the feelings involved. Existential therapists use this technique to help their clients develop the skills needed to imagine new life possibilities.

If successful I would have emerged from existential therapy with a new— mature or authentic—orientation to life, one that stressed the opportunities available to me for shaping myself and my world. I would be a new person living in a new world of possibilities that I could choose and for which I would be responsible, even if those choices sometimes proved troublesome to others.

Focus of the Study

My point in constructing these scenarios of counseling possibilities is to illustrate how all therapies inevitably involve more than treatment techniques designed to remedy people's troubles. They also include assumptions and theories about people's troubles and troubled people, as well as vocabularies for describing people and their troubles. Indeed, these aspects of therapy are quite interconnected since therapy treatments only make sense in the context of the theories, assumptions, and vocabularies associated with them. These differences are perhaps most obvious in my imagined therapists' orientations to the causes of my behavior. My psychoanalyst would have looked for these causes in my unconscious, my behavioral therapist in my social environment, and my existential therapist would have focused on my orientation to my present and future life.

Put differently, these issues involve the relationship between language and meaning, on the one hand, and therapeutic practice on the other. Therapy is a meaning-creating process involving language and social interaction. Whatever their approaches, experienced successful therapists are adept at meaning creation, and at using language in interacting with their clients. My interest in language use and meaning in therapy is both academic and practical. I am interested in the artful ways in which therapists and clients use language to create therapeutic meanings and in their practical consequences for therapists and clients. My interest in the artfulness of therapy emphasizes therapists' and clients' interactional and interpretive skills. While often taken for granted by therapists, clients, and others, these skills are vital aspects of all therapy relationships and interventions. Therapists and clients collaboratively construct meanings in their mutual interactions, and the meanings have practical implications for how clients' problems are defined and remedied.

These interests define the general focus of this study and my approach to therapy. The approach draws from aspects of sociology that stress how our knowledge of the world, and actions within it, are shaped by language and social interaction. My approach also involves qualitative research in therapy settings. As a qualitative researcher, I observe what others do, ask them to explain their actions, and sometimes tape record their interactions. My job, as I see it, is not to critique the people who grant me the opportunity to observe them as they go about their everyday lives. They—not I—are the experts on the professional significance of their activities, including whether they are doing them properly. My contribution involves describing, and sociologically analyzing, what I see and hear.

I apply and elaborate on my approach to therapy in the rest of this book by analyzing the philosophy and practice of brief therapy, a unique approach to personal troubles that does not easily fit into conventional psychotherapy and family therapy categories. As the name suggests, brief therapy is designed to remedy clients' problems as quickly as possible. Brief therapists reject the common Western assumption that people's troubles are complex disorders that require months—if not years—of treatment focused on developing insights into clients' troubled psyches, environments, and/or biographies. Rather, the focus in brief therapy is on developing short-term solutions to clients' immediate troubles. Brief therapists state that treatment that lasts longer than is necessary to solve clients' immediate troubles risks becoming a problem in itself.

The emphasis on short-term treatment in brief therapy helps to explain part of the recent popularity of this approach among many therapists in the United States. That is, brief therapy strategies fit nicely with the emphasis in health maintenance organizations and other managed care programs on minimizing the costs of mental health services (Hoyt 1996; Johnson 1995). Brief therapy promises to achieve the same or better results as other therapy approaches, but in less time and at less cost. Despite this connection, it is simplistic to think of brief therapy only as a product of recent changes in the economics and delivery of mental health services. This explanation cannot account for current interest in brief therapy in widely divergent European and Asian countries, as well as in Australia. Nor does it address the circumstances under which brief therapy first emerged and has developed over the past twenty years.

I know about these circumstances because I have had the good fortune of having observed how the philosophy and practice of brief therapy has changed over time at Northland Clinic [1], a private organization that is an internationally prominent center of brief therapy. Any serious discussion of the history of brief therapy would have to include reference to the innovative work done at Northland Clinic, as well as the international reputations enjoyed by several of its staff members. The clinic is both a center for doing brief therapy and for training practicing therapists in the philosophy and techniques of this distinctive approach to solving human troubles.

This is a case study of a radical development in contemporary therapy. I analyze both the intellectual contexts for the development of two forms of brief therapy, and how brief therapy principles are put into practice in actual therapy sessions at Northland Clinic. The approaches to brief therapy are ecosystemic brief therapy—which emphasizes the social contexts of clients' lives and troubles—and the more radical solution-focused brief therapy—which treats troubles as ways of talking about everyday life. I have observed how Northland Clinic staff members have moved from practicing ecosystemic to doing solution-focused brief therapy. Thus, there is a sense in which this book is a history of brief therapy at Northland Clinic. But it is a distinctive kind of history. This is not a chronology of significant events or roster of important people. Rather, my emphasis is on the changing language—or institutional discourse—of brief therapy.

Brief Therapy as Institutional Discourse

My approach to brief therapy and Northland Clinic is similar to that recommended by Wittgenstein (1958), who argues that the history of any group is best understood by analyzing its members' language practices. The analysis involves more than describing the new ideas and orientations that emerge in brief therapist–client interactions, although they are distinctive and important. It also asks, How are these changes constructed? This question directs attention to the practical methods used by brief therapists and clients to describe clients' lives and troubles, and to identify remedies to clients' troubles. It also requires that we pay close attention to the interactional contexts of brief therapist–client and therapist-therapist interactions.

More precisely, this is an ethnographic study of therapy as institutional discourse. Institutional discourses consist of the assumptions and concerns about social reality, vocabularies for depicting it, and the usual communication patterns associated with social settings (Miller 1994, 1997a, 1997b; Miller and Holstein 1996). They are strategies for making sense of and responding to practical, ethical, and philosophical issues. Institutional discourses may, as Merry suggests, involve specialized languages and "an explicit repertoire of justifications and explanations and implicit, embedded theory about why people act the way they do" (1990:110). Institutional discourses are also strategies for constructing selves and lives, including different types of troubled selves and lives (Foucault 1988).

Ethnography is often associated with anthropologists' practice of traveling to distant lands to observe the indigenous peoples who live there, and publishing accounts of their impressions of these "foreign" cultures. The accounts often focus on the distinctive and "exotic" values, institutions, and rituals of the people studied. Sociologists have adapted this research strategy by studying aspects of their own societies, often observing and analyzing "exotic" subcultures within Western, industrial societies. The ethnography of institutional discourse is similar to these approaches to ethnography in its emphasis on observation. It is an empirically focused approach to everyday life and relationships.

The ethnography of institutional discourse differs from other forms of ethnography, however, in at least two major ways. First, the ethnography of institutional discourse focuses on the ordinary or mundane features of everyday life. It reverses the traditional ethnographic attitude by treating practices that are usually described as commonplace—even trivial—as complex and fascinating. It involves, in other words, making the familiar strange. This orientation to everyday life is useful because, as ethnomethodologists (Garfinkel 1967; Heritage 1984; Pollner 1987) point out, it makes it possible for us to see and appreciate the many unnoticed ways in which we routinely construct and sustain social realities. Constructing social realities is a recurring accomplishment of ordinary people involved in ordinary situations and relationships.

A second difference between the ethnography of institutional discourse and other ethnographic approaches is the former's special emphasis on language use as a topic meriting study in its own right. Ethnographers of institutional discourse emphasize how we use language to construct and sustain social realities. We do so, for example, by writing about worlds that presumably exist outside our texts (such as I do in this book), and participating in conversations about these worlds. Further, these and other uses of language are political activities because they involve taking a position on what is real (at least, real for present purposes), and they are persuasive activities. Linguistically produced realities are offered as credible representations of social reality to which speakers and writers, on the one hand, and others are asked to acquiesce (Miller 1991a).

This study emphasizes how brief therapy worlds (including their distinctive social relations, goals, practices, and outcomes) are organized within and through language. I stress how personal troubles, the contexts of the troubles, and their solutions are discursively constructed by brief therapists and clients in interaction, and by those who write about them. Brief therapists and clients use these portrayals to assign new meanings to clients' life circumstances and lived experiences, and to justify changing clients' behavior, social relations, and/or perspectives. The ethnography of institutional discourse perspective is one approach to understandings brief therapists' and clients' knowledge, skills, activities, and relationships. It stresses how brief therapy is organized as a general discourse of troubles and solutions, and as a conversational art involving contributions by therapists and clients alike.

The ethnography of institutional discourse perspective also stresses how we enter into and operate within institutional discourses. We enter an institutional discourse by adopting its assumptions, using its vocabulary, and interacting with others to construct a limited array of social realities. Thus, the ethnography of institutional discourse perspective considers how social settings are organized to encourage the construction of some realities over others. Foucault (1972, 1977) makes a similar point in analyzing general, historical discourses as conditions of possibility, a concept that Shumway (1989) compares to a dice game. That is, while no one can absolutely predict what combinations of numbers will appear on any single throw of the dice, the game is organized to produce a limited number of combinations. We also know that over the course of one or more games, some combinations are much more likely to show up than others. These conditions apply regardless of the hopes and dreams of the players.

I assume that brief therapists and clients—like other people——are both shaped by the contexts in which they conduct their mutual interactions, and are artful users of the resources provided to them by the contexts. The latter resources include the assumptions, practical concerns, vocabularies, and opportunities to speak available to therapists and clients in brief therapy settings. The conversational art of brief therapy consists of the skills and knowledge displayed by therapists and clients in constructing concrete social realities and relationships. To return to the dice game metaphor, it should also be emphasized that while all players are affected by the constraints and opportunities of the game, some people understand and play the game better than others.

Overview of the Book

The rest of the book is organized into three parts. Part I—Contexts of Brief Therapy—consists of three chapters dealing with the emergence and development of this study, and of ecosystemic and solution-focused brief therapy. In Chapter 2, I discuss how I first became involved with Northland Clinic, and how I have developed my sociological analysis of it. I also discuss how brief therapy is related to the constructivist movement in therapy, and to more general postmodern developments in contemporary Western societies. These contexts of brief therapy involve major challenges to important conventional assumptions about therapy and, more generally, about contemporary social realities and relationships. While brief therapists have adapted and applied them in distinctive ways, the radical impulse and importance of brief therapy cannot be separated from these influences. Finally, this chapter deals with the ways in which brief therapy is organized and accomplished at Northland Clinic.

We turn to the background, major assumptions, and strategies of ecosystemic brief therapy in Chapter 3. It begins with the precursors of ecosystemic therapy, and later shifts to the writings and teachings of ecosystemic therapists. I draw from the texts that define this field and from my observations of the instructional activities of Northland Clinic staff members and other notable brief therapists. Much of this chapter considers how ecosystemic brief therapists use the concept of social system to define their clients' troubles, and to find solutions to the troubles. Chapter 4 shifts the discussion to the solution-focused version of brief therapy. It includes a discussion of how this approach to therapy emerged from ecosystemic brief therapy, and the intellectual shifts associated with its emergence. Most of the chapter, however, focuses on solution-focused therapists' writings and teachings about their new assumptions, concerns, and practices. Solution-focused therapists have also developed an array of questioning and related rhetorical strategies for talking their clients out of their troubles and into solutions.

Part II—Workings of Brief Therapy—is concerned with the practical side of ecosystemic and solution-focused brief therapy. Here I analyze the concrete ways in which brief therapists, clients, and others interact with one another to define clients' troubles and to identify solutions to them. The chapters in Part II are based on my observations at Northland Clinic and analyses of tape recordings of therapy sessions occurring there. Chapter 5 deals with first meetings between ecosystemic brief therapists and clients. These meetings are largely focused on defining "ecosystemic problems" for clients, and mapping clients' troubles and their social systems.

Second and subsequent ecosystemic brief therapist–client sessions are discussed in Chapter 6. These sessions emphasize creating change in clients' lives. Significant aspects of these interactions include encouraging clients to develop optimistic attitudes toward their present and future lives. In Chapter 7, I analyze the activities of ecosystemic brief therapy teams, which consist of other therapists who observe ongoing interviews from behind one-way mirrors in rooms that adjoin brief therapy interview rooms. Team members monitor both the therapists' questioning strategies and clients' answers. They sometimes intervene in ongoing interviews by telephoning interviewing therapists, and suggesting new lines of questioning or related strategies for better managing the interviews. Team members also discuss preliminary proposals for solving clients' troubles.

The final step in the ecosystemic brief therapy process involves the therapists giving advice to their clients. This is the topic of Chapter 8. The advice is given as intervention messages, which ecosystemic therapists develop during therapist-team meetings. These meetings take place near the end of each interview. The messages always include compliments for clients, which are designed to display the therapists' support for clients and to encourage optimistic client attitudes. Other parts of the messages vary depending on clients' troubles and social systems, and past attempts to remedy clients' troubles. The messages are subsequently read to clients, and ecosystemic therapy sessions end.

Chapter 9 shifts the analysis to solution-focused brief therapists' and clients' interactions. I analyze how these therapists use the distinctive questions emphasized in solution-focused discourse to persuade clients that their lives are not as bad as they think, and/or that their lives will get better in the future. The questions are designed to build new—positive and hopeful—stories of clients' lives, and to identify personal resources that clients might use in solving their problems. We also consider the intervention messages developed and conveyed in solution-focused therapy sessions.

The last section of the book—Implications of Brief Therapy—consists of one chapter concerned with the general, sociological implications of ecosystemic and solution-focused brief therapy. The issues involve the general orientation to life that is directly and indirectly conveyed to clients through brief therapists' questions and intervention messages, the cultural resources that brief therapists and clients draw upon in interacting with each other, and the political implications of brief therapy. I use these issues to further distinguish ecosystemic and solution-focused brief therapy, and to highlight some of the ways in which brief therapy—especially solution-focused brief therapy—contributes to broader cultural and political themes in contemporary Western societies. These contributions are important aspects of the recent, international appeal of brief therapy.

Note

1. The name "Northland Clinic" is a pseudonym. To my knowledge, no such clinic exists. I use this term to protect the confidentiality of the therapists that I studied and their clients. I have also altered aspects of the data to further protect the confidentiality of the clients. The client names used throughout the book are pseudonyms, and I have altered aspects of the personal information provided about clients. While retaining the analytically important aspects of the interactions, I have changed aspects of them to make identification of particular individuals—especially clients—more difficult.

PART I

CONTEXTS OF BRIEF THERAPY

CHAPTER 2

ENCOUNTERING BRIEF THERAPY

This project started in the winter of 1984 when I was invited to meet with the staff of Northland Clinic. I knew nothing about brief therapy when I first visited Northland Clinic, nor did I know why I had been invited to the clinic. The therapists explained that they wished to be "evaluated" from a qualitative research standpoint. Prior studies of the clinic had used quantitative procedures that the therapists considered useful, but unable to get at some important aspects of their work. The therapists were especially interested in the interactional dynamics of their interviews with clients. Therapy interviews are major sites for defining clients' troubles, identifying remedies to them, and assessing the effectiveness of prior definitions and remedies.

Much of the meeting focused on an edited videotape of several sessions with a client who complained that her husband was inattentive and uncaring. We watched the tape, after which one of the therapists asked me to comment on it, asking "So, what do you 'see' there?" We had a lengthy discussion of the tape, and how it might be analyzed from a sociological perspective. We also discussed the staff's rationale in suggesting to the client that she act as if she were having an affair, and why it was effective in regaining her husband's attention and affection. At the end of the afternoon, I was invited to do a qualitative research project on the clinic, which started a few months later and has—in a sense—been ongoing ever since.

The gestation period of this book has been lengthy. I neither planned nor imagined this at the outset of the research. But it has had some benefits. First, it has made it possible for me to observe several hundred brief therapy sessions, analyze the transcripts of eighty therapy sessions, and observe numerous staff meetings, seminars, and workshops conducted by the Northland staff and by other prominent brief therapists. The research has brought me into contact with a wide range of therapists, some of whom were just beginning to learn about brief therapy when we first met, and others who were more familiar with, and accomplished in using, brief therapy techniques. The therapists primarily come from Australia, North America, Asia, and Europe. They practice brief therapy in diverse institutional settings, including private practices, businesses, correctional settings, schools, hospitals, and residential treatment centers. This book is informed and enriched by my contacts with these therapists. Their diversity also points to the significance of brief therapy as an internationally emergent approach to the treatment of personal troubles.

The lengthy research period has also provided me with opportunities to observe a fascinating process of professional change at Northland Clinic. I was privy to the invention of a radically new approach to personal troubles and their solution. The approach—solution-focused brief therapy—directly challenges the fundamental assumptions of most forms of psychotherapy and family therapy by treating clients' troubles as social constructions. Troubles are, from this perspective, literally talked into existence by clients and others in their social worlds, and can therefore be talked out of existence if clients describe their lives in new ways. Solution-focused brief therapy is a strategy for encouraging clients to persuade themselves that their lives are not so troubled as they assume. Central to this rhetorical process is asking clients to imagine and describe how their lives would be different if a miracle happened and their troubles suddenly disappeared. Hence, the title of the book.

Finally, the lengthy research period has given me time to think about how developments occurring at Northland Clinic were related to changes emergent in other contemporary institutions and intellectual circles. These changes involve a shift toward constructivist perspectives, which emphasize how we create the social worlds in which we live our lives by assigning meanings to our experiences. People assign meanings as they describe social reality, and act in accord with their descriptions. We have already seen, for example, how the reality of my youthful troublesomeness changes when it is defined, described, and treated by three different psychotherapists. Constructivist perspectives may be contrasted with historically dominant Western perspectives—including many psychotherapies and family therapies—which assume that reality exists independent from people's interpretations. Viewed from the latter standpoint, social reality is a stable arrangement of "facts" that shape people's options and behavior, even if they do not recognize the existence and influence of these facts.

I develop the constructivist emphasis in brief therapy in the next four sections. We begin with general themes in constructivism and their relationship to postmodern perspectives. We then turn to how these themes and perspectives are part of brief therapy. Our focus shifts to Northland Clinic in the last several sections of the chapter. These sections deal with the arrangement of people and activities at the clinic, and my early impressions of everyday life at the clinic.

Themes in Constructivism

Constructivist perspectives are now widespread—although not dominant—within Western intellectual life. They are central to some of the most important recent developments in literary studies, philosophy, history, sociolegal studies, anthropology, sociology, family studies, and psychology. The sociology of social problems, for example, has been transformed over the past twenty-five years by the emergence of a constructivist perspective that treats social problems as claims-making activities (Spector and Kitsuse 1987). These activities consist of the ways in which individuals and groups express their dissatisfaction with putative social conditions, and call for social change. For social problems claims-makers, the conditions in question exist independent from their interpretations of reality. They just are social problems. Constructivist sociologists, on the other hand, analyze how social problems claims-makers construct social conditions as social problems by

> demanding services, filling out forms, lodging complaints, filing lawsuits, calling press conferences, writing letters of protest, passing resolutions, publishing exposés, placing ads in newspapers, supporting or opposing governmental practice or policy, setting up picket lines or boycotts. (ibid., 415)

These activities are both forms of social activism and ways of creating social realities. We also construct aspects of everyday life as social problems by doing social problems work (Miller 1992; Holstein and Miller 1993). This involves classifying events, people, and/or relationships within such social problems categories as juvenile delinquency, poverty, mental illness, and codependency. We often use these and other categories to justify actions intended to change the events, people, and/or relationships in question.

During this same time period, Emerson and Messinger (1977) developed a complementary, constructivist perspective on personal troubles. They analyze personal troubles as definitions of reality that are constructed and changed through micropolitical processes involving the portrayal of aspects of people's lives as undesirable and identification of remedies to the troubles. Personal troubles emerge as we orient to aspects of our lives as matters for concern and perhaps action. We might ask ourselves and others, for example, if we are drinking too much alcohol, gaining or losing too much weight, really happy in our marriages, and/or whether our jobs are well suited to our abilities and goals. Of course, we might decide that our concerns are misplaced and redefine our lives as untroubled. But we might also decide that our concerns are warranted and even seek professional help in dealing with our troubles. We might, for example, consult a physician, attorney, member of the clergy, teacher, or therapist.

Emerson and Messinger (1977) analyze how our involvement with such professionals transforms our troubles into new social realities. They portray this micropolitical process much as I did in imagining how my youthful troublemaking might have been redefined in my imaginary interactions with psychoanalytic, behavioral, and existential therapists. The new definitions are likely to involve new assumptions about the causes of and solutions to people's troubles, new vocabularies for describing the troubles, and new strategies for remedying the troubles. This process may become even more complicated if we decide to seek a second opinion about or different approach to our troubles. These actions may give rise to a whole new set of trouble definitions, vocabularies, and remedies.

Taken together, constructivist perspectives on social problems and personal troubles emphasize the processes—or activities—through which people define themselves and their social environments. People do so by participating in their social worlds, interacting with others in those worlds, and assigning practical meanings to aspects of their experience. Constructing social realities is an ongoing aspect of people's everyday lives and relationships. Constructivist analysts also stress the rhetorical aspects of reality construction. It is partly a process of persuading one's self and others that one rendering of social reality is more credible than other possible reality constructions (Miller 1991a; Shotter 1993).

Billig (1987) has extended this line of reasoning into psychology and social psychology by analyzing thinking as a rhetorical process, or "witcraft." Thinking is not a private or personal activity for Billig. Rather, it is a micropolitical and interactional process centered in applying social categories to aspects of everyday life, and developing arguments that justify preferred realities and courses of action. Potter and Wetherell develop a complementary—discursive—approach to social psychology in analyzing how "language orders our perceptions and makes things happen" (1987:1). They explain that

> social texts do not merely *reflect* or *mirror* objects, events and categories pre-existing in the social and natural world. Rather, they actively *construct* a version of those things. They do not just describe things; they *do* things. And being active, they have social and political implications. We have seen how description is tied to evaluation and how different versions of events can be constructed to justify or blame these events. (p. 6; emphasis in the original)

According to Potter and Wetherell, then, social problems and personal troubles are versions (or definitions) of events that people use to justify some courses of action, and—sometimes—to blame themselves, others, and/or events. Another example of how constructivist analysis may be done is recent studies of family as a social construction (Gubrium and Holstein 1990; Stone 1988). These studies detail the ways in which people discursively assign family roles, relationships, and responsibilities to themselves and others, including constructing family connections and obligations that have no standing in law. Constructivist family scholars stress that both legally sanctioned and extralegal constructions of family have real implications for persons defined as family members, and sometimes for people cast as nonfamily. Family is, in other words, a practical and political construct that we use in pursuing various ends, including justifying preferred realities and blaming others for failing to do as we wish (Miller 1991b).

Burr (1995) summarizes the constructivist approach in psychology by emphasizing seven interrelated themes that—I might add—are also central to constructivist perspectives in other fields. First and second, Burr states that constructivist psychologists reject "essentialist" and "realist" theories. That is, theories that treat people as acting from pregiven characteristics (such as universal, unconscious processes), and that treat social reality as an objective fact. Constructivist perspectives, on the other hand, emphasize how social realities—including those that assume a universal human nature and/or assume that all of us conduct our lives within the same social reality—are built up through human action and interaction. The third and related theme of constructivist psychology is an emphasis on the historical and cultural relativity of knowledge. There are many ways of defining reality, and how we define it is related to the practical circumstances of our lives.

The fourth and fifth themes discussed by Burr also stress the importance of language in constructivist psychology. It is, she states, a precondition for individual thought, and for social action. It is through language that we make sense of our experiences, and link our actions to others. Finally, Burr analyzes the sixth and seventh themes of constructivist psychology as an emphasis on social interaction and practice, and a focus on process. These constructivist concerns displace conventional psychologists' historical interest in analyzing the "internal" causes of human behavior (such as attitudes), and their penchant for defining people as "static entities," such as constellations of personality traits.

Constructivism and Postmodernism

Some commentators describe these emergent, constructivist developments as evidence that we have entered a new—postmodern—society in which old assumptions about social reality are being displaced by constructivist assumptions. Perhaps the best succinct statement of this argument is expressed in the title of Anderson's (1990) book, *Reality Isn't What It Used to Be.* Anderson explains that

> In recent decades, we have passed, like Alice slipping through the looking glass, into a new world. This postmodern world looks and feels in many ways like the modern world that preceded it: we still have the belief systems that gave form to the modern world, and indeed we also have remnants of many of the belief systems of premodern societies. If there is anything we have plenty of, it is belief systems. But we also have something else: a growing suspicion that all belief systems—all ideas about human reality—are social constructions. This is a story about stories, a belief about beliefs. (p. 3)

Reality isn't what it used to be because many members of postmodern societies recognize that there are many ways of thinking about and describing our lives. We "choose" social realities by orienting to our lives and experiences in particular ways. But we can change these arrangements by changing our orientations, thereby creating new ideas, "facts," and realities. This orientation is not, of course, universally taken by members of contemporary Western societies. Advocates of constructivism live alongside of, and even compete with, others who advocate for essentialist and realist perspectives. This is Anderson's point in stating that pre-postmodernist belief systems are evident in postmodern society.

Postmodern perspectives are perhaps best conceptualized as aspects of a largely unorganized intellectual movement in contemporary Western societies. It is an internally diverse movement that is fraught with its own distinctive contradictions and conflicts. Indeed, as Rosenau (1992) states, the biggest contradiction in this movement may be the claim that truth is always a social construction. Here we have a relativist position being advanced in an absolutist way. The contradiction is made less glaring—but still not eliminated—when constructivists hedge their argument by stating that their position is only one of many possible understandings of truth and social reality. Still, identifying one (or even many) contradiction is not necessarily grounds for rejecting a point of view. Insightful and useful perspectives frequently—maybe always—involve contradiction.

One of the most important contributions of postmodern perspectives is their usefulness in subverting conventional cultural assumptions, social practices, and relationships. Consider, for example, the subversiveness of such constructivist claims that social problems are claims-making activities, that personal troubles are social definitions, and that our families and personality traits are rhetorical constructions. These challenges to essentialist and realist orientations also suggest some of the more general subversions associated with constructivism and postmodernism. They include being serious about aspects of life and culture that most people treat as trivial and uninteresting, such as how we start and end conversations, and the figures of speech and related logics that we use in describing the mundane details of our lives.

Postmodern subversions also include seeking out, and taking seriously, reality claims that are usually treated as wrong, immoral, irrelevant, silly, or absurd. These "marginalized" reality claims are, from the constructivist standpoint, as truthful as the more "respectable" truths that we typically use to organize our lives. Indeed, some postmodern analysts take this emphasis further by arguing that embedded in every text is a variety of contradictions, omissions, mystifications, unsubstantiated claims, dubious assumptions, and ambivalences. Postmodern analysts highlight and magnify these aspects of texts by deconstructing them (Derrida 1976, 1978, 1981). This involves examining what is excluded from or concealed by written and spoken texts. Deconstructivists also critically examine the conventional—often taken for granted—cultural categories, distinctions, and hierarchies embedded in social texts. These include the distinctions between (and hierarchies of) right and wrong, white and black, male and female, mature and immature, health and illness, and reality and fantasy.

Deconstructivists ask, for example, what is left out of, or de-emphasized in, discussions of family values, democracy, mental illness, or personality types? They also ask whether conventional cultural distinctions and hierarchies are so clear-cut as they often seem when they are used to describe social realities, and whether our uses of these distinctions and hierarchies actually serve our interests? A third question asked by deconstructivists involves the internal contradictions found in texts. They ask, Might aspects of our language use be interpreted to mean something very different than what they are usually taken to mean? Deconstructivists do not raise these questions in order to offer new—superior—answers. Rather, their studies are designed to make complex what appears to be simple and straightforward by offering new possible meanings for texts. As Rosenau states, deconstruction "discloses tensions but does not resolve them" (1992:120).

Taking marginalized reality claims and practices seriously may be seen as one way in which constructivist and postmodern analysts encourage an egalitarian orientation to the various forms of knowledge making up contemporary Western societies. They also "equalize" knowledge by skeptically analyzing official understandings of social reality, which we often uncritically take as obvious truth. Official truths are radically transformed when they are analyzed as social constructions that have been developed in and that express aspects of historical, cultural, and social contexts. At the very least, these constructivist analyses suggest that official truths are not immutable, and that ordinary people—working together—have the ability to construct new truths.

These emphases, and the other constructivist and postmodern concerns discussed above, are also central to brief therapy. But the therapists of Northland Clinic and other brief therapists have gone a step further. They have developed practical, counseling techniques that put into practice many of

the abstract assumptions and claims of constructivist and postmodern philosophy. Brief therapists collaborate with their clients to create observable
changes in clients' lives by self-consciously constructing new realities. If you
don't like your current life, they will work with you to construct a new one.

Brief Therapy as Constructivism

While the constructivist movement in therapy includes a diversity of
perspectives and assumptions, all constructivist therapists emphasize the
relativity of knowledge and how social realities—including therapeutic
realities—are socially constructed (Watzlawick 1984). Indeed, Efran, Lukens,
and Lukens describe the latter assumption as "the core of constructivism,"
stating

> At root, constructivism simply represents a preference for the Kantian model of
> knowledge over the Lockean. . . . Immanuel Kant . . . regarded knowledge as
> the invention of an active organism interacting with an environment. In con-
> trast, John Locke . . . saw knowledge as the result of the outside world etching
> a copy of itself onto our initially blank, "tabula rasa" minds. . . . Thus, the
> card-carrying Lockean regards mental images as basically "representations" of
> something *outside* the organism; while the Kantian assumes that mental images
> are wholly creations *of* the organism, produced as a by-product of its naviga-
> tion through life. Thus, the images of the objectivist can be thought of as
> "discoveries" about the outside world, and the images of the constructivist are
> more like "inventions" about what is out there. (1988:28)

Brief and other constructivist therapists, then, treat their clients' and others' troubles as inventions. This is not to say that they treat others' troubles as
trivial or "unreal," but that persons' orientations to circumstances as
troublesome—or untroublesome for that matter—are social definitions that
have practical consequences for their actions and how they experience life.
Constructivist therapists take their clients' definitions of reality seriously by
listening to clients' concerns and constructing solutions that address the
concerns. Like troubles, solutions are inventions. Brief and other constructivist therapists further argue that their approach to clients' problems is respectful, meaning that they do not dismiss their clients' perspectives or
assume that they understand their clients' troubles better than the clients.
    One way in which constructivist therapists distinguish themselves from
other therapists is by portraying their interactions with clients as "a specialized form of conversation" (Efran et al. 1988:32). They contrast this
image of professional-client relations with one in which therapists act as

experts on clients' troubles, thus casting themselves as knowing more about clients' problems than their clients. In the latter therapist-client relationships, client cooperation is usually defined as providing therapists with whatever information they request and acceding to therapists' definitions and recommendations. Constructivist therapists, on the other hand, describe their interactions with clients as more egalitarian and respectful of clients because they involve greater conversational give-and-take. This interactional style, constructivist therapists state, provides clients with more opportunities to express their concerns, preferences, and perspectives on their lives and problems.

Constructivist therapists are also self-conscious in their use of trouble and solution categories. They state that some formulations of troubles are more likely to lead to solutions than others, and that part of their professional responsibility involves working with clients to define "solvable problems." One way in which constructivist therapists express their practical interest in constructing solvable troubles is through stories, such as that told about Jay Haley (a pioneer in the field), who is said to have responded to a therapist who described a family as suffering from a complex and seemingly unsolvable disorder by stating, "I'd never let that be the problem."

This response expresses constructivist therapists' emphasis on solving their clients' problems, a concern that is both practical and ethical. As a practical matter, solving clients' problems involves developing therapy techniques that effectively and quickly create change in clients' lives. Constructivist therapists cast this issue as an ethical concern by describing the quick and effective solution of clients' problems as a central moral responsibility of therapists to their clients. They argue that clients come to therapy expecting that their lives will be improved by the experience. In accepting clients' requests for help and their money, constructivist therapists enter into implicit agreements with their clients, which require that therapists show respect for their clients by helping them to get on with their lives as quickly as possible.

The dual emphasis in brief therapy on constructivist issues and keeping therapy short-term distinguishes it from other approaches to psychotherapy and family therapy, which are often more concerned with encouraging client growth and insight than creating immediate changes in clients' lives. These differences are at the center of many of the controversies that surround this approach (and its precursors), and their "bad reputation" in some therapy circles (Hoffman 1981). The following portrayal of the strategic approach of the family therapists associated with the Mental Research Institute might also be made about the brief therapists at Northland Clinic.

> For strategic therapists, the Art of Therapy becomes the Art of Rhetoric, and strategic therapists indeed have the bad reputation that the Sophists had in ancient Greece. It does not matter, our Palo Alto friends say, whether we

believe the ingenious rationale we give the client to make him change his ways; as long as he changes them, our job is done. This position has been objected to by more traditional therapists, who feel that the use of such currency debases the profession. Charges of "manipulation" and "social engineering" are heard in the land, and are cheerfully accepted by the strategic people. They claim only to be simple craftsmen, solving people's problems in the most expedient (and least expensive) way. (ibid., 277)

Here, we see the constructivist emphasis on rhetoric as an aspect of reality construction and social relationships. Language is a practical and political resource that constructivist therapists use in fulfilling their professional responsibilities to their clients. Indeed, constructivist therapists might respond to their critics by noting that rhetoric is a pervasive and inevitable aspect of all therapy—and other social interactions for that matter. Constructivist therapists differ from others only in their recognition of this circumstance, and willingness to self-consciously use rhetoric in achieving their professional ends.

Brief Therapy as Serious Play

Brief and other constructivist therapists' orientation to their professional roles and relationships with clients is perhaps best characterized as "serious play." Gergen (1991) uses this term to describe one cultural attitude associated with postmodernism. The concept of serious play nicely represents the ways in which brief therapists convey two—seemingly contradictory— messages to their clients. One message is that clients' problems are serious matters, and that the therapists appreciate the frustration and pain expressed by their clients. But brief therapists also convey to their clients a sense of optimism and humor about the clients' lives and troubles. Whether troubled or not, these therapists argue that life is not a complex problem that is beyond our grasp. Most of the time, they state, we are quite competent at managing our lives, although some of us are more elegant at it than others.

This playful and ironic attitude toward life, troubles, and therapy is also evident in the literature of brief therapy. Consider, for example, Watzlawick's (1983) book, *The Situation Is Hopeless, But Not Serious: The Pursuit of Unhappiness,* which offers "practical" advice on how to make oneself unhappy. Watzlawick explains that the advice is needed because

The modern state is in such dire need of ever-increasing helplessness and unhappiness of its citizenry that the fulfillment of this need cannot be left to the well-intentioned but inept attempts of its individual citizens. As in other walks of human life, here, too, government planning and direction is the road to success. Anybody can *be* unhappy, but to *make* oneself unhappy needs to be learned. (p. 15; emphasis in the original)

Watzlawick's statement addresses two related themes in brief therapy discourse, both of which justify an attitude of serious play. The first involves the emphasis on personal inadequacies—or deficits—in contemporary Western societies. The emphasis is evident in diverse social settings and relationships, ranging from conversations among friends to formal encounters involving professionals and their clients. It focuses on people's weaknesses, failures, and other shortcomings, thus casting their lives as troubled. The practical effect of this focus is, according to brief therapists, to undercut alternative—hopeful and positive—orientations that stress people's strengths, accomplishments, and worthiness. Brief therapists' optimism and humor are designed to counter the dominance of the language of deficits and troubles in their clients' lives.

Brief therapists' attitude of serious play is also designed to counter perspectives that define personal troubles as pathologies. So defined, troubles are symptoms of underlying disorders that must be eradicated if individuals are to regain normal statuses. Personal troubles are serious matters for advocates of this perspective, who also argue that "real" solutions to troubles require professional expertise and intervention into troubled persons' lives. Brief therapists' attitude of serious play, on the other hand, is designed to convey an image of troubles as normal features of normal lives. Troubles are not reasons for losing hope or feeling helpless. Indeed, an irony of brief therapy is that clients go to therapy seeking advice on how to deal with what they consider to be their extraordinary and unmanageable problems, only to be told that the solutions to their problems involve treating the problems as ordinary and manageable.

Brief therapists also express a postmodern attitude of serious play in preferring categories and descriptions that blur taken-for-granted cultural distinctions, including the sharp distinctions made between sanity and insanity, fact and fiction, and therapist-client roles in some approaches to therapy. They prefer, instead, to use a nonspecialized vocabulary in talking with clients, and strongly resist clients' and others' requests that they diagnose their clients' problems. Brief therapists avoid these practices by focusing on their clients' portrayals of social reality, and "playing" with their words in order to construct new understandings of the clients' circumstances, and new possibilities for the clients' lives. For example, if I had been referred to a brief therapist to deal with my youthful adventures, it is very likely that my therapist would have agreed with my portrayal of my parents, teachers, and other complaining adults as unfair and intolerant. But the discussion would not have lingered on this issue for long. Rather, my brief

therapist would have probably followed my portrayal of myself as a victim
by asking, "So, what do you need to do to get these unfair and intolerant
people to leave you alone?"

From the perspective of brief therapy, there are no deep meanings to be
discovered in clients' descriptions of their lives and concerns, only possibilities for describing clients' motives, behavior, and lives in new ways. The
possibilities are contingent commitments made by the therapists to any
particular formulation of social reality because brief therapists remain open
to reconsidering (and even abandoning) the formulation as their interactions
with clients proceed. One way in which brief therapists express their open-
ness to new definitions of reality is by deferring to clients' preferences when
misunderstandings emerge. The assumption is central to brief therapists'
willingness to apologize to clients when clients object to their suggestions,
and when clients report that the therapists' recommendations are not working. For brief therapists, life is too serious to insist that social reality must be
defined in only one way, especially if that definition is an obstacle to solving
our problems.

The constructivist and postmodern themes in brief therapy are not free-
floating ideas, however. Brief therapists draw upon aspects of these intellectual developments in addressing their clients' practical and immediate troubles. Thus, it is also important to consider the organizational contexts within
which brief therapists and clients collaborate to construct solutions to clients' problems. We turn to the social organization of everyday life at Northland Clinic next.

Northland Clinic

The Northland Clinic staff have moved the clinic twice during the research period, but most of the time the clinic has been located in a central
region of the city. Northland clients come from all parts of the city, the
surrounding suburbs, more distant communities in the state, and some clients travel great distances from other states to meet with the therapists.
While complete demographic data are not available, it is clear from my
observations that the Northland Clinic's clientele represents a variety of
social classes, ethnic groups, and age groups. The therapists describe this as
a unique circumstance, stating that most therapy centers serve more homo-
geneous populations. They also state that their distinctive approach to therapy is related to the need to address the various concerns and cultural
preferences of their diverse clientele.

The therapists work with clients who complain of a wide range of troubles. For example, I have observed sessions involving—but not limited to—family conflicts, adjusting to divorce, anorexia, bulimia, depression, children fighting in school, unsatisfactory relations at work, developing parenting skills, inattentive spouses, drug and alcohol abuse, and dating problems. While some clients independently contact the center, others are encouraged or required to seek the therapists' services. For example, clients are referred to the clinic by school officials, clergy, other therapists, local human service professionals, and former clients. Clients required to seek therapy are usually sent by the courts or correctional officials. The former are typically parents who have been found to be neglectful of their children and who are required by the courts to enter therapy in order to regain custody of their children. The latter clients are incarcerated individuals who are nearing release from correctional facilities and are required to participate in therapy sessions concerned with the clients' transition to life outside the facilities.

The size of the full-time therapy staff at Northland Clinic has varied over the research period, ranging from a low of two to a high of five. The clinic directors are long-time therapists who have practiced in diverse human service settings. In addition to teaching and conducting therapy sessions at the clinic, the directors also travel extensively throughout North America, Europe, Asia, and Australia, conducting workshops for and consulting with other therapists. The consultations often include sessions with the clients of local therapists. The full-time therapy staff has been augmented by varying numbers of part-time staff who sometimes treat clients under the auspices of Northland Clinic and at other times act as teachers and trainers. Part-time staff are drawn from a number of sources: some are college professors (most in social work), others work in local human service organizations, and a third group consists of therapists who are pursuing careers in other fields (such as management). Part-time staff members' involvement in the clinic is varied, reflecting changes in their careers and interests in brief therapy. Some have been associated with Northland Clinic for several years; others leave after a few months, although they sometimes renew their involvement at later times.

Because much of therapy training involves supervised practice with clients, the actual number of therapists working at the clinic on any given night—much of their work is done in the evening when it is easier for clients to go to therapy—may range upwards of fifty. Most of the people who come to the clinic for training are practicing therapists who wish to augment their knowledge of brief therapy. A smaller number are members of other human service professions (such as physicians and nurses) who wish to integrate counseling with their other professional activities. Therapist-trainees come to the clinic for varying amounts of time; some come for only a few days and others are in residence for a month or more. Training consists of varying combinations of seminars and workshops about aspects of brief therapy, observing and discussing—live and videotaped—therapy sessions, and conducting interviews with clients. This training procedure is related to professional certification rules, which require that therapists develop and hone their skills under the supervision of accredited therapists.

The central city office of Northland Clinic was made up of several spaces that were associated with different kinds of activities. Clients first entered the reception and waiting area, where they identified themselves to the receptionist and waited to meet with their therapists. The number of clients waiting in the waiting room varied, depending on the number of sessions scheduled for the evening and the number of people involved in each session. During much of the research period, the clinic was equipped to handle five simultaneous therapy sessions, although that circumstance was not considered desirable by the staff. Beyond the reception and waiting room were the full-time staff members' offices, which were also used as therapy rooms when needed, and the two primary interviewing rooms.

Brief therapy at Northland Clinic is a team activity. It involves interviewing therapists who meet with clients, and therapy or support teams. The teams consist of other therapists (including therapist-trainees) who observe sessions from rooms adjoining the interviewing rooms in which therapists and clients meet. The teams watch the sessions through one-way mirrors that form one wall between the interviewing and observation rooms. An in-house speaker system makes it possible for teams to listen to ongoing interviews. Also, because most sessions are videotaped (with clients' permission), team members may watch the interviews on the monitors that are kept in the observation rooms. The tapes are sometimes reviewed by Northland Clinic therapists in preparing for future sessions with clients, and are often edited and used in seminars and workshops to illustrate aspects of their approach to brief therapy.

Brief Therapy at Northland Clinic

Brief therapy sessions involve three major parts—the interview, team meeting, and delivery of the intervention message—which staff members seldom vary. Often wrapped around the sessions are presession and postsession discussions of clients, their troubles, and the impact of just completed sessions on clients. Presession discussions may take as long as fifteen minutes, but most take less than five minutes. They usually begin as descriptions given by interviewing therapists or supervising staff therapists about clients' major complaints, and how many times clients have met with their therapists. For example, "This is a couple who can't get along. They've been here a couple of times before."

If team members have no questions, interviewing therapists leave the observation room to meet with clients. The presession discussions are extended when team members have questions, which usually focus on the intervention strategies that have been tried with clients. These meetings may also be extended by interviewing therapists, who sometimes request their teams' advice on how to handle cases that are not going well. The therapists stress their previous, but failed efforts to create changes in clients' lives. The interviewing therapists usually conclude by asking team members to pay special attention to aspects of the interview, and/or to suggest new interviewing strategies.

Team members sometimes continue presession discussions after interviewing therapists leave to meet with their clients. The major discussion topic involves team members' assessments of clients' circumstances based on their initial appearances and behavior in the interviewing room. The discussions are most likely to occur with clients who are returning for their second or subsequent sessions. Team members treat such changes as clients' improved grooming and more cheerful demeanor as possible signs that they are getting better at managing their troubles. Presession discussions are always provisional assessments, which might prove to be significant in later deliberations about clients, might be completely set aside as interviewing therapists and team members focus on other issues that emerge during the interviews, or might be given some level of significance between these extremes. The discussions orient team members to subsequent interviews, but do not determine how they will interpret the interviews.

Therapy sessions formally begin with the interview phase, which takes place in the interviewing rooms and includes clients and their therapists. Perhaps the first thing that clients see upon entering the interviewing rooms are several chairs, organized in a semicircle to facilitate interaction. Each interviewing room also includes a coffee table on which a box of tissues is placed (some therapists remove it prior to their sessions), and one or more microphones. The video cameras are embedded in the walls of the interviewing rooms, but they are still visible to clients and therapists. Unlike some other therapies, Northland Clinic therapists rarely specify where clients must sit or how the chairs should be arranged. When they do, the therapists usually explain that they are trying to "shake things up" in the sessions.

The number of clients involved in therapy sessions ranges from one client to all of the members of large families, perhaps eight to ten people. The vast majority of sessions involve one to three clients. The number of clients also varies across sessions: sometimes one or more members of a client group stop coming to therapy after a while, and new members may join later sessions. Northland Clinic therapists sometimes encourage these changes by suggesting that other people be invited to attend future sessions or—more likely—stating that they do not need to meet with the entire group anymore. The suggestions are strategic moves by the therapists, often intended to gain useful information from new clients and to focus subsequent therapy sessions on the client or clients whom they assess as most committed to change.

About two-thirds of the way through each session, the interviewing therapists inform clients that they are going to take a break in order to meet with their teams. The meetings take place in the observation rooms, without clients. Even on those exceptional occasions when teams are not present, Northland Clinic therapists take breaks. They state that this makes it possible for therapists to collect their thoughts as they review the details of their interviews and helps clients shift their orientation to the next phase of the session, which involves receiving intervention messages from the therapists. The break encourages clients to take the intervention message seriously by creating an attitude of anticipation in clients.

While discussions during the break are sometimes far-ranging, the interviewing therapists and team members eventually—usually within ten or fifteen minutes—focus their interactions on the development of intervention messages. The messages are written in a style that suggests that they are summaries of the discussions during the break, although they do not mention all—or even most—of what was said behind the mirror. Upon returning to the interviewing room, the therapist gives the intervention message, which is almost always read to clients. Interviewing therapists complete this phase of the therapy process by walking clients to the clinic's waiting area, sometimes arranging for their next meetings, and bidding clients good-bye.

As these events are happening, Northland Clinic team members are watching from the observation room. A major concern of the team members is the assessment of the clients' responses to the intervention messages. They note, for example, when clients smile or otherwise "perk up" in response to aspects of the messages, assuming that the clients' responses indicate that they are positively oriented to the messages. Discussion of clients' reception of intervention messages may continue after clients have left the office, and the interviewing therapists rejoin their teams in the observation room. The discussions focus on aspects of the interviews, clients' motives or perspectives, and whether the clients will come back. Team members often elaborate on their discussions during the interviews and/or delivery of intervention messages, as well as on issues raised during team meetings with interviewing therapists. The discussions also sometimes turn to practical, ethical, and theoretical issues involving the practice of brief therapy and therapist-client relations.

First Impressions

Initially, I saw daily life in Northland Clinic as chaos. There was constant movement of people and messages from the waiting area to the interviewing rooms, observation rooms, staff members' offices, and back again to the waiting area. Yet, in the midst of this movement, therapists and clients—behind closed doors—were conducting unhurried and very personal conversations about clients' lives and troubles. The receptionist and team members were also unfazed by the diverse, simultaneous activities of the clinic. Later, I came to see these activities as related to the Northland Clinic staff's scheduling of cases as a continuous flow, especially during the late afternoon and evening hours. Full-time staff members and many therapist-trainees spend twelve or more hours a day at the clinic, usually finishing their last cases at 9:00 or 10:00 P.M.

Beginning in the early evening then, Northland Clinic therapists are engaged in clinic-based activities, making it largely impossible to take formal breaks for dinner, rest, or related activities. Thus, as the evening wears on, the observation room often takes on a surreal quality. The scene that emerges is of a dark room illuminated only by the light from the TV monitor, and filled with the hushed tones of team members' talk and the louder sounds from the therapy room. The sounds include therapists' questions, clients' descriptions of their troubles, and the occasional thumps caused by clients' accidental touching of the microphones or kicking of the table on which the microphones sit. At the same time, some observers are eating their dinner (while watching the sessions), others are calling home to check on family members or returning calls to their clients, and others are fighting fatigue by doing stretching exercises while also watching sessions.

My first impressions of the conversations between Northland Clinic team members sitting behind the mirror were also confused. Sometimes they clearly focused their attention—from start to finish—on the therapy sessions taking place in the next room. At other times, however, it seemed as though the team members had no interest in the ongoing therapy interviews. They chose instead to talk about other clients, mutual acquaintances, books they had recently read, workshops they had recently attended, new computer software and hardware, or their future plans. Two team members, in particular, occasionally spent whole sessions talking about their favorite philosophers, only sometimes linking their discussions to the cases at hand or to brief therapy. Yet, when another therapist entered the observation room and asked about the ongoing therapy session, Northland Clinic team members always had a response that summarized salient aspects of the interview.

I responded to all of this by trying to keep my mouth shut, and my eyes and ears open. I was a diligent—even obsessive—note taker, emphasizing what was said and done by others rather than my assessments of their actions or motives. During therapy sessions, I usually sat by the monitor in the observation room. I used the light emitted by the television set to see while I wrote notes about the ongoing interviews and team members' conversations about them. One of the directors of the clinic sometimes sat behind me, taking notes on my taking notes about others' activities, thereby blurring the distinction between the observer and the observed. The research scene was thus also pervaded by its own constructivist, postmodern, and subversive themes.

It is perhaps unfortunate that I have become accustomed to these aspects of the brief therapy and Northland Clinic ways of life. Brief therapists' typical activities and professional orientation no longer confuse me—at least they don't confuse me most of the time. I expect, and am comforted, to see these activities, which now define much of brief therapy for me. I still find the brief therapy process fascinating, but it is no longer mysterious. I hope to convey this attitude toward, along with my understandings of, brief therapy and Northland Clinic to you in the rest of the book. We begin with the general themes and concerns of ecosystemic and solution-focused brief therapy. They are the topics of the next two chapters, respectively.

CHAPTER 3

TROUBLES AS SYSTEMS PROBLEMS

Ecosystemic brief therapy cannot be separated from the prior emergence of family therapy in the United States. Beginning in the 1950s, this movement involved a variety of individuals located in diverse cities and work sites around the country, ranging from the East Coast to the West Coast and many points in between (Hoffman 1981). Most prominent ecosystemic therapists were trained in this approach to troubles and therapy, and some were students of the inventors of family therapy. Thus, it should not be surprising that ecosystemic therapists' writings and teachings are pervaded with traces of these early influences. The traces are quite evident in the seminars on brief therapy held at Northland Clinic, where references to the prior work of John Weakland, Milton Erickson, Jay Haley, Paul Watzlawick, Salvador Minuchin, and other pioneers in family therapy are frequently heard. Staff members cite these works in explaining both how aspects of their perspective and strategies extend prior developments in the field and how they depart from these developments.

One of the most important connections between early family therapy and ecosystemic therapy is their shared emphasis on the importance of the one-way mirror in doing therapy. Hoffman compares this technological innovation with the invention of the telescope in astronomy, because both were associated with epistemological shifts in their fields. Specifically, the one-way mirror made it possible for therapists to observe therapy sessions from two different physical and intellectual standpoints, that of the therapist in interaction with clients and of the observing team member. This innovation was epistemologically significant, according to Hoffman, because "seeing differently made it possible to think differently" (p. 3).

I discuss some of the most important contributions of two precursors to ecosystemic brief therapy in the next two sections: Ericksonian therapy and the strategic therapy approach developed by members of the Mental Research Institute (MRI). The discussions are not comprehensive, but provide a

baseline for later discussions of the concerns, logic, and strategies of ecosystemic brief therapy.

Ericksonian "Uncommon" Therapy

Erickson's major influence on ecosystemic therapy involves his experimentation with hypnotic techniques and his approach to resistance as an
aspect of the therapist-client relationship. In this case, the term *resistance*
does not necessarily refer to clients who do not want to solve their problems
or who harbor negative feelings about their therapists, although it might. The
term refers to clients' inability or unwillingness to "cooperate" with therapists by answering their questions, fulfilling their directives, or otherwise
following therapists' leading moves in their interactions. Prior approaches to
resistance treated it as a client-initiated problem and focused on the ways in
which therapists might overcome it. Erickson also viewed resistance as client initiated, but treated it as a resource that therapists might use in encouraging change in clients' lives. Erickson's logic, as de Shazer states, was "as
long as they are going to resist, you ought to encourage them to resist"
(1982:10–11). Indeed, Erickson's fame is significantly related to the unpredictable and creative ways in which he responded to client resistance to
create conditions for change, an approach that is often characterized as
"uncommon" therapy (Haley 1973; O'Hanlon and Hexum 1990).

Consider, for example, the case of a young man who was scheduled to
take a physical examination in order to enter the military. He sought
Erickson's help because he could only urinate through a metal tube, a habit
that was likely to exclude him from military service (Erickson 1967). This
habit, we are told, appeared to be related to a traumatic incident in the
man's childhood when he was caught urinating through a knothole in a
fence. But Erickson was uninterested in the history of the problem or the
psychoanalytic issues that might be raised about it. He also showed no
interest in telling the client to stop using the tube, a directive that the client
would have been unable to follow. Rather,

> Erickson induced a trance and suggested that [the client] get a twelve-inch
> tube of bamboo and substitute it for his other equipment. He was told to hold
> the bamboo with his thumb and forefinger and his other three fingers flexed
> around his penis, alternating his right hand with his left. At the same time, he
> was to try to feel the passing of the urine through the tube. He was also told to
> mark the tube off in quarter inches, and the suggestion was made that he might
> begin to consider shortening the tube but that he must not feel compelled to do
> so but let the decision happen of itself; he was to concentrate instead on what
> day of the week he might choose to shorten it. Finally, he was told that his

army physical examination would be postponed but that he would be called up for a second examination in about three weeks and would probably be accepted. (Hoffman 1981:232)

Erickson (1967) reports that, after progressively shortening the bamboo tube to about a quarter of an inch, the young man realized that his fingers could be seen as a tube, and he discarded what was left of the bamboo tube. The young man then experimented for a while with various techniques for forming a tube with his fingers—including extending his little finger while urinating—and eventually concluded that no special techniques were required.

This example illustrates several general themes in Erickson's approach to therapy that have been picked up and extended by ecosystemic brief therapists. First, notice that the client's resistance (the inability to follow a directive to change his behavior) was involuntary. He wanted to stop urinating through a tube, but didn't know how. It would have done no good to tell him to stop. Second, this case illustrates how Erickson utilized clients' resources in solving their problems. Not only did Erickson not tell the young man to stop using the tube, but he left it up to the client to decide when and how he would shorten (and eventually discard) the bamboo tube, and how he would adjust to not using the tube. The assumption was that the client already possessed the intelligence and skill needed to make these decisions and to solve his problem.

Further, Erickson's suggestion for change was not designed to eradicate the client's reliance on a tube in urinating: rather it substituted one tube for another and relied on the client to eventually figure out that he could make his own tube with his fingers. Thus, the client never had to give up urinating through a tube. This strategy, Erickson explains, is "predicated upon the assumption that there is a strong tendency for the personality to adjust if given the opportunity" (p. 417). This assumption is also related to the indirectness of Erickson's strategy and his interest in producing conditions that might persuade the client that he really didn't have a problem after all. As Hoffman states, "with an Ericksonian therapist there is no such thing as a problem, only something defined by somebody as a problem" (1981:234). Finally, Erickson's hypnotic message for the client was optimistic about the future, predicting that he would eventually be accepted into the military.

Strategic Family Therapy

Members of the MRI group extended these themes in Erickson's work, but they also recast them by linking them to new concepts, concerns, and therapeutic strategies. For example, these therapists brought a strong research emphasis to therapy, stressing the importance of studying clients and their families in their "natural" settings. Based on their observations of everyday family interactions, members of the MRI group and other early family therapists developed a systems approach to troubles and their solution. The approach treats troubles as embedded in clients' social worlds, particularly their family relationships. This view generally treats family as a set of interrelated parts that form a unitary whole that is somewhat separate from its environment. Goldenberg and Goldenberg, authors of a major textbook in the field, elaborate on this view of family:

> A family is far more than a collection of individuals sharing a specific physical and psychological space. A family is a natural social system, with properties all its own, one that has evolved a set of rules, is replete with assigned and ascribed roles for its members, has an organized power structure, has developed intricate overt and covert forms of communication, and has elaborated ways of negotiating and problem solving that permit various tasks to be performed efficiently. The relationship between members of this microculture is deep and multilayered, and is based largely on a shared history, shared internalized perceptions and assumptions about the world, and a shared sense of purpose. Within such a system, individuals are tied to one another by powerful, durable, reciprocal emotional attachments and loyalties that may fluctuate in intensity over time but nevertheless persist over the lifetime of the family. (1991:3)

It is difficult to overstate the significance of the concept of family system for the development of strategic and other early forms of family therapy, particularly in distinguishing itself from psychotherapeutic perspectives that define troubles as the products of persons' intrapsychic conflicts (Hoffman 1981; Hansen and L'Abate 1982). Early family therapists countered this imagery by treating their clients' troubles as embedded in the somewhat unique structures and processes of each client's family system. Thus, family therapists defined their clients' troubles as family troubles. One way in which they recast clients' troubles was by treating them as signs of—or even caused by—dysfunctions in clients' families.

Bateson and his colleagues' (1956) influential theory of the *double bind* provides us with an example of how one might think about troubles from a systems perspective. Developed out of research on individuals diagnosed as schizophrenic and their families, the concept refers to an internally contradictory communication pattern in which the expressed message is contradicted by the circumstances associated with it. Watzlawick, Weakland, and Fisch offer the following example, which was expressed by a mother in explaining her concerns about her son's distaste for homework:

> I think what I am trying to say is: I want Andy to learn to do things, and I want him to do things—but I want *him* to want to do them. I mean, he could follow

orders blindly and not want to. I realize that I am making a mistake, I cannot pinpoint what I am doing wrong, but I cannot agree with dictating to him what to do—yet, if a child were to be put completely on his own like that, he would eventually be mired down into a room this deep [referring to clothes, toys, etc., on the floor] or whatever—no, these are—there are two extremes. I want him to *want* to do things, but I realize it's going to be something that we have to *teach* him. (1974:62)

In this case, the double bind involves a conflict between the mother's desire that her son want "to learn to do things," and recognition that if he is ordered to do them (and follows the order), his learning will be involuntary. She elaborates on her dilemma by acknowledging that, if left on his own, her son would not choose to learn, but would become "mired down" with other interests. But, still, she wants him to choose to learn, while recognizing that "it's going to be something that we have to *teach* him." This line of reasoning might go on forever, continually wrapping the mother in a situation in which action is both called for and is inappropriate. Her logic tells her to do something about the situation and to not do anything about it, a circumstance that is impossible to achieve in practice.

While it has been extensively revised and extended over the years, the early formulation of the double bind teaches some of the most important lessons of the systems perspective for family therapists. Three of them are an appreciation for the many paradoxes embedded in clients' family systems, how clients' troubles are adaptations to these paradoxes, and why straightforward—linear—responses aren't likely to be effective. In the above case, for example, it makes sense that the mother would respond to her dilemma by doing nothing on the one hand, and by being dissatisfied with this response on the other. It is also unlikely that she would be satisfied with a straightforward directive from the therapist to leave her son alone or to order him to study. The solution must be indirect, circular, and outside the logic of the paradoxical system in which she is ensnared.

Thus, a major emphasis in family therapy is with developing techniques and strategies for indirectly disrupting troublesome (often paradoxical) patterns and cycles in clients' family systems. Indeed, many of the techniques and strategies developed by these therapists are distinguished by their reliance on irony. The intervention strategy of "prescribing the symptom," for example, assumes that if a trouble is directly eliminated (or even greatly reduced) from a family system, new troubles may emerge to replace it. Like Erickson, who assumed that personalities adapt to practical circumstances, these therapists assume that social systems are also adaptive.

The technique of prescribing the symptom anticipates this system tendency by asking clients to do more of what is troubling them and others in their social systems. It is a counterparadoxical strategy that also reminds clients that their troubles are, in a sense, choices (Watzlawick et al. 1974). If clients can choose to do more of something, they might also be able to choose to do less of it. Thus, strategic therapists also share Erickson's interest in utilizing clients' resources in solving their problems, and his reliance on rhetorical strategies in encouraging clients to utilize the problem-solving resources available to them. Strategic therapists are famous for developing some of the most important and cleverest pattern interruption strategies in family therapy, strategies intended to produce conditions that would indirectly persuade and help clients solve their own problems.

However, these achievements should not be allowed to obscure the general and radical challenge that these therapists presented to the more conventional psychotherapists of their day (particularly psychoanalysts). The challenge involved the strategic therapists' rejection of individualistic models of schizophrenia and other "mental illnesses." These models treat schizophrenia as a distinctive property of the schizophrenic person (or personality), and are associated with etiology, the search for the causes of these personal disorders. Strategic therapists challenge this view by treating schizophrenia (and other troubles) as adaptations within family systems. It is a learned response to practical conditions. Therapists who wish to look for the causes of their clients' problems should focus on the organization and operation of clients' family systems. This shift in focus is also associated with many strategic therapists' rejection of formal diagnostic categories of mental illness and other troubles. Their focus is instead on the mundane operations of clients' family systems. Consider, for example, the following statement made by John Weakland (a prominent member of the MRI group) in a seminar:

> I think the important thing is that all I care about is what's happening in the family and what are people saying to one another. I don't care how it's been labeled, whether it was the wife or a professional. I just want to know what they are doing . . . observable things that are going on in the family and how they are talking to each other. For me, that's the bedrock of this approach that separates this approach from all the others. That's what I want when I ask them what brought them here. It's real different from what other people want.

The focus of strategic family therapy, in other words, is on patterns of action and interaction, not with identifying underlying psychopathologies.

The Emergence of Ecosystemic Brief Therapy

Traces of these precursors to ecosystemic brief therapy will be evident in the discussions that follow. Perhaps the most obvious is ecosystemic therapists' interest in assessing their clients' social systems and in developing indirect (often paradoxical) intervention strategies designed to persuade clients that they already have the personal strengths and other resources needed to solve their problems. Ecosystemic brief therapy, like its precursors, is very much a rhetorical enterprise and might even be described as a process of talking clients out of their problems. Ecosystemic therapists also sometimes use hypnosis in treating their clients, although they are more inclined to adapt hypnotic techniques in order to make them usable in therapy sessions in which clients are not hypnotized.

However, just as strategic therapy recast prior developments in Ericksonian and other forms of psychotherapy, so ecosystemic brief therapy is a distinctive approach to defining and remedying troubles. A major difference involves ecosystemic therapists' interest in the ways in which they are linked to their clients and the clients' social systems. Keeney (1979), for example, argues that the therapist-client relationship is itself an ecosystem that is related to clients' social systems. As members of the same social system, therapists and their clients inevitably influence one another in various recognized and unrecognized ways, such as by collaboratively constructing images of clients' family systems in order to make sense of clients' troubles. Family systems constructed in therapy are patterns of action, interaction, and perception that link family members, and that therapists and clients seek to change in positive directions.

One way in which ecosystemic therapists pursue this interest is through research. The literature on ecosystemic therapy done by ecosystemic therapists includes, for example, studies of the therapists' effectiveness in remedying clients' troubles, studies designed to isolate the most important techniques of this therapeutic approach, and philosophical works that examine the assumptions associated with ecosystemic strategies. At least one group of ecosystemic therapists attempted to construct a computer program that other therapists might use to guide them through the various phases of the ecosystemic therapy process. Also, participants in seminars and workshops conducted by the Northland Clinic staff are encouraged to think about their professional activities and relationships from a research standpoint.

The ecosystemic orientation to research might be contrasted with that of the strategic therapists, who focused their research on the families that they treated. For example, they sometimes videotaped the families in nontherapy settings and used information gleaned from the tapes in assessing and treating their clients' problems. At Northland Clinic and other major ecosystemic therapy settings, on the other hand, videotapes are routinely made of therapy sessions, and the tapes are reviewed by members of the clinic's research committee as well as others involved with the clinic. While ecosystemic therapists' interests in the tapes include solving their clients' problems, most of the information that they use in pursuing this interest involves therapist-client interactions, not interactions between clients and their significant others.

Ecosystemic therapists' focus on the therapist-client relationship as a social system is also reflected in their orientation to clients who might be described as resistant or uncooperative (de Shazer 1984, 1985). For ecosystemic therapists, clients' behavior in therapy sessions is best understood as messages sent to therapists about clients' reactions to therapists' behavior and suggestions. Clients' so-called resistance is a major way in which they signal to therapists that the therapists have misunderstood them, their troubles, and/or family systems. Client resistance is not initiated by clients, but is an interactional development involving both therapists and clients. Clients' seeming resistance is a reaction to therapists' prior actions, and is a positive contribution to therapist-client relationships. It is a message to therapists that they are not meeting their professional obligation to address their clients' desires and needs.

In sum, the emergence of ecosystemic brief therapy involved both a break with and extension of the language and philosophy of early family therapy. While retaining the general concept of family system, ecosystemic therapists also defined the therapist-client encounter as a relevant social system. The new focus justified a "cooperative" therapist attitude toward clients, one that assumed that the purpose of therapy is to collaborate with clients in finding mutually agreeable definitions of and responses to clients' troubles. I discuss how ecosystemic brief therapists cooperate with their clients to construct troubles and remedies in the next four sections.

Change, Maps, and Skeleton Keys

Ecosystemic therapists describe their approach to therapy as non-pathologizing because they focus on positive aspects of clients' lives in helping them create changes in their lives. Indeed, ecosystemic therapy might be characterized as a normalizing discourse because it assumes that clients already possess the necessary skills to effectively manage the changes and difficulties that inevitably arise in the course of day-to-day life. Ecosystemic brief therapists assume that there is more that is "right" with their clients than is "wrong" with them. As a clinic staff member stated in a seminar,

> I think therapists talk too much about families not having problem-solving skills. What they mean by that a lot of times is that they don't agree with what the family is doing. They do have problem-solving skills. Just think about what it takes to have a baby and raise it to, say, six months. That takes a lot of

problem-solving skills to just get to that point. So, they have problem-solving skills and we shouldn't minimize that, but its just they don't use the right method.

Ecosystemic brief therapists stress that positive changes in clients' social systems do not necessarily involve large-scale changes, or even changes in those aspects of clients' lives that therapists consider most troubled. They argue, instead, that small changes reverberate through clients' social systems, initiating other changes in clients' lives and social systems that may result in radically new patterns of thought and relationship. In this way, big changes result from little changes. Consider, for example, the following lesson taught by a Northland therapist in a seminar. It emerged during a discussion with members of a family in which the daughter complained of stomachaches, the husband/father complained of backaches, and the husband and wife complained of marital problems:

> What the girl's stomachaches have to do with the marriage or the man's backaches, I don't know. But family patterns are connected, I believe that. So, to change one pattern is to change all of 'em. It's like we say to clients, I don't know which solution will solve which problem.

Ecosystemic therapists' interest in small changes is related to their assumption that change and adaptation are normal and inevitable features of everyday life and social systems. While troubled individuals and families act in ways that perpetuate their troubled circumstances, people's behavior does not "naturally" tend toward stability. Rather, both effective individuals and families are—to varying degrees—sensitive and adaptive to ongoing changes in their surroundings.

For ecosystemic brief therapists, the troubles that bring clients to therapy are the result of clients and others in their social systems having become "stuck," temporarily unable to effectively adapt to ongoing changes in their environments. One indicator that clients are stuck is their primary focus on the troubled aspects of their lives, making it impossible for them to interpret their lives in positive ways. Thus, a major responsibility of ecosystemic therapists is to help their clients use already developed skills at managing their lives to get "unstuck." Small changes that disrupt clients' existing trouble-focused patterns of action, thought, and/or relationships are often sufficient to achieve this goal.

Ecosystemic therapists also emphasize the circularity of social systems. That is, the various aspects of social systems are linked to one another in a variety of direct and indirect ways that make it impossible to isolate a single cause for clients' troubles. Troubles emerge as complex patterns that cannot be adequately understood by searching for a single causal factor. They can, however, be mapped as recurring interpretive and behavioral sequences that

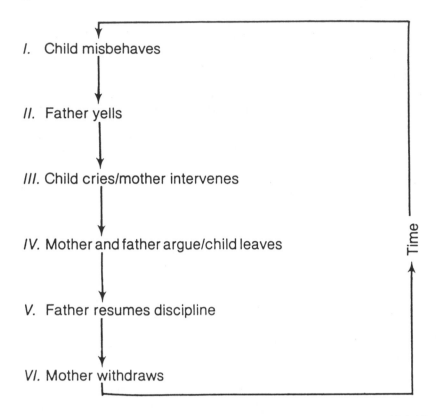

sustain clients' focus on their lives as troubled. For example, de Shazer (1982:41) offers this map (Figure 3.1) of a behavioral sequence involving a misbehaving child and his or her parents.

Each of the aspects of this behavioral sequence may also be associated with an interpretive pattern that sustains the behavioral pattern and further divides family members. For example, the father's response to the child's misbehavior may be related to his interpretation of the child's behavior as the result of the mother's coddling of the child. And the mother's response to the father's yelling may be related to her interpretation of him as impatient, insensitive, and/or overly strict with the child. The child, of course, is also interpreting the parents' behavior, and perhaps learning how to use the pattern to play one parent against the other in order to get his or her way with them.

For ecosystemic brief therapists, this example illustrates one of their most important practical decisions, i.e., where should they intervene in the troublesome behavioral sequence to create change? While they might intervene at any point in the sequence, all interventions are not likely to be equally acceptable to clients or effective in altering the troublesome pattern. For example, the therapists might tell the father to stop yelling at his misbehaving child, or tell the mother not to intervene when the child begins to cry. In both cases, however, the therapists risk having the husband or wife interpret their instructions as taking sides in the disagreement and even blaming them for their family troubles. On the other hand, the therapists might suggest a change that clearly does not take any family member's side, but is totally foreign to their perspectives and experiences. This strategy risks having clients ignore or even reject the therapists' advice.

Ecosystemic brief therapists note these and other intervention possibilities in explaining their concern for "mapping" the most important aspects of their clients' social systems. While they sometimes literally draw maps of clients' social systems, it isn't necessary in order to do this type of therapy. It is sufficient, they argue, to construct mental maps by asking questions that encourage clients to concretely describe troublesome behavior sequences and the family systems in which the sequences are embedded. One way in which ecosystemic therapists obtain information about troublesome behavior sequences is by asking clients to describe the behavior as if they were video cameras. They ask that clients disregard their own and others' motives, and describe what happens to initiate the troublesome sequence, who does what next, and so on.

Ecosystemic brief therapists use this information to assess their clients' and others' perspectives, and to identify intervention strategies that both disrupt troublesome behavioral sequences and "fit" with clients' perspectives. The therapists' strategy is related to Bateson's discussion of binocular vision as a necessary condition for creating change. He states that "it takes at least two different somethings to create a difference" (1979:68) because new visions of reality only emerge in people's creative synthesis of several compatible—but different—images. Thus, one way in which ecosystemic therapists encourage change in their clients' lives is by offering them compatible, but different understandings of their troubles and circumstances. De Shazer calls this goal *isomorphism,* and explains how it can be achieved:

> The concept of isomorphism can thus be applied to therapy as the ability of the team to describe the family's patterns (A) in such a way that their reframed description (A_1) can serve as a guide for designing an intervention that can be mapped onto the pattern the family has described and shown (A). The elements of the team's description need to correspond to the elements of the family's description and the patterns it has shown the team in the therapy session(s). Furthermore, the team's description (A_1) needs to be from a different angle so that the family (at least potentially) can receive the news of a difference, a perceptual shift, which promotes change in the family patterns.

The resultant behavioral change will create a different subjective experience. (1982:9)

While ecosystemic brief therapists state that effective interventions must "fit" with their clients' perspectives and social systems, they also stress the development of general intervention strategies that will be effective with diverse clients and troubles. One metaphor used by ecosystemic therapists to explain the latter goal involves describing clients' circumstances as a lock that needs to be opened, if change is to happen (de Shazer 1985). Therapists have two choices in choosing a key to open the various locks presented by their clients. One strategy is to search for the unique keys that fit each and every client circumstance and trouble, a strategy that promises to be both time and energy consuming. The second, and more efficient strategy is to find one or a few skeleton keys that may be used to open several different locks. As de Shazer states,

> [T]he therapist need not know many details of the complaint in order to at least initiate the solution of the problem. The interventions, therefore, need only prompt the initiation of some new behavior patterns. The exact nature of the trouble does not seem important to effectively generating solutions, because the intervention needs only to fit. Just a skeleton key is called for, not the one-and-only key designed to specifically match the specific lock. (p. 119)

Ecosystemic brief therapists state that the latter strategy is preferable when possible. Hence, much of the Northland Clinic staff's instruction of other therapists is concerned with identifying strategies that might be used as skeleton keys in defining and responding to diverse client troubles. We turn to these issues in the next several sections, which focus on the trouble defining and remedying strategies of ecosystemic therapy.

Ecosystemic Strategies

The significance of practical considerations in ecosystemic brief therapy cannot be overstated. The ideas and techniques proposed by ecosystemic therapists are judged by how well they advance the therapists' interest in creating change in their clients' lives. Techniques that advance this goal are retained and refined, those that are judged ineffective are discarded. The axioms taught by ecosystemic therapists stress the priority that they give to practical concerns. One of the most frequently repeated is, If it isn't working, do something else. Ecosystemic therapists argue that even when clients and therapists are not sure of how best to change troublesome patterns, they still know that more of the same won't work. On the other hand, once change has started, clients should do more of the same.

Ecosystemic brief therapy is designed to be a simple and efficient approach to human troubles. Preferred interventions are those that are isomorphic with clients' perspectives and family systems, involve as few therapy sessions as possible, and make realistic demands on therapists' time and other resources. Ecosystemic therapists further argue that achieving their goals often involves rejecting conventional assumptions about troubles and their solution. They explain that conventional assumptions often don't work, involve complex treatment protocols, and are unduly time-consuming. One such assumption is that the more information therapists have to work with, the more likely they are to understand clients' realities and develop isomorphic interventions. Ecosystemic therapists state, on the other hand, that it is possible to have too much information, which ends up confusing therapists, not clarifying clients' perspectives or the therapists' options in developing useful interventions. When they are confused about how to respond to clients' troubles, ecosystemic therapists often assume that they have too much information, and respond by discarding as much of it as necessary in order to simplify and clarify their task.

The practical focus of ecosystemic strategies is also related to the rhetorical emphases in ecosystemic brief therapists' writings and teachings. They describe persuading others as both a major criterion for distinguishing between effective and ineffective therapists, and—in a sense—as a major ethical responsibility of therapists to their clients. Central to any brief therapist-client relationship are the related "promises" made by therapists to help their clients change their lives in positive directions and to do so as quickly as possible. The responsibility is an aspect both of therapists' and clients' economic relationships (that is what the clients are paying for in seeking the therapists' services) and of the ecosystemic discourse that defines therapists as agents of change. As Cade and O'Hanlon state, politics and ethics are inextricably linked in therapist-client interactions:

> Brief therapists typically make frequent use of direct suggestions and tasks and, therefore, must become adept at the art of persuasion. It is arguable that the art of therapy, whatever the approach used, has much in common with the art of persuasion. For many, this will be an unpalatable fact. Yet, whether we like it or not, we are a profession concerned primarily with encouraging people, directly or indirectly, to change their attitudes or their behaviors. (1993:64)

A Northland Clinic staff member makes the same point, although in a different fashion, in the following statement made in a workshop.

> Once you get the client to say yes to you, then getting him to do something that you want him to do . . . he's more likely to say yes if he's already saying

yes. . . . You don't have to say nice things about them to get them to agree with you, but the simplest way to get them to agree with you is to agree with them.

Cade and O'Hanlon (1993) elaborate on these instructions by specifying six conditions associated with effective persuasion in brief therapy. The conditions might be stated as the following instructions to therapists.

- Clients are more likely to be persuaded by therapists when they feel that the therapists understand and respect their concerns, values, and experiences.
- Persuasive therapists' suggestions and directives are usually congruent with clients' perspectives, experiences, and desires.
- Clients are most likely to implement ideas for change that they generate, or that they believe were their own.
- Persuading clients to make "big" changes is best achieved incrementally, beginning with little changes and later moving to suggestions for more dramatic changes.
- Clients are more likely to accept undesired suggestions from therapists if the suggestions are presented as "an illusion of alternatives in which two suggestions are made, both of which might be rejected if presented singly, but where one might be attempted if its rejection is made dependent on the acceptance of the other" (Cade and O'Hanlon 1993:77).
- Therapists should pay close attention to clients' reactions to their suggestions and directives, treating them as signals that therapists should continue or develop new persuasive strategies.

These instructions are both practical and ethical matters to which ecosystemic brief therapists orient in managing their participation in therapy sessions. They address aspects of therapists' interrelated obligations to be credible, helpful, and persuasive counselors. The instructions also cast cooperative ecosystemic therapist-client relationships as including therapists who closely attend to clients' language, concerns, and reactions to their suggestions, and who use information gleaned from their observations to devise effective strategies for creating change in clients' lives.

The strategies are responsive to three major practical problems: transforming clients' complaints into problems that therapists might help clients solve, developing intervention strategies that disrupt existing troublesome patterns in clients' lives, and encouraging clients to imagine new behavioral and interpretive patterns. The problems are interrelated; thus the techniques associated with therapists' response to one problem may also be helpful in responding to the other. We consider these aspects of ecosystemic brief therapy in the next two sections.

From Complaints to Problems

Ecosystemic brief therapists state that most clients bring complaints to therapy. Complaints are vague portrayals of clients' circumstances, their feelings about the circumstances, and how they want to change their lives. They are trouble definitions that do not point to solutions. For example, married couples sometimes describe their troubled relationships as without love, but love is a concept that is open to widely varying definitions. What love is, when and how it is expressed, and how it is evident in our everyday worlds are only a few of the questions that might be asked about this concept. They are also questions about which reasonable people might disagree. Complaints, in other words, are trouble definitions that are not amenable to therapeutic remedying. Ecosystemic therapists further state that dwelling on complaints too long unnecessarily extends the therapy process, and risks making clients' troubles worse.

But complaints are still important to ecosystemic brief therapists. They express aspects of clients' worldviews, and the circumstances that have led to their decisions to request therapy (de Shazer 1985). Complaints are depictions of how clients see social realities, both the reality of their present circumstances and what they hope for in the future. Complaints are partly vague because clients often express their worldviews in figurative language, such as through metaphors that link otherwise different concepts or aspects of life. Clients' complaints also frequently involve stark contrasts. One contrast is between clients' exclusively negative evaluations of their present and future lives, on the one hand, and their utopian hopes for the future on the other. Clients' complaints also frequently involve a contrast between those who are to blame for clients' troubles and their victims (this category often includes the clients). For ecosystemic therapists, both of these contrasts are aspects of clients' troubled circumstances.

Complaints suggest how clients have ended up in therapy because, according to ecosystemic brief therapists, clients respond to their troubles by doing whatever seems logical within their worldviews. For some clients, there is only one "right" response to their troubles, whereas others may try several related responses prior to choosing therapy. In both cases, however, clients' decisions to seek therapy suggest that they are trapped in feedback loops (perhaps the language of vicious circles is more descriptive of the experience) in which their failed attempts to remedy their troubles give rise to further responses that are also likely to fail. Indeed, clients often respond to failed remedies by returning to them time and again, on the vain hope that they will eventually work because, from the clients' perspective, the remedies should work.

Ecosystemic therapists distinguish complaints from problems, which are trouble definitions that suggest ways in which clients' lives may be concretely and positively changed. To say, "My spouse doesn't love me," is a complaint. But to say, "I know my spouse doesn't love me because he or she doesn't listen when I talk," is the beginning of a problem. The latter statement suggests that the trouble involves a behavioral and maybe an interpretive sequence. It also suggests that the trouble might be remedied by a change in the existing pattern. Problems are circumstances that clients can evaluate as present or absent in their lives, and as getting better or worse. Problems also imply goals, which are improved future circumstances toward which therapists and clients might work. Goals—like problems—are concrete circumstances that clients can assess as present or absent, and nearer or further from realization.

A major responsibility of ecosystemic brief therapists involves helping their clients move beyond their complaints and to begin to formulate problems. Indeed, there is a sense in which ecosystemic therapy cannot be done without properly formed problems. Consider, for example, the following instructions given to seminar and workshop participants at Northland Clinic about the importance of properly formed problems. In this case, the therapist casts the double bind as a malformed problem.

> Therapists make a lot of messes for themselves by having poorly stated problems. We'll call them malformed problems. They're [clients are] saying, "Johnny has to go to church because he wants to" is an example of a malformed problem. You can't make him like it, so you have to get them to a solution. You know, you could say, would it be good enough if he just went to church? If they agree to that, then you have a properly formed problem, one you can solve. You can change his behavior, but not his mind.

But constructing proper problems is not just the responsibility of therapists in interaction with clients: team members observing in adjoining rooms also share in this professional responsibility. Further, this responsibility may be conceptualized in a variety of ways. Therapists and team members may, for example, ask, Does the client's trouble description suggest an observable remedy? Are the client's desires for change realizable? Does the client really want to change his or her life? Can we remedy this problem within the typical time frame of brief therapy (preferably, in no more than three sessions)? A "no" answer to any of these questions is, for ecosystemic brief therapists, evidence that they have not yet developed a workable problem, and perhaps that the therapy session is moving in the wrong direction. As a Northland therapist explains,

> So, the basic rule, whether you're back here or in front of the mirror, a question you have to be able to answer is, "How long are we going to continue meeting like this?" If you don't have any answer to that, you have a malformed prob-

lem. Until you can answer that, you don't know what you're doing. That's a basic rule that you have to always follow.

In sum, ecosystemic brief therapists describe problems as trouble definitions that are constructed out of clients' complaints. They are negotiated within therapist-client encounters (Cade and O'Hanlon 1993), particularly during the interview phase (Lipchik 1988; Lipchik and de Shazer 1986). Further, the problems that are eventually constructed by therapists and clients must "fit" with clients' perspectives and social systems; otherwise clients will not accept them or make the changes that are needed to solve their problems. A Northland therapist described this process as "focusing family complaints down to problems that have solutions." She explained that this is done through "purposeful interviewing" that helps clients develop new understandings of their complaints, focuses on problems that clients can see, and for which therapeutic interventions can be developed.

Constructing Problems

Constructing problems out of complaints involves paying close attention to clients' complaints, which often include information about troublesome behaviors and how clients interpret them (de Shazer 1985). Ecosystemic brief therapists may help clients construct workable problems and goals by asking them to further specify the troublesome sequences and their contexts. When a client says, "I know my spouse doesn't love me because he or she doesn't listen when I talk," for example, the therapist might ask the client to describe the circumstances when the spouse does or doesn't listen, and about the concrete behaviors that the client takes as signs of listening and not listening. The client's response to the question provides the therapist and team with useful information about the client's perspective and expectations.

Purposeful interviewing also involves establishing control over the pace, content, and direction of interviews. Seminar participants are taught that while it is important to establish rapport and be sympathetic with clients, this is insufficient in itself. They must learn to direct interviews away from complaints and toward problems and goals. The techniques for managing interviews are varied, depending on clients' troubles, perspectives, and behavior in interviews. For example, workshop participants are taught to ask clients with many complaints which of them is most serious or important. The therapists should respond by asking questions that focus on the clients' chosen complaints, attempting to construct problems out of them. With depressed clients, who often have many complaints, Northland Clinic staff advise that therapists "mirror" their clients' depression by slowing the inter-

Table 3.1 Types of Purposeful Questioning

Detective Questions	Constructive Questions
Individual	Individual
Systemic	Systemic

view to the pace of the clients' speech, acknowledging that clients have good reasons to be depressed, and by asking how it is that the clients are still able to accomplish as much as they do when faced with such daunting and depressing circumstances.

Ecosystemic interviewing is a complex process that requires that therapists pay close attention to both the content of clients' statements and the patterns of interaction within which the statements are being made. To aid others in developing ecosystemic interviewing skills, the Northland staff divide purposive interviewing into two general types of questions (detective and constructive questions) and the four subtypes that are represented in Table 3.1.

Detective questions are intended to "detect" presently existing situations. They ask, Why is it a problem and how did it come about? Individual detective questions are concerned with clients' opinions about their circumstances. An example is, Why do you think that this is a problem? Systemic detective questions deal with the relationships among persons in clients' social systems. Such questions might ask, What do you think your spouse thinks about the troubled circumstance, or Who in the family is most upset about this situation? Constructive questions are concerned with goal setting and solutions. Thus, they are always future oriented. Constructive systemic questions ask about possible future developments in clients' social systems, such as, Who do you think will notice it first when you don't have a problem any more? Constructive individual questions, on the other hand, ask about clients' future behavior or perspectives on the future, for example, How will you know when this problem is gone?

Seminar and workshop participants at Northland Clinic are taught to move to constructive questions as quickly as possible, thus moving the interactional focus of interviews away from the troubles at hand and toward future goals. They are also encouraged to alternate between individual and systemic questions. According to Northland therapists, a major difference between ecosystemic brief therapy and many other therapy approaches is their emphasis on systemic questioning. Two advantages of systemic questions are that they are nonconfrontive (clients aren't likely to find them hostile or judgmental), and they may disrupt dominant system patterns and assumptions. Often, for example, family members do not discuss what they think others think about issues of mutual concern. Rather, they assume consensus when family members really disagree, or disagreement when family members actually agree. Northland therapists explain that an important early step toward change may occur when clients realize that their assumptions about others in their social systems are wrong.

Systemic questioning also serves ecosystemic brief therapists' interest in managing therapy sessions, and creating new insights into clients' perspectives and skills. Northland Clinic staff members state, for example, that systemic questions may be useful in dealing with conflicts between clients during interviews. The questions shift the interaction away from disputed "facts," and toward others' interpretations that may not be matters of dispute. The questions may, in other words, help to build the cooperative interactions that ecosystemic therapists state are necessary for therapy to be effective. Systemic questioning is also useful in avoiding the pathologizing tendencies of other therapy approaches, which often involve only individual and detective questions. Systemic questions ask clients to shift their perspectives as they discuss, for example, how others might interpret or react to possible changes in their behavior. These questions move therapy away from clients' fears, unlikely claims, or other actions that might be interpreted as signs of pathology. The questions also provide clients with opportunities to display their competence and skills at interpreting aspects of their social systems.

Seminar participants at Northland Clinic are especially encouraged to use systemic questions in interviewing clients who might be classified as mentally ill. Northland therapists explain that such clients are often treated by psychotherapists as lacking the skills and insights that are needed to do effective family therapy. Systemic questioning may, however, reveal that such clients are more capable than therapists assume. The problem is not the clients, but the language in which they are forced to speak in response to therapists' questions. Northland therapists often make this point in seminars by showing and commenting on videotapes of clients who have been or might be diagnosed as mentally ill. As a Northland Clinic staff member stated about one such videotape,

> Did you notice how she answered [the therapist's] questions? She really sounded crazy, didn't she? In most other therapies, they would have pursued that and her feelings, and she'd have gotten crazier and crazier. The systemic questions shifted her frame and she sounded saner.

Ecosystemic brief therapists' purposeful interviewing is also designed to initiate changes in clients' lives by encouraging them to think about their lives in new ways. Such reframings, as ecosystemic therapists call them, may open new possibilities for clients by allowing them to consider behavioral possibilities that they might have previously considered illogical or doomed to failure. Reframings are one way in which ecosystemic therapists encourage binocular vision in clients, forcing clients to reconcile the differences between their old perspectives and the alternative possibilities suggested by the reframings.

Opening Possibilities for Change

Ecosystemic brief therapists use two major questioning strategies in opening alternative possibilities for clients. One technique involves asking clients if positive changes have occurred in their lives since their last sessions, or between the time when they scheduled their first therapy sessions and the actual sessions. As Weiner-Davis, de Shazer, and Gingerich state, "Many times people notice in between the time they make the appointment for therapy and the first session that things already seem different" (1987:306). When clients report that positive changes have taken place, ecosystemic brief therapists focus their questions on the details of the changes. They ask clients to specify the circumstances of the changes, including the behaviors involved, and when and how the changes are evident to clients. A Northland therapist explains this strategy by stating that when clients report positive change since their last sessions,

> That's the solution right there. Just build on it. You don't need all this other crap. That's the solution. What we do in the following session, it may not look like it, but what we're doing is building on it. . . . [H]ow can you keep it going and questions like that, that's building on it. You don't need to know a whole hell of a lot to solve it.

Indeed, finding change in clients' lives is sufficiently important that ecosystemic therapists often begin interviews by asking clients, "So what has changed since we last met?" When clients report that nothing has changed, the therapists continue to ask about possible changes until they are satisfied that the clients are fully convinced that their lives have not changed. Consider, for example, the following advice given by a Northland staff member:

> If clients say that nothing is good, then you should accept what they say, but don't believe it. [laughter] You know, ask for more information. You should listen to the negative information, but ask if anything positive happened between the bad things. You can also ask if it is as bad as in the past.

The strategy of focusing on change is consistent with ecosystemic therapists' interest in creating change as quickly, efficiently, and simply as possible. As they frequently remind others, "If it ain't broke, don't fix it." Troubled circumstances that are, from the client's point of view, getting better are no longer "broken." A Northland staff member explained the rationale for, and importance of, this strategy in a seminar by stating,

> If the clients say that things are better this week, but they're still bad, you forget all the other stuff and go right for that. Ask them how things are different this week, and why they think that things are different now. This is what we are trying to do, to build on change, and you focus on it whenever you can. In a case like this, maybe all you need to do is reinforce the change.

Ecosystemic brief therapists also assume that when clients report positive changes in their lives, they now have a goal toward which they and their clients might work. The goal specifies the concrete behaviors that are needed (i.e., more of the same) and raises clients' expectations that their lives will get better. According to ecosystemic therapists, expecting life to get better is an important part of getting out of the troublesome cycles and patterns in which clients find themselves stuck. Troubled clients expect life to be unsatisfactory, and help to make it so by interpreting virtually all aspects of their everyday lives as signs of trouble. Change breeds change, because clients' interpretations of many aspects of their lives become more positive when they see some aspects of their lives as getting better.

Ecosystemic therapists also encourage new client expectations by using the crystal ball technique (Erickson 1954; de Shazer 1978). It involves asking clients to imagine themselves looking into one or more crystal balls and projecting themselves into future times when their current troubles are absent. Originally developed as a hypnosis technique, ecosystemic brief therapists use it with unhypnotized clients. Crystal ball questions may be asked in various ways. One approach taught at Northland Clinic consists of therapists requesting that clients project themselves into a future time when their lives seem to have improved. The therapists follow up on this question by asking clients to describe how they will know whether the changes are real and lasting improvements. Ecosystemic therapists might ask, for example, "How are you going to know when you've had sex three, four, five times, or whatever that it's not a fluke?"

Ecosystemic therapists state that the crystal ball technique is effective because clients are asked to both imagine and describe new—untroubled—lives. The technique changes clients' expectations about the future, and identifies concrete goals toward which therapists and clients might work. Therapists and clients may also measure their effectiveness in achieving their goals in future sessions by comparing clients' present life circumstances with the images that they "saw" in their crystal balls. We next turn to how ecosystemic brief therapists use information gleaned in interviews to develop recommendations and suggestions (they call them intervention messages) for clients.

Intervention Strategies

The skeleton key metaphor is most appropriate for describing ecosystemic brief therapists' orientation to intervention strategies that are developed during therapists' meetings with team members. They use the meetings to assess clients' perspectives and social systems, while also suggesting how clients might initiate changes in their lives or build on existing changes. The responses are given as messages from therapists and/or team members. They are designed to be isomorphic with clients' perspectives and systems, but also to initiate changes in clients' behavior or perspectives. When they are effective, ecosystemic interventions help clients begin to get "unstuck" from the muddles in which they find themselves.

A crucial ecosystemic intervention strategy is the list of compliments given to clients at the outset of messages. The compliments stress how impressed therapists and team members are with clients' actions, motives, and/or strengths in managing their troubles. Compliments are designed to fit with clients' perspectives, and communicate a respectful and nonjudgmental attitude toward clients. They may also reframe aspects of clients' lives, making positive what was once seen as troublesome. Compliments sometimes create a client orientation that is similar to a hypnotic trance, thus making clients more likely to accept and follow through on the concrete suggestions that are offered later in intervention messages. As de Shazer states,

> The purpose of compliments is to build a "yes set" . . . that helps to get the client into a frame of mind to accept something new—the therapeutic task or directive. These directives, tasks, and suggestions are essentially designed to be posthypnotic suggestions and frequently are linked up with inevitable events which can serve as "triggers" that help the client do something different. (1985:95)

Ecosystemic brief therapists sometimes elaborate on the hypnotic aspects of compliments by including embedded commands in their intervention messages. Such commands are indirectly given by stressing some words and including pauses in sentences that set off some phrases from the rest of the sentences. The pauses call attention to the phrases, and transform them from suggestions or descriptions into commands. The result is sentences that may seem poorly structured or badly read by therapists, but that may be suggestive to clients who are highly focused on and positively oriented to the therapists' words. Consider the following example and explanation of an embedded command that is part of a question. Notice that the therapist stresses the italicized words, and that the command ("Joan take a calm and reasonable approach to your children") is preceded by a pause (indicated by the comma):

> "What sort of thing do you think *will* happen *when* you start to, Joan take a more calm and reasonable approach to your children?" Several messages are implicit here: (1) the idea or suggestion that Joan should take a more calm and reasonable approach (the second part after the comma), (2) the expectation that Joan will take this approach (the "when" before the comma, not an "if"), and (3) the expectation that a more calm and reasonable approach will make a difference that Joan can notice (things will happen). (ibid., 35)

In addition to being adaptations of hypnotic techniques, compliments and embedded commands are also Ericksonian in their indirectness. Compliments are used to establish positive contexts for the messages that follow and that might otherwise be experienced by clients as undesired directives. Embedded commands are also designed to direct clients while not explicitly doing so. Compliments and embedded commands are two ways in which ecosystemic therapists play with language in persuading clients to change their behavior and/or perspectives.

Another major intervention strategy used by ecosystemic brief therapists involves disrupting the behavioral and/or interpretive patterns in which clients are stuck. The strategy often involves a version of the reframing technique, i.e., suggesting that clients pay attention to previously ignored aspects of their lives and/or thinking about the positive aspects of their lives. An example is the "first session task," which is the Northland Clinic staff's most frequent response to new clients. The task involves the following request:

> Between now and next time we meet, we (I) want you to observe, so that you can tell us (me) next time, what happens to your (life, marriage, family, or relationships) that you want to continue to have happen. (de Shazer and Molnar 1984:298)

The Northland Clinic staff state that one of the reasons that their approach may be accurately called brief is because this task is often all that clients need to "get them started again." Disrupting an interpretive pattern is often enough to create new behavioral patterns and social relationships.

Other reframing tasks involve disrupting troublesome behavior sequences. The therapists sometimes suggest, for example, that clients change their normal routines by not responding when their children throw tantrums, by altering the "rules" that govern their fighting, by sleeping on different sides of the bed, and by flipping a coin each morning to determine which of two different ways of managing their troubles clients will use that day. Of course, these strategies may be elaborated into complex pattern interruptions. When clients complain that their spouses are spending great amounts of time away from home, for example, the therapists sometimes suggest that the clients break this pattern by challenging their spouses' assumptions that they will always be waiting at home. The therapists suggest that clients act as if they are developing independent lives of their own, including acting as if they are involved in adulterous affairs of their own.

While varying in their details, all ecosystemic interventions designed to disrupt troublesome patterns are also designed to remind clients that they and others in their social systems are making choices. Troublesome patterns are sustained through clients' choices, and thus change requires that clients make different choices. Indeed, ecosystemic brief therapists sometimes challenge clients to make new choices by stating that they have doubts about whether clients' lives will ever improve or whether they will follow through on the therapists' suggestions. They sometimes tell clients, for example, that the team is divided. Half of them believe that clients will follow the suggestions, and half do not. Sometimes the therapists side with one half of the team and other times they state that they can't know what will happen. Clients are next told to do as they wish, and to inform the therapists and team members of their choices at their next sessions.

Ecosystemic brief therapists also use symptom prescription or paradoxical interventions by advising clients to continue (even increase) troublesome patterns, or to slow the changes that are occurring in their lives (de Shazer 1985; Cade and O'Hanlon 1993). As might be expected, paradoxical interventions are often used with clients who seem unlikely to do whatever tasks that therapists and team members might suggest, but they are also used under other circumstances. For example, ecosystemic therapists use paradoxical interventions to reframe behaviors that clients describe as spontaneous and beyond their control. By telling clients to continue these behaviors, the therapists redefine the behaviors as choices that clients make and can control, and create a double bind. The new definition is affirmed no matter what clients do between sessions. If they change their behavior, the clients have shown that the behavior was a choice. If clients report that they did not change their behavior, therapists congratulate them for being able to resist the impulse to change—another choice.

CHAPTER 4

TROUBLES AS LANGUAGE GAMES

The solution-focused approach did not suddenly emerge at the clinic, nor did it involve an immediate transformation in therapist-client relations or therapists' practices. Rather, this discourse emerged over the course of several years, and involved both the development of new ideas and techniques and the elaboration of prior assumptions and practices. The shift might be characterized as a reconfiguration of therapeutic assumptions, practices and orientations. The new configuration has made some prior assumptions and practices irrelevant, and assigned new practical significance to others. Thus, solution-focused discourse retains traces of the ecosystemic discourse, while providing therapists and clients with new resources for constructing and remedying clients' troubles.

The development of solution-focused therapy was a substantial shift in the constructivist direction by the Northland Clinic staff and other therapists working along similar lines. The shift is constructivist because it focuses therapists' attention on the relativity of their own and their clients' knowledge, and on how both forms of knowledge might be used to construct and remedy clients' troubles. It also provides therapists with opportunities to reorient to language as an aspect of therapy, to clients' and their own positions within therapeutic relationships, and to observe how change is embedded in the processes of everyday life.

We begin this overview of solution-focused discourse by considering the interrelated practical and intellectual contexts within which the solution-focused brief therapy emerged. Later sections consider how these influences are evident in the professional orientations and practices of solution-focused therapists.

Ecosystemic Practice as a Context of Change

A major context for the development of solution-focused brief therapy is the organization and practice of ecosystemic brief therapy. This context includes the various mutual adjustments made by therapists and clients to one another in therapy sessions. Nor should the potential significance of ecosystemic teams in facilitating change be underestimated. They are an ever-present, professionally informed, and interested audience for refining existing ecosystemic techniques and inventing new ones. Not only do team members suggest new lines of questioning and intervention strategies to therapists, but they observe and assess therapists' techniques, including moves that team members consider to be effective. Team members also sometimes question ecosystemic therapists about their rhetorical moves during team meetings or after sessions.

An example of how ecosystemic brief therapists and their teams develop new techniques in the process of doing therapy is the history of the *miracle question.* This question—which is discussed more fully later in the chapter—is perhaps the most important innovation associated with solution-focused brief therapy. The question is partly significant because it is a way of bypassing ecosystemic discussions of complaints and problems, thus moving directly to the definition of goals. It asks clients to describe how their lives would be different if a miracle occurred and their troubles suddenly disappeared. Berg and Miller suggest that the question be asked in the following way:

> Suppose that one night, while you are asleep, there is a miracle and the problem that brought you into therapy is solved. However, because you are asleep you don't know that the miracle has already happened. When you wake up in the morning, what will be different that will tell you that this miracle has taken place? (1992:13)

While practicing ecosystemic brief therapy, the Northland Clinic staff sometimes described changes in clients' lives as miracles, but their development of the miracle question was unrelated to this usage of the term. Rather, the question was first used in an interview in which the client and therapist were having difficulty specifying a goal toward which they might work. The client responded to the question by offering the beginnings of a workable ecosystemic goal, a development that was noted by both the therapist and his team. The clinic staff tested and refined the question by asking other clients to imagine and describe their postmiracle lives and by adjusting the ways in which they asked the question to fit their distinctive styles of interacting with clients.

The Northland Clinic staff's response to the initial use of the miracle question points to another major context in which the solution-focused discourse emerged. It involved the therapists' reflecting on the general implications of their practices and assumptions. One way in which they did so was in the regular meetings of the research committee in which committee members sought to identify effective therapeutic techniques by watching videotapes of prior sessions and live ones. They also discussed their ideas about effective therapy, and "tested" them by observing past and ongoing therapy sessions. The therapists sometimes tested ideas emergent in the discussions by applying them in their therapy sessions. The clinic staff also reflected on their past and changing practices and assumptions in their ongoing training activities, which involved demonstrating their techniques to other therapists and explaining why they were effective.

Each of these activities addresses the therapists' interest in developing a "minimalist" approach to brief therapy. The therapists stress that brief therapy should involve as few sessions as possible, and that the best responses to clients' troubles involve minimal intervention by therapists into clients' lives. They further argue that, to the extent possible, clients should determine how their troubles are to be remedied and what constitutes an acceptable way of life. As exemplified by the miracle question, a major shift in solution-focused therapy is toward the identification of solutions to clients' troubles and away from extended discussions about the definition of clients' troubles, social worlds, and perspectives.

Indeed, solution-focused brief therapists treat extended discussions of clients' troubles as part of the problem that they wish to remedy. They explain that lengthy discussions about clients' troubles divert therapists' and clients' attention away from developing solutions and may actually make clients' troubles worse. Trouble-focused talk or stories worsen clients' troubles when they are treated as master narratives that define the most important aspects of clients' lives and selves. Such narratives act as self-fulfilling prophecies that both predict that clients' lives will be troubled and encourage clients to interpret their lives as filled with signs of trouble. By emphasizing solutions, solution-focused therapists avoid stories that they consider to be part of clients' problems, and may begin to build alternative stories within which clients are competent and leading satisfactory lives.

Put differently, the stories initiated in solution-focused brief therapist-client interactions are progressively oriented (Gergen and Gergen 1983, 1986). Progressive stories emphasize how clients are moving toward desired goals; thus they are designed to justify hope and optimism. The progressive stories constructed in solution-focused brief therapy may be contrasted with the "stability" and "regressive" stories (ibid.) that clients bring to their initial meetings with solution-focused therapists. The latter stories emphasize how clients' lives are not changing (stability stories) or are getting worse (regressive stories).

While the minimalist theme in solution-focused brief therapy may be understood as a desire to become more technically efficient, the therapists describe it as also related to two other major professional concerns. One concern is ethical and involves the therapists' moral obligation to respect their clients by helping them "get on with their lives" as quickly as possible. Notice, for example, de Shazer's (1991) choice of words in the following statement in which he characterizes solution-focused therapists' efforts to "restory" clients' lives as a professional responsibility. For de Shazer, stability and digressive stories are trouble-focused, and progressive stories are oriented toward positive change.

> Therapists' concerns and responsibilities in therapy conversations also vary depending on the types of narratives or stories that dominate in their interactions with clients. Their major concern and responsibility in conversations dominated by stability and digressive narratives is to help clients construct new stories that signal and are sources for desired change. . . . Therapists' major concern and responsibility in therapy conversations dominated by progressive narratives are to help clients elaborate and "confirm" their stories. (ibid., 93)

Solution-focused therapists' concern for efficiency is also related to their rejection of complex (especially pathologizing) theories of human troubles and troubled persons. They argue that such theories are usually associated with long-term treatment programs that focus on the causes of (not solutions to) clients' troubles, and justify therapist-client relations that are dominated by therapists who often make moral judgments about clients and their lives. Thus, solution-focused therapists also justify their rejection of complex theories of troubled persons and circumstances on intellectual grounds. We turn to these intellectual issues in the next several sections.

Poststructuralism as a Context of Change

The Northland Clinic staff reflected on and recast their practices and assumptions by bringing new philosophical assumptions, concerns, and perspectives to bear on them. A particularly important shift was the therapists' adaptation and incorporation of ideas associated with poststructuralism into their therapy (Eagleton 1983; Harland 1989). As the name suggests, a major defining feature of poststructuralism is its relationship to structuralism, a school of thought that has had profound implications for Western culture and institutional practices. Structuralist assumptions and concerns are especially prevalent in psychotherapy, which was literally built on them.

For example, structuralist analysis generally assumes that culture, language, and thought are shaped by universal—but unseen—structures (Caws 1988). A major preoccupation of structuralist theorists is with identifying the deep structures that underlie surface appearances, and specifying the laws that regulate them. In psychotherapy, such deep structures might involve the organization and operation of the unconscious as a source for our desires and behaviors, including those that we or others might describe as troublesome. Poststructuralists challenge structuralism in a variety of ways, including by questioning the usefulness of structuralists' search for deep structures, their belief in the universality of the structures, and their faith in science as a privileged form of knowledge.

Northland Clinic staff members use poststructuralist perspectives as intellectual vehicles for both criticizing and elaborating on their ecosystemic assumptions and practices, some of which might be analyzed as structuralist. The perspectives also provide the therapists with a context for formulating new understandings of their therapeutic practices and relationships. Of special significance are the ways in which the Northland Clinic staff use poststructuralist perspectives to extend and reformulate their prior constructivist assumptions about the definition and remedying of clients' troubles. These changes are also associated with the development of a new— solution-focused—orientation to therapist-client relationships.

We consider three—interrelated—poststructuralist themes that have informed the development of solution-focused brief therapy in the next three sections. It should be noted, however, that these intellectual influences are inseparable from the practical contexts of solution-focused therapists' dealings with their clients. Aspects of poststructuralism provide the therapists with useful ways of thinking about their professional activities and responsibilities, but their poststructuralist ideas are always subject to "test," based on their practical experiences with clients.

Social Realities as Local Constructions

A major theme in poststructuralism is the rejection of the past, dominant assumption that social reality can be understood and comprehensively represented within a single theoretical scheme or metanarrative (Lyotard 1984). Poststructuralists argue, instead, that social realities are diverse and local constructions that are inextricably linked to the circumstances within which they are produced. Social realities—including troubled realities—are narratives that make sense within particular social, cultural, or historical circumstances but are not necessarily generalizable to or useful under other circumstances. Viewed from this standpoint, all knowledge is relative and contingent on the diverse local circumstances associated with its construction and use.

Solution-focused brief therapists express this poststructuralist theme in rejecting highly abstract and generalized theories that categorize, explain, and/or remedy human troubles. They stress instead the variety and indeterminacy of life and troubles, and therapists' responsibility to accept this "fact of life" in orienting to their therapeutic relationships and practices. This is not to say that solution-focused brief therapists use no general techniques and strategies in working with clients, only that the usefulness of the techniques and strategies vary from one therapy session to another. They are resources that solution-focused therapists might use, not rigid recipes that must be strictly followed in each and every session. A prominent solution-focused therapist makes this point in his seminars and workshops when he routinely concludes his discussions of solution-focused techniques by stating, "This works every time, except when it doesn't."

Solution-focused brief therapists' rejection of grand theories is perhaps most explicitly expressed in Berg and Miller's (1992) book on solution-focused strategies for dealing with problem drinkers. They reject approaches that treat problem drinking as alcoholism—a term that assumes that all problem drinking behavior is the same, stems from the same sources, and can be remedied in the same ways. Also, while the first chapter deals with the principles and assumptions of the solution-focused approach, Berg and Miller begin the chapter with the following caveat:

> We worried that this chapter might give the reader the mistaken impression that one needed to first understand these principles and assumptions in order to successfully practice the approach described in the book. Our experience has always been the opposite: those students *least* burdened with abstract theoretical notions are usually the *most* capable of learning solution-focused therapy and, for that matter, therapy skills in general. (p. 1)

Cade and O'Hanlon (1993) further develop this linking of practical and poststructuralist concerns in solution-focused brief therapy by noting its implications for therapist-client relations. They state that "since we have no general explanatory models or normative models to guide us" (p. 60), solution-focused therapists must turn to their clients for guidance on how to conduct therapy sessions. Further, the guidance provided by clients is interactional. Solutions to clients' troubles emerge as therapists and clients interact with one another within therapy sessions, constructing distinctive, local relationships and—in the process—goals. The interactions involve utilizing clients' resources in constructing "images of future goals and possibilities for clients" (Dolan 1991:25). This focus further localizes the practice of solution-focused therapy, because each client might utilize different resources within the therapeutic relationship. As Walter and Peller (1992) note, it is within concrete therapist-client interactions that these resources are made available to and put to use by therapists and clients in solving clients' troubles.

Troubles as Uncaused Realities

Solution-focused brief therapists' interest in developing techniques and strategies for utilizing clients' problem-solving skills and resources takes on added significance when we consider that—unlike most psychotherapists—solution-focused therapists deal with troubles that have no causes. Causal explanations involve penetrating surface appearances of reality, and finding their genesis (and "true" significance) in previously invisible factors that lie behind or underneath the surface. They are, to use Weakland's terminology, iceberg theories, which assume that what we see is only a small part of the "real" problem (Weiner-Davis 1993). Causal theories also encourage therapists and clients to confuse explanations with solutions.

According to solution-focused brief therapists, causal explanations are a major source of conventional psychotherapists' power in their dealings with clients. They are experts who know better than clients about the causes of and solutions to clients' troubles (de Jong and Berg 1996). Structuralist psychotherapy discourses also encourage therapists to see signs of problems in virtually all aspects of their clients' behavior, perspectives, and relationships. Berg and Miller, for example, describe how they previously oriented to troubles as pervasive in everyday life and related to deep structures:

> True to our initial training, we were both, at one time, expert in problem detection and description. So expert were we that we could detect mental health problems at a distance. While creeping along the interstate during rush hour, we were able to diagnose those drivers suffering from "low self-esteem" from their slumped posture and sagging shoulders. The supermarket provided an even greater opportunity to observe complex and varied human problems ranging all the way from parents lacking adequate child-rearing skills to shoppers with serious eating disorders. Alas, it seemed that we were therapists in search of problems, and, not surprisingly, we found them everywhere we looked. (1992:2)

Solution-focused brief therapists state that structuralist psychotherapy approaches also provide therapists with resources for assigning pathological significance to their clients' troubles. As a practical matter, the search for root causes to clients' troubles is often organized to produce definitions of clients as suffering from disorders (or deficits) of various types (Furman and Ahola 1992). Solution-focused brief therapists counter this perspective by emphasizing how troubles are embedded in the stories that therapists and clients tell about clients' lives (Cade and O'Hanlon 1993). If there is a cause to clients' troubles, it is a narrative construct. The causes of clients' troubles are, in other words, embedded in the plots, figures of speech, and related narrative devices that therapists and clients use to describe—and give coherence to—clients' lives.

De Shazer (1994) further contrasts the solution-focused approach with structuralist psychotherapy approaches by characterizing solution-focused brief therapy as an attempt to get "to the surface of the problem." From this standpoint, troubles are not hidden below or behind surface appearances, and attempts to penetrate the surface to locate the causes of clients' troubles will only confuse therapists and clients. Becoming a solution-focused therapist, then, involves learning to resist one's trained urges to penetrate surface appearances and to assign pathological significance to clients' troubles. It involves, instead, learning to accept "things as they are" (ibid., 31). Accepting surface appearances is a beginning step for solution-focused brief therapists in developing new stories about clients' lives, stories that are change-oriented, not trouble-focused.

Accepting surface appearances is also one way in which solution-focused brief therapists display respect for their clients, and utilize clients' resources in defining and remedying their troubles. Solution-focused therapists display respect for clients by treating clients' concerns, experiences, and portrayals of social reality as sensible and adequate. There are no "root causes" of clients' troubles separate from clients' portrayals of their lives and hopes for the future. Further, because solution-focused therapy deals with surface appearances about which clients are as expert as therapists, solution-focused therapists may utilize clients' resources in constructing therapeutic goals and strategies for achieving them (de Jong and Berg 1996; Dolan 1991; Walter and Peller 1992).

Language Use as a Reality-Creating Activity

Perhaps the most culturally radical aspect of poststructuralist perspectives is their orientations to the relationship between language and social realities. For example, poststructuralists challenge the dominant Western assumption that language is a neutral medium for conveying thoughts and ideas to others. The latter—"correspondence theory of language"—assumes that the categories that make up language are labels for aspects of social realities that exist separate from the categories. Thus, our use of language may be assessed as more or less accurate because our words can be tested against the objective reality that they describe.

Poststructuralists offer a very different view of language. They treat social realities as constructed and sustained through our use of language, and emphasize the ways in which our thoughts are shaped by the words that we use. This reversal of what might be called the commonsense understanding of language is related to poststructuralists' image of language as a weblike structure and process (Eagleton 1983). In using language, we construct complex signs that are linked in ways that are similar to spiders' webs. That is, as spiders weave their webs, it becomes increasingly difficult to answer such seemingly simple and straightforward questions as, Where do the webs begin? Where are the web-building projects going? and To what extent are the projects shaped by the spiders' choices and by the constraints provided by the emergent webs?

Poststructuralists argue that these questions are not answerable in any absolute sense and only lead to "conceptual puzzlement" (Wittgenstein 1958) if seriously pursued. Conceptual puzzlement is the distinctive confusion that inevitably accompanies serious efforts to get at the origins, essences, or transcendental purposes of words. What, for example, is the "real" meaning of such trouble categories as schizophrenia, anorexia, and dysfunctional families? Answering this question necessarily involves asking and answering other questions, such as how are we able to recognize instances of these troubles in our own and others' lives? Or, are these categories always best defined as troubles, and might they be usefully defined in other ways? The questions go on and on.

Wittgenstein (1958)—a major influence on poststructuralism—argues that the best way to avoid the endless pursuit of such questions is to focus on the ways in which we use language in our everyday lives to construct meanings and achieve practical ends. To be sure, these meanings are unstable and shifting. Sometimes we categorize our own or someone else's behavior in one way, and other times categorize it quite differently. This is not a problem for Wittgenstein, however. Indeed, he treats this aspect of ordinary language use as one of its most important qualities. The meaning of things is always contingent on the contexts and language games within which they are described and/or categorized. As de Shazer states,

> Language games are culturally shared and structured activities that center on people's uses of language to describe, explain, and justify. Language games are activities through which social realities and relationships are constructed and maintained. The signs (or moves) during the game consist of sentences (or signs), which are made up of words, gestures, facial expressions, postures, thoughts, etc. Since this is a system complete in itself, any particular sign can only be understood within the context of the pattern of the activities involved. Thus, the meaning of any one word depends entirely on how the participants in the language game use that word. If the context were significantly different, that game would not be played; it would be a different game altogether. (1991:73)

In applying the concept of language games to their professional practices, solution-focused brief therapists stress that clients' troubles and solutions to them are constructed within therapist-client interactions in therapy sessions. Solution-focused therapists state that everything that is needed to construct solvable troubles and initiate changes is available within therapist-client interactions, because solutions are interactionally constructed realities. The realities emerge as therapists and clients negotiate the terms of their relationships, particularly the vocabularies and logics that they use in assigning meaning to clients' descriptions of their lives.

This emphasis in solution-focused brief therapy raises yet another challenge to conventional approaches to personal troubles. That is, since problems and solutions are different language games, they need not be related. Our usual linking of them is a matter of convention, albeit one that is justified by structuralist assumptions about deep structures and root causes. For solution-focused therapists, on the other hand, it is possible to solve clients' troubles without ever specifying a problem to be solved. This is not to say that they never link problems and solutions; rather, the linkage is established within the context of their interactions with clients. Sometimes they collaboratively construct both problems and solutions, and other times only solutions.

Becoming Solution-Focused

Becoming solution-focused involves entering a new discourse that provides brief therapists with new assumptions about social reality and therapeutic relationships, new practical concerns about therapeutic processes and therapists' responsibilities within them, and new strategies for constructing change in clients' lives. Thus, while traces of the ecosystemic approach are still evident in solution-focused brief therapy, the significance of these apparent continuities is different in solution-focused therapy. Solution-focused discourse, for example, involves a reflexive orientation that is not associated with the practice of ecosystemic therapy. Therapists adopt a reflexive orientation by treating their interactions with clients as sites for self-consciously constructing social realities, not just for describing them. Indeed, from a reflexive standpoint, the descriptions are themselves reality-creating activities (Garfinkel 1967; Heritage 1984; Pollner 1987).

The reflexive emphasis in solution-focused brief therapy is perhaps most evident in the therapists' greatly reduced interest in mapping their clients' family systems. While solution-focused therapists ask questions that ecosystemic brief therapists might interpret as mapping questions, their practical significance is different in solution-focused therapy. Clients' answers to mapping questions asked in ecosystemic therapy provide therapists and their teams with information for assessing aspects of clients' lives that exist outside the ongoing interaction. Similar questions asked in solution-focused interviews, on the other hand, are rhetorical moves for restorying clients' lives. Their relationship to social worlds that presumably exist outside the ongoing interaction is unclear, and not a matter of concern for solution-focused therapists.

The reflexive emphasis in solution-focused brief therapy also provides therapists with opportunities to make choices about the social realities that they interactively construct with their clients, and about how they are going to construct them. One such choice is whether to stress problem definition (that is, turning complaints into problems) or constructing solutions to whatever problems clients might have. Solution-focused therapists prefer to construct solutions and not define problems (Furman and Ahola 1992). The choice is partly practical, because solution-focused therapists argue that a focus on solutions is the quicker route to change. But it is also related to the solution-focused assumption that change is an ever-present aspect of life (George, Iveson, and Ratner 1990). Clients are not so much stuck on their complaints as they are unable to see that the solutions to their problems are already present in their lives. As Berg (1994: 10) explains,

> Solution-focused brief therapists believe that it is easier and more profitable to construct solutions than to dissolve problems. It is also easier to repeat already successful behavior patterns than it is to try to stop or change existing problematic behavior. Furthermore, they believe that activities that center around finding solutions are distinctively different from problem-solving activities. For example, the activities a worker may engage in to "protect a child" from his abusive or neglectful parent are quite different from those designed to "build safety" for the same child. What the worker does becomes even more different when he looks for and finds instances when the parent is already successful in ensuring the safety of the child, even a little bit and even if it occurs only occasionally. Getting the client to repeat her successful method of child rearing is easier than trying to teach her totally new and foreign skills. This clearly is an easier and simpler type of solution.

A related difference between the discourses of ecosystemic and solution-focused brief therapy is solution-focused therapists' treatment of therapist-client interactions as the primary contexts of clients' troubles. This is a major epistemological shift in brief therapy. Clients' troubles are both constructed and solved in therapy. Troubles and solutions have no reality outside this context for solution-focused therapists. Thus, a major practical and ethical responsibility of solution-focused therapists is to aid clients in developing therapy goals and solution strategies that are mutually agreeable and achievable within the context of their relationships (de Shazer et al. 1986; Cade and O'Hanlon 1993; O'Hanlon and Weiner-Davis 1989).

De Shazer (1991) offers a postmodern understanding of this epistemological shift in arguing for a "deconstructivist" perspective on therapeutic processes and realities. His approach assumes that the meaning of any reality claim lies in the relationships associated with it. These relationships include the ways in which aspects of the claim are linked, and in which readers and authors of the claim interpret it. De Shazer further argues that therapists' and clients' interpretive activities in therapy sessions are best described as "misreadings," because there is no way in which anyone can determine the ultimate meaning of clients' descriptions of their lives and concerns. He explains,

> [T]he reader can never know what the author might have meant because he cannot know what the author brought to the meaning of what he wrote. Similarly, the author himself cannot read what he wrote; he too can only misread. Misreading is not a problem to be solved, just a fact to be lived with. . . . Rather, each misreading creates a new version of the text and increases both its potential usefulness and potential misunderstanding. (p. 51)

Viewed as a deconstructivist process, solution-focused brief therapy involves the self-conscious and reflexive development of misreadings of clients' lives and options in solving their troubles. The issue is not discovering an ultimate truth (be it root causes to or the real meanings of clients' troubles), but developing effective strategies for misreading clients' lives and troubles in change-oriented ways. Since, we are always misreading social reality anyway, solution-focused therapists ask, Why not misread it in positive ways?

Solution-Focused Strategies

Like ecosystemic therapists, solution-focused brief therapists stress that effective therapy is a simple process. It involves only a few—uncomplicated—assumptions and practices. But solution-focused therapists go further than ecosystemic therapists in their pursuit of a minimalist brief therapy. In their instructions to readers and workshop members, for example, solution-focused therapists emphasize how getting at the surface of clients' problems involves setting aside complex theories about how clients' troubles are embedded in social systems, and overly clever intervention strategies designed to interrupt troublesome patterns in clients' social systems. They state that, instead, everything that is needed to solve clients' troubles will emerge in the course of the therapy interview, if therapists ask solution-focused questions and work at reading (or misreading) clients' answers as solutions.

De Shazer (1991), for example, describes the case of a married couple who came to therapy seeking a cure for the wife's "nymphomania." She stated that she had recently developed a need for sex at least once a day or she couldn't sleep. Both the wife and husband complained of the circumstance. She stated that she felt controlled by her compulsion, and he complained of becoming a "stud" whose only function was to service his wife. The clients also reported at subsequent sessions that the trouble was getting worse. A significant shift occurred, however, when the husband stated that he believed that the problem was not sex, but a sleeping problem. The wife responded by asking the therapist, "Do you have any cures for insomnia?" (p. 65).

De Shazer explains that this shift in focus opened the discussion to a variety of new possibilities, such as that the problem might "really" be the wife's new exercise regimen, which started at about the same time as her need for daily sex emerged. Equally important for solution-focused therapists, the shift in language recast the trouble as nonpathological (lots of "normal" people have sleeping problems, whereas the language of nymphomania suggests mental illness) and made a variety of new solutions available for consideration. The shift in terminology, in other words, provided the therapist and clients with a new theme for constructing a new story about the clients' lives and trouble.

This example illustrates how solution-focused brief therapists look for solutions at the surface of their own and their clients' talk. While accepting the couple's characterization of the problem as nymphomania, the therapist did not question them about the causes of the wife's recently increased sexual desire. To do so would make nymphomania the only available definition for the clients' problem. Indeed, the therapist managed the interview to facilitate the possibility of other definitions emerging, definitions that might be more easily solved than nymphomania. Notice, also, that the therapist did not provide the alternative definition for the clients, but waited for it to emerge within the interview.

This example also shows one way in which solution-focused brief therapists misread troubles (de Shazer 1988, 1991). That is, the husband's characterization of the problem as a possible sleeping disorder might have been dismissed as irrelevant or inappropriate, but the therapist responded by asking the clients to seriously consider it and its implications for solving their troubles. A related deconstructivist strategy involves therapists' misreading clients' problems by expressing confusion. The confusion is designed to normalize clients' lives by suggesting that their seeming problems are normal aspects of life. For example, solution-focused therapists sometimes ask clients to explain why their problems are problems. O'Hanlon and Weiner-

Davis discuss how Weiner-Davis broaches this issue by asking, "So what else is new?" They give the following example:

Client: My eight-year-old and I have some problems as a result of his chronic illness. I like him . . . periodically. (laughter)
Michele: You like him periodically?
Client: Yeah.
Michele: So what else is new?
Client: Periodically I don't like him.
Michele: Well, so what else is new? (1989:95)

Solution-focused brief therapists also misread their clients' lives and problems by accepting and pursuing the practical implications of clients' claims and logic. The therapists sometimes misread by asking questions designed to reveal to clients the unsatisfactory assumptions and conclusions that clients' logic entails, and to consider other—more satisfactory— possibilities. An alternative misreading strategy involves describing clients' lives for them based on the clients' complaints. The descriptions are de- signed to suggest new understandings of clients' problems and how they might be solved. O'Hanlon and Weiner-Davis, for example, discuss how O'Hanlon sometimes responds to clients complaining of depression by tell- ing them that depression is something that he really knows how to do, because he has learned from former clients who were really good at doing it. Next, O'Hanlon describes the various depressed behaviors and attitudes that he has learned to do.

> By the time he is through with this litany, most people are smiling or nodding with recognition. They do not realize that they have inadvertently accepted the definition of depression as a "doing" and, therefore, as something they can do something about. From there, if that intervention has not been enough, it is a simple matter to ask the person which technique he or she specializes in and to use that as a focus for intervention. (p. 98)

These solution-focused brief therapy strategies are also associated with solution-focused therapists' orientation to therapy sessions as conversations about change (de Shazer 1991; Walter and Peller 1992). Defined as conver- sations, the sessions are collaborative encounters in which therapists and clients make equal—although different—contributions to their interactions (de Jong and Berg 1996; Furman and Ahola 1992). This imagery also sug- gests that solution-focused therapy sessions involve give-and-take between therapists and clients. The concerns of all participants are relevant to the conversations, which may go in a variety of directions, some of which might be unanticipated by therapists and/or clients. The conversational image of therapist-client interactions is also related to solution-focused brief therapists' interest in finding solutions that fit with their conversations with clients, not with clients' perspectives and social systems. Consider, for example, de Shazer's discussion of the above misreading of nymphomania as the couple's problem:

> Of course the therapist cannot just pick a new meaning or a new label at random. The new meaning must fit . . . within the context, within the pattern of conversation. In this particular context, fit was a simple matter because the new name for the complaint simply gave precedence to what was seen as secondary (the sleep disturbance) over what had been seen as primary (the sexual disturbance); this is a move typical of post-structuralist thinking and deconstructivist endeavors. (1991:66)

We next turn to solution-focused therapists preferences for their conversations with clients.

Conversational Preferences and Narrative Guidelines

Perhaps the most obvious conversational preference of solution-focused brief therapists is their preference for talking about solutions, not problems. This preference is partly related to the assumption that in talking about problems and solutions, we construct self-fulfilling prophecies. Berg and Miller (1992) make this point in contrasting the solution-focused approach to problem drinking with conventional approaches to alcoholism. The latter approaches assume that clients can only solve them through total abstinence. These approaches also predict that clients who do not "cooperate" with their psychotherapists will continue their excessive drinking until they "hit bottom," because their problem is beyond their control.

Solution-focused therapists argue that when conventional psychotherapists teach this theory of alcoholism to their clients, they create social conditions that—unintentionally—justify uncontrolled drinking by clients who "fail" in therapy. That is, these therapies "fail" their clients because they give nonabstaining clients no hope for the future, including the possibility that they might figure out how to drink in moderation. Solution-focused therapists argue that a conversational focus on solutions creates social conditions that encourage clients to assume that there is hope for change.

Dolan (1991) stresses this point in advising solution-focused brief therapists to use supportive group therapy sessions with care in treating clients suffering from sexual abuse. She states that while hearing others' stories of victimization may help clients manage their feelings of self-blame, isolation, and stigmatization, creating change involves getting beyond victim stories and developing hopeful stories about better future lives. One way in which solution-focused therapists encourage their clients to develop hopeful stories is by complimenting them. Compliments may be given at any point in solution-focused therapy sessions, not just during the intervention message phase (O'Hanlon and Weiner-Davis 1989). Further, as Berg and Miller emphasize,

> Complimenting the client is not the same as condoning her destructive behavior. It simply acknowledges and gives credence to her view of her world, affirming her view of herself, accepting her "story," and soothing her frustration at having to admit to failures. (1992:102)

While solution-focused brief therapists' frequent use of compliments might be interpreted as a procedure for not holding clients accountable, there is a sense in which the opposite is true. Solution-focused therapists do not blame their clients for their problems, but they do contend that clients are responsible for helping to construct solutions to the problems. As a prominent solution-focused therapist explained in a workshop, "[C]lients own their problems by taking responsibility for solving them." She also cautioned the workshop participants that allowing therapy conversations to dwell on clients' motives and feelings about their troubles and/or theories about the causes of the troubles "lets clients off the hook." In other words, because these topics focus on problems, they end up allowing clients to avoid taking responsibility for proposing solutions to the problems.

Solution-focused brief therapists' interest in complimenting clients is related to this concern. The therapists explain that compliments may help to build clients' faith in their problem-solving abilities and encourage them to see how they already possess the personal and social resources for changing their lives (de Jong and Berg 1996). Clients in solution-focused therapy also take ownership of their problems by defining the goals of therapy. Solution-focused therapists state that—within limits—it does not matter how clients wish to solve their problems. They also explain that encouraging client-initiated goals gives clients "a voice in determining the course of their lives" (Berg 1994:61). It also helps to build solution-oriented self-fulfilling prophecies by providing clients with an initial success that they and their therapists might use to build expectations of change.

Defining therapy goals, in other words, can be the first step in constructing progressive stories about clients' lives. Indeed, solution-focused brief therapists provide their readers and workshop members with narrative guidelines for constructing progressive stories. Three of the most frequently mentioned are

- The goal must be stated as the presence of something rather than the absence of something (ibid., 73).

- The goal must be described as a beginning of a new behavior, not an end of undesirable behavior (ibid., 76).
- The goal must be viewed as taking a lot of "hard work" by the client (ibid., 77).

These guidelines express some of the most significant solution-focused assumptions about change-oriented stories. First, each of them assumes that change involves striving for something new; this is, after all, what makes clients' new stories progressive. Solution-focused brief therapists further argue that constructing new lives for clients should appear to require great effort by clients, and that their efforts should be honored by both the clients and therapists. Central to this assumption is the solution-focused emphasis on hope as an elemental component of change. Solution-focused brief therapists explain that emphasizing the hard work of change implicitly acknowledges the many frustrations that clients have already encountered in trying to deal with their troubles. If change were easy, clients wouldn't be asking for the therapists' help. Emphasizing hard work is also a way of blaming clients' problems on the problems, and not on the clients. Berg explains:

> When you emphasize how difficult it is to solve the particular "problem" the client has, you are "blaming" the problem, not the client's lack of intelligence. When you are on the side of the client looking at the "problem" together it seems awesome to handle. This approach not only enhances the team spirit but also acts as a "face saving" device. That is, it is not the client's shortcoming but the enormity and stubbornness of the problem that is the challenge. (ibid., 78)

A related solution-focused assumption is that progressive stories should not emphasize how change involves giving up something. There is a sense in which solution-focused brief therapists treat the absence of troublesome behavior and trouble-related concerns as creating a void in clients' lives. Change will not be sustained if the void is not filled with something new. Solution-focused brief therapists explain that stories that only emphasize giving up troublesome behaviors actually direct clients' attention to that which they are supposed to avoid. Clients' troubles are, once again, the focal point of their lives, which are now defined as resisting temptation. One practical effect of this focus, solution-focused therapists explain, is that clients are more likely to "give in" to their troublesome desires, habits, or urges.

Solution-focused brief therapists are taught that therapists should never take something from their clients (such as their troublesome behavior or reasons for the behavior) without replacing it with something new. Telling a problem drinker that there are no good reasons for binging or an unhappy couple to just stop fighting leaves them with no direction for the future. They have no goals to work toward and no basis for developing hopeful, progressive stories. This advice may cast the problem drinker as making excuses and the unhappy couple as unable or unwilling to control their hostile emotions. It may also be taken by clients as suggesting that their problems are easily solved. Clients are further demeaned by their inability to solve their problems on their own.

Solution-Focused Questions

The questions asked of clients by solution-focused brief therapists are designed to get at the surface of clients' problems, and to misread clients' lives as progressive stories. These stories emphasize how the solutions to clients' stories are already present in their lives. What is gained, solution-focused therapists ask, by asking questions that inevitably complicate therapy and confuse both clients and therapists, when the solutions to clients' problems are already present at the surface of clients' lives? Berg, for example, describes a case involving a single mother who was having great difficulty managing her children. Officials of several local human service agencies had complained that she was contributing to her children's problems by being inconsistent with them and not holding them accountable to household rules. In the course of the therapy interview, the client stated that she worked as a supervisor, and that she was quite successful at it. Thus,

> The team decided to help her see herself as a supervisor of her children. Effective "supervision" of children requires basically the same skills and approaches as those involved in her job: being clear about expectations in concrete and behavioral terms, reinforcing positive behaviors, giving frequent and consistent feedback, and when appropriate, enforcing the natural consequences. The result was very positive. (1994:62)

Solution-focused brief therapists state that getting at the surface of clients' problems and restorying their lives are best achieved by emphasizing a few simple questions. I discuss these questions in the next four sections as "getting-by," exception, scaling, and miracle questions.

"Getting-By" Questions

"Getting-by" questions focus on the ways in which clients are already managing their problems and how they might build on present successes in the future. These questions are useful to solution-focused brief therapists because they report that roughly two-thirds of their clients have already begun solving their problems prior to their first sessions with therapists (Berg 1994; Weiner-Davis 1993). Thus, asking about presession changes is a way of speeding up the therapy process by focusing the conversation on changes that are already working. It is also a way of helping clients redefine themselves as problem-solvers (Dolan 1991). Further, clients' descriptions of their recent successes make lengthy discussions about goals unnecessary. The goals are provided ready-made in clients' descriptions of presession changes, and provide therapists and clients with tested strategies for solving clients' problems.

Positive answers to questions about presession changes also give solution-focused brief therapists a chance to compliment clients, and a chance to ask clients how they accomplished their successes (George et al. 1990). The latter queries—which might be termed "How did you do that?" questions—emphasize how clients already possess the personal and social resources needed to solve their problems and competently manage their lives. The questions are one way in which solution-focused therapists assign responsibility for clients' successes to clients. It is difficult for clients to deny that they are responsible since they have already said that their lives are getting better. "How did you do that?" questions are similar to "Do more" questions, which solution-focused therapists use to focus interviews away from past client successes and toward better future lives for clients (Berg 1994; Berg and Miller 1992). "Do more" questions ask clients how they plan to do more of whatever is working for them. These questions assign responsibility to clients for solving their problems, and assume that clients possess whatever resources are needed to solve their problems. In other words, these questions assume that there are many effective ways of solving problems.

Solution-focused brief therapists pursue the same goals in dealing with clients who complain that their lives are filled with troubles by asking "coping" questions (Berg 1994). These responses involve two parts. First, the therapists agree with their clients' descriptions of their lives as deeply troubled, and then they ask how the clients are able to manage under such difficult conditions. Solution-focused therapists use coping questions as alternatives to the "pep talks" frequently given to clients by well-meaning family and friends, but that solution-focused therapists describe as counterproductive (Berg and Miller 1992; Weiner-Davis 1993). Pep talks don't work, solution-focused therapists state, because they demean clients' realities by arguing that clients' lives aren't as bad as clients say. Solution-focused therapists' coping questions, on the other hand, acknowledge the seriousness of clients' troubles, but also assume that clients possess the personal resources needed to deal with them. These questions are also useful to solution-focused therapists because they may elicit information from clients that justify asking "Do more" questions.

Questions about Exceptions

One way in which the beginnings of solutions are present in clients' lives is as variations from the problem patterns reported by clients (de Shazer 1991; Cade and O'Hanlon 1993; O'Hanlon and Weiner-Davis 1989; Weiner-Davis 1993). Thus, a major emphasis in solution-focused brief therapy is on identifying when problems are absent from clients' lives or less troublesome to clients (de Jong and Berg 1996; George et al. 1990). Dolan discusses this questioning strategy as "following the client's easiest path" (1991:166). Such questions take for granted that clients' lives are not always the same and that change is an ever-present aspect of everyday life (Berg and Miller 1992; Berg 1994; de Shazer 1994). Solution-focused brief therapists state, for example, that no one abuses drugs every minute of every day of their lives. Thus, focusing attention on the times when troublesome patterns do not exist or are less troublesome can be helpful in reframing clients' understandings of their circumstances and options in managing their troubles. It is also a useful procedure for constructing goals toward which clients and therapists might work. The goals involve increasing the number of exceptions in clients' lives until clients no longer view them as exceptions.

There is a sense in which solution-focused therapists' interest in exceptions is similar to ecosystemic therapists' interest in change. Once clients report on either circumstance, the therapists redirect interviews, asking about the details associated with the changes or exceptions, and how clients might build on them. A major difference between them, however, is many clients' greater ability to describe exceptions. Thus, a shift to the language of exceptions fits with solution-focused brief therapists' concern for quickly, efficiently, and simply moving away from talk of clients' complaints and toward talk of goals and solutions. Walter and Peller (1992:95–96) provide the following example of how exception talk can be elicited with a client who hears voices:

Therapist: So I am a little confused. How are these voices a problem for you? . . .

Client: Well, these voices tell me that people are after me and that I'd better be careful.

Therapist: That could be good advice in some cases. So how are they a problem? . . .

Client:	Well, people at my residence hall are telling me that I am acting pretty weird and paranoid.
Therapist:	Oh, so the problem is that you act differently and then people treat you differently? . . .
Client:	Yeah, they are getting real suspicious of me.
Therapist:	So, are there times when you do not listen to the voices or you do not act that way? . . .
Client:	Well, the voices are there all the time.
Therapist:	So, do you listen to them all the time? . . .
Client:	No, not all the time. Sometimes, I am just too busy or I trust my own opinion rather than the voices.
Therapist:	So, sometimes you trust your own opinion and you act differently. Those times go more the way you like? . . .
Client:	Yes
Therapist:	How do you do that? . . .

This exchange illustrates how solution-focused therapists use questions about exceptions in combination with other solution-focused strategies and techniques. The interaction begins with the therapist expressing "deconstructive confusion" ("How are these voices a problem for you?") and offering a normalizing response to the clients' statement that the voices tell him to be careful because other people are after him ("That would be good advice in some cases"). The therapist uses this conversational line until the client offers the beginning of a problem (others in his residence hall are telling him that he is paranoid). The therapist responds to the client's answer by moving to questions about exceptions (asking about the times when the client does not hear the voices and when he doesn't listen to them). Once the client notes that exceptions do occur, the therapist asks a "How do you do that?" question.

Scaling Questions

While it is not a brand new development in brief therapy, solution-focused brief therapy is distinctive in its emphasis on scaling questions (Berg and Miller 1992; Berg 1994; Cade and O'Hanlon 1993). These questions ask clients to rank aspects of their lives on ten-point scales. A therapist might ask, for example, "On a scale of zero to ten, with zero being the worst things have ever been and ten being when everything is better, where are you today?" Scaling questions may be asked in a number of different ways and for different purposes, such as to elicit comparative information about clients' perceptions and relationships. This involves asking all the members of the same client group the same scaling question, or asking the same question of a client (or clients) across several sessions. The first approach is useful in eliciting several different stories about clients' problems and relationships. Solution-focused therapists ask the latter type of scaling question in encouraging their clients to reorient to their lives as progressive stories (de Shazer 1994).

Scaling questions have several advantages for solution-focused brief therapists. First, they concretize clients' troubles, and make it possible to gauge whether clients believe they are getting better or worse (Walter and Peller 1992). Scaling questions are also helpful in constructing exceptions. When clients rate other times of their lives as less troublesome, for example, the rating provides a justification for therapists to ask about the details of the previous times (O'Hanlon and Weiner-Davis 1989). Other times, solution-focused therapists use scaling questions to focus therapists' and clients' attention on future solutions and to construct concrete signs of future change. A scaling question frequently asked by solution-focused therapists, for example, is, "So what will you [or other people] notice about you when you have reached [a higher number on the scale]?" Dolan (1991) describes how she uses scaling questions in helping survivors of sexual abuse identify signs of safety and danger in their lives. She states that identifying these signs gives clients a greater sense of control in their lives.

Each of these uses of scaling questions is related to the general emphasis in solution-focused brief therapy on encouraging clients to determine how their lives should change. As Berg and Miller state,

> The more the client repeats what she wants during the conversation, the more convinced the client is that these goals are exactly what *she* wants for herself. This increases her motivation and her confidence that the change is something she can carry out and maintain. (1992:85)

For solution-focused brief therapists then, problems, solutions, and the motivation to solve them are interactional accomplishments that are achieved within therapeutic conversations. A major step in this process is constructing miracles in clients' lives.

The Miracle Question

The miracle question is the most obviously future-oriented question asked by solution-focused brief therapists because it asks clients to imagine that their lives have changed in desired directions and to describe how they will know that their lives have changed (Berg and Miller 1992; Berg 1994; Cade and O'Hanlon 1993; de Jong and Berg 1996). The question can be asked in several different ways. Some solution-focused brief therapists cast the miracle as something that just happens (such as while clients are sleeping), and others cast it as a therapeutic accomplishment. O'Hanlon, for example, sometimes asks his clients, "If I pulled out a magic wand and were able to perform magic on your situation, what will be happening that is different from before?" (O'Hanlon and Weiner-Davis 1989:106).

The miracle question is deceptively simple. On the surface, it is answerable by any client, but answering it requires that clients consider possibilities that they are unlikely to have thought about in some time. It is difficult to think about miracles when you are focused on your troubles. It also asks clients to think about what they want added to their lives, not just what they would like to see eliminated. This, too, is an issue that many clients stop thinking about when they become problem-focused. Thus, one way in which solution-focused therapists use the miracle question is to elicit concrete goal statements from clients about their hopes for the future and for therapy. Dolan (1991:34) states, for example, that

> one survivor of sexual abuse responded to the miracle question by saying "I'd be spending more time with my husband and daughter, I'd be taking good care of my body instead of overeating all the time and I wouldn't be thinking about the past all the time. I'd be thinking about my life *now*. I'd really believe that what happened wasn't my fault."

Dolan further explains that once clients have specified concrete goals, solution-focused brief therapists might ask about the times when clients are achieving their goals. Clients' answers to the latter question might open opportunities for therapists to ask "How did you do that?" and/or "Do more" questions. In this way, solution-focused therapists and clients begin to construct progressive stories of clients' lives.

But the miracle question involves more than this. Its development was a signal event in speeding the radical turn in solution-focused therapy. The question makes it possible for clients and therapists to separate problems from solutions (de Shazer 1991, 1994). Problem definition becomes superfluous once clients have specified the details of their miracles. The relevant task at hand is figuring out how the miracle might be made to happen, or—as solution-focused brief therapists prefer—figuring out how the miracle is already evident in clients' lives. Thus, Northland Clinic staff members encourage their colleagues to ask the miracle question early in therapy sessions. They explain that when clients respond with workable miracles, it is not necessary for therapists to ask about clients' problems.

Solution-Focused Interventions

A major change accompanying the shift from ecosystemic to solution-focused brief therapy is therapists' orientations to therapy interviews as sites for constructing solutions. The solution-focused questions discussed above are designed to facilitate this shift. Extended discussions about clients' social systems become unnecessary when the solution to clients' problems involves constructing new stories about their lives. Clients' social systems are relevant only to the extent that they are aspects of clients' stories. Extended discussions of clients' social systems are also unnecessary when clients respond with detailed information about how they are getting by, about exceptions to troublesome patterns, and about how their lives might be miraculously changed.

Solution-focused brief therapists' stress on defining and solving troubles in interviews greatly reduces the importance of intervention messages for creating change. When the process works as planned, the solutions to clients' problems have already been identified well before solution-focused therapists' meetings with their teams. Nevertheless, solution-focused therapists continue to take breaks for team meetings and to devise intervention messages. They may even use intervention strategies associated with ecosystemic brief therapy from time to time, although for somewhat different reasons (Berg and Miller 1992; de Jong and Berg 1996). Solution-focused brief therapists also sometimes ask clients to pretend that a miracle has happened and to observe what happens that is different in their lives (Berg 1994). Most of the time, however, solution-focused therapists' intervention messages highlight and affirm positive developments in interviews, such as clients' discussions of exceptions and how they might do more to increase the exceptions (George et al. 1990). The solution-focused intervention message is, in other words, constructed to fit with therapists' and clients' ongoing conversations.

We consider how the Northland Clinic staff and their clients entered into and operated within the discourse of ecosystemic brief therapy in the next four chapters. The chapters emphasize the artful ways in which ecosystemic brief therapists, clients, and team members relate to one another and achieve their practical ends within different aspects of the ecosystemic brief therapy process.

PART II

WORKINGS OF BRIEF THERAPY

CHAPTER 5

CONSTRUCTING ECOSYSTEMIC PROBLEMS

This chapter considers the first encounters between therapists at Northland Clinic and their clients. The interviews involve putting into practice the philosophy of ecosystemic brief therapy and its various techniques and strategies. Thus, the interactions are concerned with the details of each client's or client group's circumstances and how the therapists and team members might respond to them. Ecosystemic brief therapists' and team members' focus is on fitting with clients, which involves assessing the significance of clients' statements and demeanor in therapy sessions as well as identifying general ecosystemic principles that apply (or might be modified to apply) to the clients' circumstances.

First sessions also involve interactional contingencies that, to some extent, cannot be anticipated by therapists and clients. They include clients' orientations to the typical organization of ecosystemic brief therapy sessions, relations between members of client groups in the sessions, the composition of therapy teams and their involvement in the sessions, and the possible influences of absent parties on sessions. The latter contingency is most relevant to sessions in which clients are referred to the clinic by outside organizations. The referrals are sometimes involuntary and have practical consequences for clients, such as court requirements that parents found to be neglectful participate in therapy in order to regain custody of their children.

Ecosystemic Interviews

Ecosystemic brief therapy interviews involve several parties who share a practical concern for remedying the problems at hand, but their related interests and understandings are often very different. One difference involves the languages (both vocabularies and assumptions) preferred by therapists and clients in describing clients' troubles and how they might be remedied. Ecosystemic therapists' distinction between complaints and problems is one way of conceptualizing this difference. For the therapists, only one of them (the problems language and orientation) leads to effective remedies to clients' troubles. Clients, on the other hand, sometimes assume or prefer otherwise. A critical aspect of first interviews in ecosystemic brief therapy, then, involves therapists' and clients' entrance into a problems language within which they might construct mutually agreeable trouble definitions and remedial strategies.

While clients are active participants in these negotiations, the therapists' role and actions are critical. Ecosystemic brief therapy interviews are organized as question-answer exchanges within which therapists usually ask the questions and others answer them. Dingwall (1980) characterizes this interactional arrangement as *orchestrated encounters,* meaning that the interaction turns on the central role of one party. Ecosystemic brief therapists' orchestration of interviews involves virtually all aspects of the interactions, beginning with the introductory comments at the opening of sessions with new clients to announcing when the team meetings will take place. The therapists use their questions to move from one topic to another and to specify who should speak in response to them. They also use their central role in the interactions to gloss over undesired comments by clients.

We first consider how ecosystemic therapists and clients enter the discourse of ecosystemic brief therapy. Later sections discuss how therapists and clients construct definitions of and contexts for clients' troubles, and open possibilities for positive changes in clients' lives. It bears emphasizing, however, that while I discuss these moves as discrete aspects of ecosystemic interviews, they are very much interconnected within ongoing interviews. There is no single, rigid format for conducting the interviews. Rather, troubles contexts, definitions, and remedies are recurring and shifting topics in the interviews. Therapists and clients may discuss one issue, shift to another, only to return to the first, and move on to yet another over the course of any particular interview. While all of the ecosystemic interviews that I observed involved the moves discussed here, each interview was a unique event involving its own arrangement of interviewing practices.

The orchestration metaphor, then, is an apt characterization of the ecosystemic brief therapy interviews conducted at Northland Clinic. Like orchestra leaders, the therapists conduct the sessions. They use the same basic format in most interviews, but they still must take account of and adjust to their clients, who bring different interests and abilities to the interviews as well as other contingencies that might emerge during the course of their interviews. Just as orchestra conductors depend on others to help them make music, so ecosystemic therapists depend on (and must adjust to) their clients if therapy is to be successful.

Opening Moves

There is a sense in which ecosystemic brief therapy interviews start when Northland Clinic therapists go to the waiting area to invite clients to join them in an interviewing room. The therapists usually introduce themselves at this time. If not, they do so shortly after being seated in the interviewing room. Therapists might also discuss insurance or related matters at this time. They also make certain that clients understand that they are being observed by a team with whom the therapist will consult later in the session and that the session is being videotaped. Occasionally, clients ask that their sessions not be taped. In every session that I observed at Northland Clinic, the therapists complied with clients' requests to not record their sessions. Clients sometimes have questions of their own, usually about the therapy process or how referring agencies are to be informed of the sessions.

At this point, Northland Clinic therapists usually ask clients about themselves. Often the therapists' questions focus on clients' occupations or school experiences, asking how long they have been at their jobs, if they like the jobs, what grade they are in in school, and what subjects they like the best. The therapists also often ask new clients about their families, such as how many people are in the household, their ages, and interests. Ecosystemic brief therapists describe these questions as aspects of "joining" with clients. The questions show clients that their therapists are concerned about their lives, and can be trusted to work with clients to solve whatever problems they might have. The following exchange is an example of how first sessions usually begin. Please note that I designate pauses with [. . .] in this and subsequent interactional exchanges.

Therapist:	You know this is a one-way mirror and I have some staff behind the mirror, my team.
Client:	Uh, huh.
Therapist:	And they listen to what we are saying and then they phone and ask a question. All right, if they want to?
Client:	So, who runs the session?
Therapist:	Oh, I do [. . .] And um in about forty-five minutes I'll go and consult with them. And then I'll come back and tell you what we're all thinking.

Client: OK.
Therapist: So, let me see, and you work at . . .

While therapists' and clients' introductory or joining remarks sometimes take as long as ten minutes, entrance into the ecosystemic brief therapy discourse usually occurs when the therapists ask clients about their reasons for coming to therapy. The question might be asked in a variety of ways, as in the following examples:

- [After discussing the client's complaints about his work situation, the therapist states,] OK. All right [. . .] Anything else? Um, OK, um, what, uh, what can we help you with this morning?
- [After discussing the father's occupation, and how he includes the family on his trips out of town, the therapist states,] So, what brings you here?
- [After describing how the therapy process works, the therapist states,] OK, so now it's back in your court, and you can tell us what problem we can help you with.

I observed two exceptions to this pattern at Northland Clinic. Both involved clients who initiated the shift to talk of clients' troubles. In one case, the client had been to the clinic several years earlier and came prepared with a written statement about his concerns, when and how his life was troubled, and what he wished to get from therapy. The client shifted the interaction toward his troubles by removing the statement from his pocket and reading it to his therapist—the same therapist who had worked with him previously. The client's statement both initiated a shift toward talk of troubles and anticipated many of the questions that the therapist would have normally asked later in the interview. The other atypical shift occurred when the client responded to her therapist's usual opening questions by stating, "OK, here's the situation," and then described the reasons why she had requested the therapy session.

However it is raised, movement to the reasons why clients have come to therapy refocuses interviews on "troubled" aspects of clients' lives. These questions might be interpreted as requests that clients justify their presence at the clinic by providing the therapists with problems on which they and the clients might work. Thus, I refer to them as *problem questions* in the rest of the chapter. While clients often speak of troublesome aspects of their lives during the "joining" period prior to the therapists' problem questions, clients do not always mention these troubles as matters that they wish to pursue with their therapists.

The question of why clients are in therapy, then, is a significant move within ecosystemic brief therapy interviews because most clients treat it as a signal that the therapists now wish to discuss "serious" troubles. The question also initiates a shift in the therapist-client relationship, moving it from friendly interchanges to a working relationship focused on defining and solving problems. The shift is often accompanied by a change in clients' demeanor, such as adjustments in their gaze, facial expressions, and posture. Each of these responses is also part of therapists' and others' entrance into the discourse of ecosystemic problems and solutions.

While entrance into this discourse is initiated by therapists' questions, how they move into and work within it is contingent on clients' responses. Ecosystemic brief therapists orchestrate—but do not determine—the therapy process. Indeed, the route into the therapists' preferred discourse is sometimes circuitous, involving various twists and turns.

Client Responses

Clients respond to questions about their reasons for coming to therapy in a variety of ways. A few describe ecosystemic problems without hesitation and with minimal context. More typical, however, are somewhat halting client replies that include pauses prior to beginning to answer the question and within the answers. Some clients reply with several answers, the latter being elaborations and/or correctives of prior ones. The following interaction illustrates this pattern:

Therapist: So, what prompted you to come here, you know?
Client: Well, everyone's been telling me to go and get counseling.
Therapist: For what?
Client: Well, I guess because my husband left me.
Therapist: To help you adjust?
Client: I guess.
Therapist: To his being gone?
Client: Yeah, but now, since he told me the truth and because of the way he's been acting, the major reason I'm here is to try to figure out how to handle my kids . . .

This exchange is typical of many (perhaps most) clients' reluctance to "jump into" discussions of their troubles. These are sensitive issues, and clients express their sensitivity in their responses to the therapists' opening questions. In this interaction, the client's orientation to her troubles is expressed through the evolution of her answers, beginning with the claim that she has come to therapy because others have told her to get counseling and ending with an expression of concern for her children. Also, notice how the client hedges her responses to the therapist's questions by beginning them with "Well," and suggesting that she can only guess about why others have advised her to seek counseling.

Other clients respond to ecosystemic brief therapists' problem questions with historical accounts of how they have come to see their lives as troubled, constructing troubled biographies in the process. For example, one client replied to her therapist's request for a problem by stating, "I'm thinking that I don't want to stay in this marriage anymore." She then described how she had arrived at this conclusion while participating in therapy concerned with her child's problems in school. The client explained that in the course of the prior counseling, she realized that her child's problems were related to long-standing tensions in her relationship with her husband:

> Client: In fact, I would say from the beginning it's been a troubled relationship, and it's worked. [. . .] It's worked for a long time, in many ways, but it doesn't work so much for me anymore.
> Therapist: Uh, huh.
> Client: I don't think it's going to, I don't think it's going to work anymore. I put up with a lot for a long time, 'cause I thought I could change things.
> Therapist: Uh, huh.
> Client: Ignoring stuff, I thought I could change it.
> Therapist: Uh, huh.
> Client: But I'm not sure I want to.

This exchange illustrates how some clients respond to therapists' questions by offering the beginnings of what ecosystemic brief therapists classify as problems. In this case, the client offers the problem of deciding whether to divorce her husband, and initiates discussion of it by offering a history of how she has come to see divorce as a viable possibility. She states that "from the beginning it's been a troubled relationship," and that she has lost her desire to change the relationship. Notice also that the Northland Clinic therapist offers minimal responses ("Uh, huh") to the client, once she identifies and starts to describe a problem. The client treats the responses as invitations to continue to talk.

Not all client responses to therapists' initial queries are so focused, however. Frequently, clients respond with what ecosystemic brief therapists regard as complaints. Usually, these are statements that do not obviously point to therapeutic solutions because they are extremely vague and/or are extended histories of events that do not define a problem on which clients wish to work. For example, one client responded to a Northland Clinic therapist's invitation for a problem by stating that he and his wife had "a hard time communicating." Ecosystemic therapists respond to such statements by asking clients to explain themselves. They usually ask for concrete examples of the troublesome circumstances, thereby maintaining their focus on eliciting problem statements from clients and beginning to map clients' troubles. In this case, for example, the therapist asked, "The two of you do, OK, what form does that take, how, what's that like or what happens here?"

Ecosystemic brief therapists employ a similar strategy in responding to client histories that do not suggest problems. The strategy sometimes produces immediate problem statements from clients—as in the above example—and other times initiates more extended interactions. The latter interactions often eventuate in the specification of problems, but not always. Sometimes clients continue to focus on what the therapists classify as complaints, as well as sometimes asking for assistance that the therapists are unwilling to give. Consider, for example, the case of a married couple who came to Northland Clinic seeking help in dealing with their daughter, granddaughter, son-in-law, and ex–son-in-law.

The clients first responded to their therapist's question about why they had come to therapy by describing the history of their relationship with their daughter, who divorced the father of their grandchild and later married another man. They emphasized how they had remained friends with their ex–son-in-law since the divorce, but that their relationship with their daughter had greatly deteriorated and that they did not approve of their new son-in-law. Between them, the two clients spent the first twenty to twenty-five minutes of the session detailing these events and how they negatively affected their relationship with their grandchild, with whom they wished to have a close and loving relationship.

At this point, the therapist offered a different version of the earlier question by asking the clients, "How do you see our working here together?" The clients replied that they were not sure what they wanted from therapy, but that they were interested in knowing what the therapist thought of their handling of the situation. Before the therapist could respond, however, the clients returned to their prior complaints, and then described their daughter as unassertive in her relationship with her husband. This line of talk eventually resulted in a conclusion by the clients that the person with the "real" problem was their daughter, and they asked how she might become more assertive in her relationship with her husband.

The therapist did not accept this as a problem, however. He rejected it by stating, "I don't see how I can help you with that at this point." The therapist did not elaborate on his position, nor did the clients ask for an explanation. Rather, the clients responded by shifting the interactional focus to their legal right as grandparents to spend time with their grandchild and to their great dislike for their new son-in-law. This discussion was interrupted by a call from the therapy team. The therapist restated the team's question, which the clients took as a proposal of a problem to be remedied. As the following negotiation shows, the clients quickly rejected the proposed problem:

Therapist: There seems to be a question in their [team members'] heads about how badly you want to exercise your constitutional rights, if you will, versus, you know, trying to fuse or change this situation somehow.

Client 1: It's a problem that we don't want to solve.

Client 2: I think that sums it up.

Client 1: Because we don't want to have anything to do with that guy [the son-in-law].

Eventually, one of the clients asked if their handling of their conflicts with their daughter and son-in-law might be hurting their grandchild. The therapist responded, "Yeah, it's a good question. I was going to ask you the same one." Roughly thirty-five minutes into the session then, we see the beginnings of a problem that both the clients and therapist express an interest in pursuing. It bears emphasizing, however, that a problem has not been specified, only that the therapist and clients have agreed that the question of how the grandchild might be hurt by the conflict was a good one. The clients then spent the rest of this phase of the session—about ten minutes—discussing the question, but also elaborating on their prior complaints about their daughter and son-in-law.

In sum, while entrance into the therapeutically preferred language of problems is a critical step in ecosystemic brief therapy, when and how this shift occurs is greatly dependent on clients' understandings of and responses to therapists' questions. The above session is typical of how Northland Clinic therapists usually respond to clients who prefer to talk of complaints. The therapists allow the clients to speak at length of their concerns, occasionally asking questions and offering suggestions that focus the interactions on problems. When clients ignore or reject the proposed problems, the therapists pursue other possibilities. The above session also shows that when clients offer possible problems on which the therapists are willing to work, the therapists quickly focus their questions on the proposed problems. The new focus includes questions for mapping the dimensions and contexts of clients' problems.

Mapping Clients' Problems

Problems may be located within a variety of social contexts in ecosystemic brief therapy, including clients' family systems, social relations at work or school, and involvements with neighbors and friends. Indeed, eco-systemic brief therapists and clients sometimes construct complex troubles contexts that include aspects of one or more of these social systems. The therapists defer to clients' preferred contextualizations of their troubles by first allowing clients to describe their concerns and then questioning them about the concerns. Later in the interviews, the therapists sometimes ask about other aspects of clients' lives, thereby extending or even reformulating the social systems within which clients' troubles might be understood.

In mapping clients' problems and social systems, ecosystemic brief thera-pists and clients become increasingly enmeshed in the language of prob-lems. Central to the process are questions about the behavioral and interpretive sequences associated with clients' problems. Ecosystemic thera-pists treat clients' descriptions of these sequences as useful information about clients' problems and social systems, and use the information in de-veloping responses to clients' problems. The responses are designed to fit with clients' perspectives and circumstances and to interrupt the trouble-some patterns described by clients. Ecosystemic therapists also use mapping questions to encourage clients to orient to their troubles as concrete and changeable circumstances.

Depending on clients' responses to therapists' initial questions about their reasons for coming to therapy, the mapping process might begin very early in ecosystemic brief therapy interviews. Consider, for example, the follow-ing exchange, which includes a father and his three children (Sarah, David, and Jim). It is partly distinctive because the father offers the beginnings of a problem in his initial response to the therapist's question. The interaction is typical of how clients' troubles are initially contextualized in ecosystemic brief therapy interviews at Northland Clinic:

Therapist:	OK, so how can I help? [. . .]
Father:	Well, we have some problems, we [. . .] seem, like between them [the children] a lot of times, they don't like to mind and they [. . .] are given instructions, they question everything we tell them [. . .] and . . .
Therapist:	All of them or one of them or . . .
Father:	Uh, some more than others.
Therapist:	Some more than others, OK [. . .]
Father:	And there seems to be an awful lot of anger at times. [. . .] And, . . .
Therapist:	How can you tell this anger?
Father:	Shouting, um crying [. . .] tantrums.
Sarah:	When do we cry? [. . .]
David:	All the time, Sarah.
Sarah:	I never cry.

Therapist: Are they angry at each other or at [. . .]
  Father: I really don't know what they get angry at other than their
           parents.
Therapist: At their parents [. . .]
     Jim: And each other too.
Therapist: And each other too.
    Sarah: Yeah, as much so [. . .]
Therapist: Anything else?
  Father: Well, it's gotten to the point where [. . .], we as parents find
           ourselves being kind of unhappy. [. . .] Uh, [. . .] we're
           having a hard time coping with it. [. . .] I was brought up on
           a farm and [. . .] we, as kids, always showed a lot of respect
           to our parents and [. . .] and it doesn't seem like my wife
           and myself get the same kind of respect. [. . .] That bothers
           me. [. . .] And the anger bothers me too [. . .]

This negotiation is interesting for several reasons. First, notice that the
father's specification of the problem involves constructing a social context.
His response casts the problem as a family trouble involving parental author-
ity, the children "don't like to mind," and "they question everything we tell
them." The therapist follows the father's lead by asking about the details of
his complaint, to which he responds by further specifying its dimensions.
That is, the problem involves some of the children "more than others," "a lot
of anger," and has produced unhappiness and coping problems for the
parents. The therapist continues to ask for details (such as "How can you tell
this anger?") to which the father replies, "Shouting, um crying [. . .] tantrums." The father's last statement specifies yet another dimension of the
problem: that his children's attitude is partly troublesome because it is so
different than the more respectful attitude that he and his wife showed their
parents when they were children.

    In the first few minutes of this interview the therapist is provided with
information for beginning to map the children's "troublesome" behavior and
the father's usual way of interpreting the behavior. The problem at hand is
no longer any sort of family problem, but one that is embedded in a distinctive family system. Finally, notice how the therapist orchestrates the interview by focusing on the father even though other family members question
and comment on his statements. Later in the interview, the therapist invites
other family members to voice their perspectives on these issues, thus providing family members with an opportunity to construct a more complex
social context for their problems. But the invitation was not open-ended:
rather the therapist asked other family members to respond to the details
provided by the father at the outset of the interview.

    Ecosystemic brief therapists do not always need a problem prior to asking
mapping questions, however. They often use mapping questions in order to

move interviews toward problems. In these interactions, clients' problems are defined as clients specify the social contexts of their troubles. This might be characterized as an indirect strategy for constructing problems, because clients provide the needed information in response to various therapist moves, not just in response to questions. Consider, for example, the following exchange, which followed the therapist's question about why a married couple (Marie and Art) have come to therapy:

Marie: Well [. . .], we have two children at home.
Therapist: Uh, huh.
Marie: A girl and a boy [. . .]
Therapist: Right.
Marie: And now, [. . .] I have been taking him [the son] in to a psychologist for two years [. . .] and he doesn't seem to be that much better, and they have recommended that we all come as a family for therapy.
Therapist: Uh, huh. [. . .] And what do you think about that?
Marie: Well, I like it. He [indicating Art] doesn't care for it.
Therapist: Uh, huh. OK. [. . .] And you're saying the boy's been visiting therapy of some sort?
Marie: Uh, huh at Cedarview.
Therapist: Uh, huh. [. . .] [Turns to Art] Do you agree, she said that it didn't seem to do him much good? Do you agree?
Art: Right [. . .]
Therapist: OK [. . .] Well, what sorts of things does this, uh [gestures to the clients]?
Marie: Well, now I only had a meeting at school again today.
Therapist: Uh, huh.
Marie: And they're gonna fail him . . .

Here the therapist offers minimal responses to Marie's opening remarks about the children at home, finally asking a question when she gives a reason for coming to therapy ("And what do you think about that?"). Within the discourse of ecosystemic brief therapy, this is a detective question. Such questions are used to elicit information about the clients' perspectives, and might be elaborated to construct systemic contexts by asking about others' perspectives. Indeed, Marie offers a beginning for such an elaboration by contrasting her attitude toward coming to therapy with Art's. The therapist then shifts the interactional focus by first asking about their son's involvement in therapy, and then asking Art to give his opinion on the therapy. In this way, the therapist includes both parents in the interaction, and further develops the construction of a family system for the clients' problem.

Notice, however, that the clients do not offer a problem on which they would like to work with the therapist. Nor does the therapist insist that the clients give him a problem. Rather, Marie starts to specify a problem in response to the therapist's question of "Well, what sorts of things does this, uh?" and the therapist's wave of his hand. Marie treats the therapist's statement and gesture as an invitation to speak of her son's difficulties in school, although it might have been interpreted in a variety of ways. The full specification of a problem took most of the session.

In sum, mapping questions are pervasive in ecosystemic brief interviews. They are partly ways of obtaining details about clients' lives and perspectives that might be useful in solving their problems, including developing strategies for interrupting troublesome interpretive and/or behavioral patterns. But they might also be seen as rhetorical moves designed to persuade clients to orient to and describe their lives and troubles in therapeutically preferred ways. Indeed, this shift in clients' discourse might be seen—from the ecosystemic perspective at least—as therapeutic in itself. It provides them with a new standpoint for interpreting their lives and troubles, one that allows them to speak of problems, not complaints.

Three aspects of mapping clients' troubles in ecosystemic brief therapy merit special discussion. They involve the therapists' interest in clients' prior efforts to solve their problems, use of systemic questions to contextualize the problems, and use of constructive questions to focus on the future. I discuss them in turn in the next three sections.

Mapping Remedies

Ecosystemic brief therapists display two general interests in questioning clients about their attempts to solve their problems. One interest involves identifying how clients have previously thought about and responded to their problems. The information is helpful in mapping clients' troubles and eliminating from further consideration remedies that have already proven to be ineffective. The pragmatic focus of ecosystemic brief therapy stresses that doing something different is always preferable to continuing to respond to problems in ways that have proven to be ineffective. Indeed, these therapists state that a major reason that problems persist is because we continue to respond to them in the same ineffective ways.

Ecosystemic brief therapists' questioning of clients about their prior efforts to solve their problems might be seen as an indirect way of discrediting failed remedies, and suggesting to clients that they need to think about their problems in new ways. They are techniques for getting clients "unstuck" from troubled patterns. But these therapists are not always so subtle or indirect as this. They sometimes offer their own evaluations of clients' prior

efforts to solve their problems, and encourage clients to abandon therapeutically dispreferred remedies that clients report as working. The following excerpt taken from the interview with Marie and Art about their
misbehaving son illustrates this aspect of ecosystemic brief interviews. The
interaction begins after Marie describes the various ways in which school
officials have tried to modify her son's behavior:

Therapist: Doesn't seem to do much good, huh?
Marie: Huh, Nothing. We have taken his television set away, his
stereo away, his privileges away. He won't even work to get
them back. [. . .] Now we had a long talk the other night
and my husband said "Now this has to, to end [. . .], you
cannot be getting these detentions." And one of them was for
mimicking a teacher. Now, this is completely uncalled for,
lack of respect. [. . .] And the next day he had a detention.
And I said [. . .]
Therapist: What did you do with him? [. . .]
Art: Give him a couple of cracks across the ass.
Therapist: Uh, huh. OK, does that help? [. . .]
Art: He hasn't got any detention since then, now.
Therapist: OK.
Art: He'll get that way for a week or so.
Therapist: OK. But you obviously don't like to do that.
Art: No.
Therapist: No [. . .]
Art: Helped for a week.
Therapist: Well maybe [. . .], maybe we need to find something that
works a little bit better than that, I guess. OK?
Marie: I think we've tried everything.

Notice that while the therapist clearly evaluates the remedies described
by the clients, he does not tell them how their problems should be solved.
Rather, he comments on the remedies by asking questions that simultaneously evaluate the remedies and invite clients to agree with his assessments. This is evident in the therapist's first ("Doesn't seem to do much
good, huh?") and last ("maybe we need to find something that works a little
bit better than that, I guess. OK?") statements. The therapist also softens (or
hedges) his negative evaluation in the last utterance by beginning with "Well
maybe [. . .] maybe." In between these statements, the therapist offers a
different, but still nondirective evaluation ("But you obviously don't like to
do that") to which the client agreed.
    Two other features of this negotiation also warrant mention. First, notice
how the therapist uses mapping questions in conjunction with his evaluations,

asking the clients to report on attempted remedies and their effectiveness. Evaluation and mapping are not always separate aspects of ecosystemic brief therapy interview. Second, the therapist frequently expresses acceptance of the clients' answers by stating "uh, huh" and "OK" early in his responses—once "OK" is his entire response. The therapist's only negative utterance—"no"—is actually a statement of agreement with the client's prior utterance, which was also "no." From the ecosystemic perspective, these responses also show clients that the therapist is cooperating with them.

The second, and more frequent, interest that ecosystemic brief therapists display in questioning clients about remedies is in identifying problem solutions that are already present in clients' lives. According to ecosystemic therapists, most clients are quite competent at managing their lives most of the time. When they become stuck on one or a few complaints, however, clients often lose their ability to recognize their competence and/or lose confidence in their problem-solving judgments. Mapping questions, then, offer the therapists opportunities to point out to clients how aspects of their lives actually contradict their claims to being helpless in dealing with their troubles. As in the following exchange, ecosystemic brief therapists' responses often focus on clients' most mundane competencies. The interaction is concerned with the client's inability to make career decisions:

Therapist: Well, where are you making decisions, in what areas in your life? [. . .]
Client: Uh, [. . .] none very well, I guess.
Therapist: Well, how did you get here tonight?
Client: Well, I can handle that decision. [. . .] But I'm just, uh, I don't know.
Therapist: You did make a decision to come in.
Client: I guess so.
Therapist: How did you get dressed?
Client: Huh?
Therapist: How did you get dressed today? [. . .]
Client: Same way I always do.
Therapist: You made a decision to wear those clothes?
Client: I guess.
Therapist: Nobody else told you that that's what you should wear? OK? So, in some areas you are still making decisions.
[The therapist asks about how the client is making decisions in other mundane areas of his life.]
Therapist: All those routine kinds of things, you're still making those decisions. [. . .] OK? What's different about making those kinds of decisions and making a decision about your career? [. . .]

Here the Northland Clinic therapist combines mapping questions with more directive statements asserting, "You did make a decision to come in" and "So, in some areas you are still making decisions." These statements and the therapist's questions that focus on the successful choices being made by the client are reframing devices. They are rhetorical moves used by the therapist to construct patterns of competent behavior and to argue for an alternative understanding of his life. The new understanding stresses the client's ability to make good choices. The reframing suggests that the client is not as stuck as he thought. Finally, the therapist highlights the purpose of her comments and questions by asking, "What's different about making those kinds of decisions and making a decision about your career?"

On other occasions, ecosystemic brief therapists are less direct—even paradoxical—in mapping clients' competencies and reframing their lives. An example is the following interaction, which follows the client's discussion of how she thinks she might help her children deal with the dissolution of her marriage. The exchange begins with the therapist's relaying a question called in by the therapy team:

Therapist: Well, you seem to have some pretty clear ideas, [. . .] simple ideas, what you think they ought to know and [. . .] what you think they hadn't ought to know. The team is wondering what you think is wrong with the ideas that you have? [. . .]

Client: Well, [. . .] it isn't that I think they are wrong. I'm just afraid of what repercussions there's going to be. Like I said, I'm afraid if I tell them Daddy doesn't love me, they are gonna blame me.

Therapist: Uh, huh.

Client: So I guess, uh.

Therapist: So, maybe, maybe you wouldn't want to say that.

The team's question might be understood in at least two ways. It might be heard as asking for information about the client's perspective. That is, information that could be used in identifying responses that fit with her perspective. The question might also be understood as an indirect way of saying, "Since you know what to do, why don't you just do it?" A client response based on either interpretation serves the therapist's and team's interests in the session. Also, notice that the client's response to the team's question ("if I tell them Daddy doesn't love me, they are gonna blame me") creates an opportunity for the therapist to evaluate this possibility without directly instructing her on how she should handle the matter. Again, the therapist hedges his response by beginning, "So, maybe, maybe," and then instructing her by stating "you wouldn't want to say that."

In sum, ecosystemic brief therapists use questions about remedies to elicit useful information about clients' lives and problems. And the questions are potential intervention strategies. If mutually agreeable responses to clients' troubles can be developed in the interviews, then the change process is greatly facilitated. The mapping questions that we have mostly considered to this point have asked about the behavioral patterns and the perspectives of individuals. We next consider how ecosystemic brief therapists use systemic questions to define, contextualize, and respond to clients' problems.

Mapping Clients' Social Systems

Ecosystemic brief therapists' interests in systemic questions are generally similar to their interests in mapping remedies. Clients' answers provide useful information about their lives and perspectives, and the questions are sometimes useful in refocusing clients' attention away from complaints and toward therapeutically preferred aspects of their lives. Systemic questions are distinctive, however, in their focus on clients' relationships with others. Thus, the questions might be seen as rhetorical moves for constructing social worlds within which clients' problems are embedded and within which possible solutions to the problems might be identified.

One type of systemic question asked by ecosystemic brief therapists focuses on troublesome patterns involving several different family or group members. For example, Northland Clinic therapists often ask family members which of them is most troublesome, or who is the most upset about the problem at hand. As the following interaction shows, clients' answers often provide information about their perspectives, including how they see their problems embedded in their ongoing social relationships. The exchange is part of the previously discussed interview with a father and his three "disrespectful" children. Prior to this excerpt, the children state that they are all sometimes crabby, but that Sarah is the crabbiest:

Therapist: So how come Sarah is the crabbiest? [. . .]
Jim: I know.
Therapist: Why?
Jim: She has a bad temper [. . .]
Therapist: She always has? [. . .]
Jim: Yes, pretty much, she takes after my dad [. . .]
Therapist: She does what?

Father: I have a bad temper too [. . .]
Therapist: So, everyone agrees that Sarah's the crabbiest?

Thus, in shifting his focus to other family members and how they are implicated in the problem, the therapist invites information for elaborating on the father's prior claim. The invitation is offered without the therapist knowing what information will be forthcoming. While not discrediting the father's earlier description of the problem, the exchange shows how problems are elaborated by others in response to systemic questions. It also shows how new therapeutic possibilities are created through such questioning. That is, this interaction opens the possibility of treating the problem as involving the father's and Sarah's bad tempers, not "disrespectful" children.

Ecosystemic therapists also use systemic questions to shift the tone and standpoint of the interviews. These systemic questions differ from those asked in the above exchange because they focus on system members' perspectives, not their behaviors. Therapists ask clients to take the standpoint of others in their social systems, and to describe the others' perspectives on the issues at hand. For example, a Northland Clinic therapist asked a client who was referred to therapy to deal with his troubled relationships with his mother, "What do you think your mother would say about repairing the relationship if she were sitting here?" The question shifted the focus of the interaction away from the client's concerns about his life and troubles, and toward his mother's concerns and desires, which the therapist treated as aspects of the client's family system.

In seminars conducted at Northland Clinic, participants are advised to ask systemic questions when clients persist in giving "inappropriate" answers to their individual questions, that is, client responses that do not address the therapists' interest in constructing solvable problems, such as those who state that they do not have a problem or who persist in offering complaints. Ecosystemic brief therapists state that in considering others' standpoints, clients are sometimes able to describe their lives and troubles in more concrete, coherent, hopeful, and/or detached ways. Even when clients do not respond with such answers, ecosystemic therapists stress that clients' answers are still useful because they often provide therapists with new information about clients' troubles and social systems.

Ecosystemic brief therapists also state that systemic questions make it possible for therapists to do family therapy even when only one or a few family members are directly involved in therapy. Achieving this goal, however, requires more than systemic questions. It also requires that clients be able and willing to speak from the standpoint of others. The requirement might be characterized as adopting an interlocutor standpoint, which involves acting as an intermediary between the therapists and absent others.

While all clients are not willing or able to act as interlocutors, those who do open a variety of therapeutic possibilities for therapy. The following negotiation illustrates how ecosystemic brief therapists may explore these possibilities with client/interlocutors. The session is concerned with ongoing conflicts between a mother and her daughter. Indeed, the mother has informed her daughter that she is considering severing their relationship. The session involves the daughter and her grandmother with whom the daughter once lived:

> Therapist: All right. Do you have any idea of what her mother would say as to what she has to do to stay with her mother.
>
> Grandmother: I think she would say to pick up after herself, and to clean her room and do her chores.
>
> Therapist: That's it? [. . .]
>
> Grandmother: And let her know where she is [. . .], you know, keep her mother informed so she knows where she is. Um, [. . .] let's see, what else would she say? Um, not to lie, [. . .] that's it.
>
> Therapist: That's it? [. . .] Do you think she is able to follow through with what her mother wants? Is she capable of doing that? [. . .] Capable of looking after herself, of not lying, of telling her mother where she is.
>
> Grandmother: I don't know. [. . .] Because when she was living with me, she was having difficulty with these things too.

First, notice the grandmother's detailed answers, which focus on the daughter's concrete behavior—picking up after herself, doing her chores, keeping her mother informed, and not lying. These details may be contrasted with the daughter's responses to the therapist's prior systemic questioning about the same issue. The daughter stated that she would have to be "perfect" in order to satisfy her mother and declined, when asked by the therapist, to explain—in concrete terms—what being perfect meant. Unlike her grandmother, the daughter refused to speak for her mother. Also, notice how the therapist invites the grandmother to provide further details by twice asking, "That's it?", and then waiting for a response before moving on. The grandmother's detailed responses, then, are part of a collaborative effort involving both the client and therapist.

Finally, this interaction is instructive because the therapist follows the grandmother's description of the mother's concerns by asking her to assess the daughter's ability to change her behavior. The question asks the grandmother to shift her role and perspective within the ongoing interaction, moving from speaking for the mother to speaking for herself based on her experience with the daughter. The seeming ease with which the therapist and grandmother manage this shift belies the complexity of their interactional moves and collaboration.

Mapping the Future

Ecosystemic brief therapists signal their interest in the future and change by asking constructive questions that focus clients' attention toward better future times, and away from their troubled past and present lives. The therapists use constructive questions to both reorient clients' time frames, and to focus the interactions on solutions to problems. The following exchange displays both of these aspects of constructive questions. It also illustrates three other major themes of ecosystemic brief therapy questioning (i.e., identifying positive signs of change, imagining untroubled future circumstances, and describing those circumstances), which will be discussed later in this section:

Therapist: What do you think would be a sign to you that you are, uh, leaning in one direction or another, or that you are beginning, your mind is beginning to clear toward, uh, one decision or another?

Client: I don't know. I don't know what the sign would be?

Therapist: Will you be feeling something or would you be behaving differently?

Client: I think mine would be a behavior. Yeah, I think I would be behaving stronger, you know, with more purpose.

Therapist: OK, when you're behaving stronger what would you do?

Client: Well, when I'm behaving stronger, I, I can have fun, and I want to take care of things. I'm not as anxious and I'm certainly not as self-destructive.

Not all clients are willing or able to make the shifts asked for by ecosystemic brief therapists, however. These clients continue to speak in ways that ecosystemic therapists classify as complaints. The therapists respond by stressing their interest in the future. They also ask clients how they might alter their behavior and/or perspectives to improve their lives. Consider, for example, the following negotiation, which began when a Northland Clinic therapist asked the client, "Well, what do you think would have to happen for things to be better, you know, how, what would have to happen in order for you to know that things were getting a little better?" The client responded by redescribing his negative feelings toward his mother, and how his prior experience in other forms of therapy had made his relationship with her worse:

> Therapist: OK, and that's what's happened in the past?
> Client: Right.
> Therapist: OK, well how can you talk and get along in the future? How are you gonna manage to do that?
> Client: We just, [. . .] I'll manage, you know. I can get along with her, but for a while.
> Therapist: How do you do that? How do you manage to do that?

Here we see how ecosystemic brief therapists continue to ask constructive questions even when clients' initial responses are unsatisfactory. The therapist asserted her interest in the future by first characterizing (by way of a question) the client's prior answer as "that's what's happened in the past," and then asking about the future. Notice also that the therapist's constructive questions focused on the concrete ways in which the client might change his behavior and/or perspective in order to create a better relationship with his mother in the future, and how he had done so in the past. The questions assumed that the client possessed the skills, insights, and power to change the relationship.

These questions might also be understood as rhetorical devices for helping clients assert control over their lives by becoming "unstuck" from their complaints. For ecosystemic brief therapists, clients often become unstuck when they realize that they already have the skills and insights needed to manage their problems, or can imagine themselves doing so. Indeed, Northland Clinic therapists sometimes described their clients as stuck during therapy sessions. The following interaction is an example. It followed a question about what the client might concretely do to positively change his life. He concluded his response by stating, "I'm just nuts, nuts."

> Therapist: Well, I don't think you're nuts. I think you're kinda stuck at the moment.
> Client: Yeah, but I feel like I'm going deeper, getting [. . .], I don't know, it just seemed like I'm losing more control. I'm not, uh, [. . .] I just don't feel like I'm [. . .]
> Therapist: How would you know if you hit bottom?
> Client: I don't know. There was a number of times when I thought I'd already hit it but I'm kind of wondering if maybe all the idle time I've had hasn't added to it, but then again, heck, I can think of all kinds of excuses and it doesn't solve my problem. I can't blame that on the whole problem 'cause the problems

> have been here for ten, eleven years, [. . .] in varying degrees.
>
> Therapist: Well, I think the clue may lie there in that last statement. Somehow, in varying degrees, and that's what, what we are still trying to figure out is what makes that difference.

This exchange is also instructive because when the client continues to offer complaints in response to the therapist's questions about how he might change his behavior, the therapist asks, "How would you know if you hit bottom?" Like her other constructive questions, the question maintains the therapist's prior interest in the future and focus on the details of the client's life. One way of understanding the concept of hitting bottom is that it is a turning point, things will get better after bottoming out. Thus, being able to recognize when the problem is at its worst may be part of the problem-solving process.

Another major feature of ecosystemic brief therapists' orchestration of initial interviews is their encouragement of clients to attend to the details of their lives as positive signs, even when the signs are not easily discernible. In the above negotiation, for example, notice how the therapist responds to the client's statement that he has suffered from the same problems for many years, although to varying degrees. The therapist focuses her reply on the client's qualifying phrase by stressing that the variations in the intensity of his problems are "the clue," and "what we are still trying to figure out is what makes that difference." Even in interviews with clients who offer little information about their problem-solving abilities then, ecosystemic brief therapists stress the hopeful aspects of their statements.

The major exception to this practice involves interviews with clients who state that they are depressed. Here, ecosystemic brief therapists pursue a more paradoxical—but positively oriented—strategy. First, they emphasize all of the good reasons that make the clients' depression warranted, and then ask, "How come you're able to do everything that you do?" under such depressing circumstances. In these interviews, ecosystemic therapists treat virtually any mundane client activity as a positive sign, including getting out of bed, going to work (even if only for a short time), and coming to therapy.

When clients respond to the therapists' constructive questions by describing what the therapists consider to be the beginnings of problems, the therapists shift the temporal orientation of their questions by asking about past times when clients' problems might be seen as absent or less intense. The questions are both sources of information for the therapists and ways of instructing clients on ecosystemic brief therapists' preferred understandings of the events reported by clients. The latter aspect of the therapists' questions is perhaps most easily seen in interactions in which the clients continue to describe their lives as troubled.

Consider, for example, the case of a client who complained that he and his wife were no longer having sex. Early in the interaction, the Northland Clinic therapist asked, "So, uh, [. . .] what would tell you that, um, she wants to have contact with you, that she wants to have sex with you, that she wants to be close to you?" The client answered by describing two recent times when he and his wife had had sex. He also stated that his wife had initiated the contact on both occasions. The client insisted, however, that his wife didn't really want to have sex with him. Rather, she was doing it to please him. From Bateson and his colleagues' (1956) perspective this client is stuck in a double bind. Having sex with his wife only seems to be a sign of positive change, but—because he is certain that her advances are insincere—having sex with his wife is actually a sign that their sexual difficulties are not improving.

The therapist then asked the client to describe the signals that his wife might send him that would convince him that she truly wanted sex. The client answered by describing the history of his marriage, suggesting that he now interpreted all of her romantic advances as insincere. At this point, the therapy team telephoned the therapist and asked the client to justify his interpretation, thus raising the possibility that his problem might be solved if he changed his perspective. The therapist restated the team's question in the following way,

> It's, um. [. . .] The team is confused about [. . .] your [. . .] impression that she does not want [. . .] to, to be with you. There were signs, [. . .] when she asks you to dance, she hugs you, she does a lot of things. So, um, we want to know, [. . .] how do you, how you, how can you be sure about this? What's, what is, how are you coming to this assumption?

Notice that while the Northland Clinic therapist and team raise the possibility that the solution to the problem involves the client's perspective, they do not tell him that he is mistaken or instruct him on how he should interpret his wife's behavior. They raise the issue more indirectly by describing themselves as confused, the client's interpretation as an impression, and stating that "there were signs" of his wife's affection. They also ask him "how can you be sure about this," and to consider how he was "coming to this assumption."

Finally, the therapist's use of pauses in the above excerpt illustrates how ecosystemic brief therapists often use pauses to set off and highlight aspects of their questions and statements. Ecosystemic therapists explain that assessments and instructions are sometimes most effectively conveyed in this way, as indirect statements embedded in information seeking questions. In the above exchange, for example, the Northland Clinic therapist's pauses before and after "you" might be understood by the client as an assignment of personal responsibility for his "impression," one that the team finds confusing. The therapist also uses a pause to set off her assertion that "there are signs" of affection from the client's wife. Finally, this excerpt illustrates how ecosystemic brief therapists often announce their upcoming questions ("So, um, we want to know"), and then pause in order to invite clients' full attention and highlight the significance of the questions that are about to be asked.

Another major technique used by ecosystemic brief therapists to map alternative futures is to ask clients to imagine future times when they have solved, or have begun to solve, their problems. At other times, these therapists simply ask clients to imagine themselves in new situations. The following interaction is typical of this variation on the crystal ball technique. It involves a client who is trying to decide whether to divorce her husband:

Therapist: . . . , I mean can you project yourself divorced or away from it totally living separate from your husband, the relationship, and that it would be a great loss to you?

Client: Yes.

Therapist: So, now, if, project ourselves into the future and you're, you're away from it, what would be the greatest losses and what would be the things you are feeling best about?

This line of constructive questioning might be understood as a procedure for helping the client make an "informed" choice about her future. That is, the Northland Clinic therapist not only asks the client if she can imagine herself divorced, but also to describe the benefits and costs of such a choice. The latter question focuses on the practical consequences of divorce as a solution to the client's troubles. The therapist further develops this focus by later asking the client, "What do you do instead of having to worry about him, and hold him up?" and "How do you picture you, support yourself, by having emotions, how are you going to find new ways of supporting yourself emotionally when he is gone?" These questions illustrate how ecosystemic brief therapists' constructive questions ask for more than wishful thinking by clients. The questions are designed to construct concrete problems and remedies for clients, as well as to offer clients hope for the future.

CHAPTER 6

CONSTRUCTING CHANGE IN ECOSYSTEMIC BRIEF THERAPY

Second and subsequent interviews in ecosystemic brief therapy differ from first interviews in their primary focus on creating and assessing changes in clients' lives and social systems. The shift is part of a change in the therapist-client relationship. Henceforth, the therapists show greatly decreased interest in clients' complaints and problems, preferring to talk about positive changes in clients' lives instead. One way in which the therapists express their orientation is by describing clients as having moved past these issues, thus making them irrelevant to the issues at hand. Consider, for example, the following therapist response to a client who responded to a future-oriented question by analyzing the history of his business troubles: "That's in the past. Now you're, you're well on your way to correcting that, uh?"

The changes of interest to ecosystemic brief therapists include those that might be attributed to their prior intervention messages, but also other developments in clients' lives. The therapists' questions are designed both to identify concrete changes that they and their clients might build on in constructing other desired changes and to encourage the development of positive client attitudes. These are interrelated aspects of change for ecosystemic brief therapists. They assume that observable changes in clients' lives are likely to encourage the development of optimistic and hopeful client attitudes that are central to keeping the cycle of positive change going. Further, clients who are without hope and primarily focused on their troubles lack the perspective needed to see and understand how their lives are getting better.

While ecosystemic brief therapists emphasize change in second and subsequent interviews, they also ask questions about clients' troubles and social systems. The questions are designed to elicit information that the therapists and team members might use in assessing the significance of the changes reported by clients and to encourage further changes. Further, like first-session interviews, these interactions are not organized as rigid formats.

They involve a variety of related practical concerns, rhetorical moves, and opportunities for constructing distinctive definitions of social reality and therapist-client relationships. They also sometimes involve surprises. For example, I observed a few sessions at Northland Clinic where clients reported that they were sufficiently uncomfortable with the suggestions made by their therapists in prior sessions that they had not taken the therapists' advice. The following is an example of how Northland Clinic therapists responded to these client concerns: "OK, well, I mean, I'm glad, certainly glad you didn't do it. You obviously know better than I do in that." The therapists then turned to questions that were similar to those associated with first interviews, that is, questions that might be useful in constructing solvable problems and in mapping clients' troubles and social systems.

Another unique circumstance involved clients who reported rapidly changing troubles in their lives. Northland Clinic therapists responded by asking clients to describe pertinent changes since their last sessions and to discuss how they planned to deal with their rapidly evolving troubles and social systems. Defining a problem on which clients and therapists might work was an ongoing process in these interviews, and was subject to re-specification from session to session. Therapist-client relationships also sometimes changed when new parties participated in later interviews or when former participants stopped coming to therapy.

In one case, for example, a married couple—largely at the behest of the wife—came to Northland Clinic seeking help in salvaging their marriage. After several sessions, however, the wife announced that she was no longer coming to therapy, stating that their marital problems could only be remedied if her husband changed. The subsequent several interviews with the husband also involved a number of twists and turns as the client and therapist first focused on what the client needed to do to repair his troubled marriage, then on the practical implications of the wife's decision to seek a divorce, and finally on beginning to develop a new, postdivorce life for the client.

Even in these unique cases, however, ecosystemic brief therapists still ask questions about how clients' lives have changed and encourage the development of optimistic client attitudes. The therapists usually avoid telling clients what changes they should make, preferring to work more indirectly by encouraging clients to see and anticipate positive changes, and to identify how they might modify their lives to fulfill their change-related goals. We consider both ecosystemic brief therapists' and clients' participation in these interviews in the rest of the chapter. We begin with their initial entrance into the ecosystemic language of change, and then analyze how therapists and clients construct, elaborate on, and negotiate change. Finally, we consider how clients' participation in therapy ended.

Opening Moves

While clients occasionally initiate movement into the ecosystemic language of change, ecosystemic brief therapists usually initiate this shift in their interactions. The therapists do so in a variety of ways, thus offering clients different opportunities for defining the initial topics of the interviews and for establishing linkages between prior sessions and ongoing interviews. Ecosystemic brief therapists' opening moves might also be interpreted as strategies for holding clients accountable for implementing the changes discussed in prior interviews. The opening strategy most frequently used by Northland Clinic therapists involved the following or similar questions: "So, uh, how did it go for you?" "How goes it?" "OK, [pause] the obvious first question is how are things going between the two of you?"

First, notice the generality of these questions, suggesting that the therapists' interest in clients includes many aspects of clients' lives. Even the last question, which focuses on the clients' relationship ("How are things going between the two of you?") invites a range of responses and might be understood by the clients as signaling a broad-based interest in their circumstances. These questions also invite clients to define the initial topics of discussion. The extent to which these client-defined topics are developed in the subsequent interactions is, of course, contingent on a variety of factors, particularly therapists' responses to the topics. Finally, these questions make no mention of the issues discussed in prior interviews or intervention messages.

Other times, however, Northland Clinic therapists open with questions or statements that suggest the topics in which they are most interested. The questions and statements invite a more limited array of client responses and define a less encompassing therapist-client relationship. For example, Northland Clinic therapists sometimes begin by asking clients to report on positive developments in their lives, asking such questions as "So, it's been good for you this week?" "So, what have you been doing that's good for yourselves?" "What's been happening that you want to continue to have happen?" While more focused than the therapists' typical opening moves, clients might still respond to these questions by discussing any number of positive changes, including changes that are unrelated to developments in prior interviews.

Accountability is more evident in a different version of this opening strategy. It starts with Northland Clinic therapists reviewing aspects of prior interviews. The reviews, which vary in length, establish explicit links between aspects of prior and present interviews, and define therapist-client relationships as—initially at least—concerned with these linkages. Clients collaborate in the exchanges by treating the therapists' statements as invitations to speak to the issues raised by the therapists. For example, in a session with a child who was having trouble in school, a Northland Clinic therapist began by stating, "Well, let's see. Last time I saw you, you were the student of the week." Through their responses, the child and his mother completed the shift initiated by the therapist. The child did so by looking away, squirming in his seat, and stating "uhm," actions that might be interpreted as signs of discomfort with the topic shift. The mother replied, "That's totally changed now," and described the child's recent disciplinary problems in school.

A related strategy employed by another Northland Clinic therapist begins with an opening statement by the therapist that she wants to review the last session so "we can get back into it." This remark casts the present interview as linked to the previous one. As the example reproduced below shows, the therapist then offers a detailed review of the prior interview, which focuses on the ways in which the client is satisfactorily dealing with her troubles, such as by feeling clear, seeing herself as competent, and making her own decisions. Notice also that the client signals her involvement in the interview by replying with "uh, huh" to the therapists' review of their prior discussion, and the therapist invites the client to speak by pausing at the end of her review of the client's prior successes.

Therapist:	Uh, you had about a week and you felt clear, [. . .] and, uh, you've come to the conclusion that whatever choice you make it doesn't have to be terrible.
Client:	Uh, huh.
Therapist:	It can be OK.
Client:	Uh, huh.
Therapist:	And that you're a competent person. [. . .] Uh, and you've been clearing up odds and ends.
Client:	Uh, huh.
Therapist:	Which gives you sense, gives you a sense of competency and control. [. . .] And, uh, you've been working on your trip to Arizona. And making all the decisions yourself. [The therapist pauses and the client begins to talk about recent events in her life.]

Finally, Northland Clinic therapists sometimes use task assignments given in prior sessions to justify asking highly focused opening questions. The questions link the present interviews with prior ones and focus the interactions on therapeutic interventions designed to create change in clients' lives. As the following examples show, the therapists broach this issue in several different ways, ranging from somewhat vague and hedged questions to very direct ones:

- Um, can I ask you how it went, the last couple of weekends? What we asked you to do?
- OK, well, let's see, last time you were here, I guess I asked if you'd noticed, and take note of, what happens between the two of you when you get together, and see each other, which you want to keep happening. What did you come up with?
- Well, [pause] did you follow our suggestions?

The first two questions display how ecosystemic brief therapists sometimes hedge their inquiries about matters that clients might take as holding them accountable to prior discussions and agreements. Notice how, in the first example, the therapist asks permission to ask about the clients' experiences with their task, and never specifies what the task involved, thus allowing the clients to define it with their response. The therapist in the second example is more specific about the task, but still hedges his question by stating that he *guesses* that the clients were asked to notice "what happens between the two of you when you get together," and concludes by asking them to report on what they have "come up with."

These questioning practices may be contrasted with the more direct approach displayed in the third example. While the differences between these opening moves might be explained as differences in Northland Clinic therapists' professional styles, ecosystemic brief therapists sometimes use more direct questions to signal their concerns and frustrations with clients, and to move the interviews in preferred directions. The moves include defining therapist-client relationships in new and more precise ways, such as by specifying the therapists' expectations for clients within their ongoing relationships. Ecosystemic therapists might raise these issues at any point in the interviews, including at the outset. We return to this issue later in the chapter.

Clients' Responses

Clients respond to ecosystemic brief therapists' opening moves in several different ways. The responses display clients' orientations to present and prior interviews, including their orientations to past suggestions made by therapists and team members for dealing with their problems. In one case at Northland Clinic, for example, the client responded to the therapist's opening question, "Well, did you follow our suggestions?" by asking, "Did you make a suggestion?" Thus, while therapists occupy a central position in brief therapy interactions, their ability to move the interactions in preferred directions is always contingent on clients' ability and willingness to collaborate with them.

When clients move in alternative directions, ecosystemic brief therapists adapt their questions and comments, thereby orchestrating different kinds of interviews than they might have expected prior to the sessions. In one case, for example, a Northland Clinic therapist responded to a client's interest in continuing to talk about her troubles by treating the interview as a second "first session." That is, the therapist shifted her questions to focus on the client's perspectives, social system, and how her complaints might be turned into problems. In another case, a male client stated at the outset of the session that he wanted to know why his wife (who had previously participated in the sessions) had decided to end her participation. His wife had told him that she would call the therapist with her reasons and that he would have to go to therapy to hear them. Here, too, the therapist adapted by first discussing the wife's decision with the husband and then asking questions designed to construct a new problem for the client.

The majority of clients respond to ecosystemic therapists' opening moves in three major ways. They state that (1) their lives have improved since their last interviews, (2) some aspects of their lives have gotten better but others have not, and (3) their lives are not improving. Each of these responses has implications for therapist-client interactions, including the rhetorical moves available to ecosystemic therapists in encouraging clients to describe their lives as changing.

Client reports that their lives are improving provide therapists with opportunities to elaborate on and extend the changes by focusing their questions and comments on the various ways in which clients' lives are changing and might change in the near future. These opportunities are not so clearly available when clients describe some aspects of their lives as changed and others as unchanged or getting worse. And they are even less available when clients state that no aspects of their lives are improved. While maintaining their interest in emphasizing positive change in clients' lives and encouraging optimistic client perspectives then, ecosystemic brief therapists vary their strategies based on the opportunities provided by clients. We consider these strategies in the next three sections.

Elaborating and Extending Change

Ecosystemic brief therapists readily accept clients' claims that their lives are improving, often expressing their approval by congratulating clients on

and/or expressing amazement at their successes. Team members also sometimes call to ask the therapists to convey their congratulations and/or
amazement to clients. In these ways, ecosystemic therapists elaborate on
their clients' reports by emphasizing the positive significance of the changes.
They stress the hard work, personal strength, and/or courage displayed by
clients in making the changes. Consider, for example, the following exchange, which followed a Northland Clinic client's (Eva) report that she had
found and started a job since the last interview:

Therapist:	So this is a big change for you, working?
Eva:	Yes, it is. Yes, it is. I've already got done furnishing and remodeling our house. That's all done.
Therapist:	You got all that done!
Eva:	Yeah, that's all done. Got the carpeting in, all the woodworking done.
Therapist:	Wow, you're an industrious person.
Eva:	Energetic, I'm energetic.
Therapist:	Pretty hard that first week or two to, uh,
Eva:	[interrupting] Yeah, I got the, the body's got to get adjusted to it. . . .

In this interaction, Eva elaborates on the changes in her life by shifting the
discussion topic in response to the therapist's question about work. She first
agrees that working is "a big change," and then describes her successes in
furnishing and remodeling her home. Notice also that the therapist responds
by first expressing her amazement ("You got all that done!"), then offering
the client a new positive identity ("Wow, you're an industrious person"), and
finally casting the changes as involving difficulties—that is, as "pretty hard"
at the beginning. The therapist invites Eva to further elaborate on these
changes in her life by first asking Eva about aspects of her new job, and then
turning to the systemic implications of the changes by asking, "So, how
would you say Curtis [the client's husband], . . . , has he noticed differences
about your new job?"

These therapist moves are aspects of a general questioning strategy employed by ecosystemic brief therapists throughout second and subsequent
interviews. Once a change has been identified, ecosystemic therapists use it
as a basis for further questioning of clients, asking such questions as "So,
what else has changed?" or "What else has gotten better?" Ecosystemic brief
therapists seldom ask, however, *if* anything else has changed in clients' lives
because, they explain, this question makes it too easy for clients to reply that
nothing has changed. Ecosystemic therapists also highlight other positive
changes reported by clients as the interviews proceed, often stating "That's
good" or "So, that's another change."

A related ecosystemic brief therapist response to clients' initial reports of positive change involves making clients responsible for the changes. This response is similar to the assignment of positive identities to clients because both are designed to convey to clients a sense of personal significance in their social worlds. In assigning positive identities to clients, ecosystemic therapists cast clients as members of respected person categories, such as the category of industrious people. Responses designed to make clients responsible for positive changes cast clients as consequential actors in their social worlds, thus anticipating and undermining possible client claims that the changes are random or caused by factors beyond clients' control.

For example, Northland Clinic therapists sometimes respond to clients' reports of positive changes by asking, "How did you get that to happen?" At other times, they take a more circuitous route, such as by asking clients to elaborate on how, and/or to explain why, they think their lives have improved. Northland Clinic therapists then ask, "Well, what have you done differently?" This question might be taken by clients to suggest that the changes are related to the clients' changed behavior or attitudes. Therapists at Northland Clinic often use clients' answers to this question to shift the interview focus toward the systemic contexts of the changes, thus beginning to map how the changes are evident in several aspects of clients' social systems.

Ecosystemic brief therapists orchestrate these discussions by asking clients to describe how others are responding to the changes that they describe, and by asking clients to identify and discuss other ways in which their lives are improving. These questions are designed to elaborate on the clients' prior reports of change, and to further the emerging cycle of positive change. The questions also elicit information that ecosystemic therapists and team members might use in developing new intervention messages and strategies. Two possible messages are that the therapists believe that further meetings with clients are unnecessary and that they want clients to think about when the meetings will be unnecessary.

A related turn sometimes taken in these ecosystemic discussions is the development of new problems on which therapists and clients might work. Often, the new problems are matters that have previously been discussed as complaints, or that clients have described as less pressing than those on which they initially wished to work. Other times, the new problems emerge as therapists and clients discuss the clients' options for the future, particularly given the recent changes reported by clients. However they emerge, ecosystemic brief therapists' inquiries about new problems focus on when and how clients might decide to deal with the problems, and how their lives would be changed if the problems were remedied.

An example of how this process might unfold is the interview with Eva discussed above, which included her report about having started a new job, and remodeling the home she shares with her husband, Curtis. In discussing these issues, Eva states that while Curtis has responded to her new job by doing more housework, she would like him to do more around the house. Eva's therapist then asks, "So, how do you, so what can you do to get him to help out?" This question might be understood as an invitation to define a new problem, but Eva does not take it. Rather, she first replies that Curtis must change in his own time, and then tells of a recent incident involving Curtis that angered her but in which she was able to control her temper. The Northland Clinic therapist shifts her questions to further develop this topic by asking Eva, "How did you manage to not lose your temper?" and "What do you do in place of that to kind of keep things mellowed out?" Both questions assign responsibility for this positive change to Eva, and the second suggests that change may involve finding new behaviors to replace troublesome ones.

Eva's therapist follows this discussion with a series of questions designed to map this change in Eva's social system. She first asks, "What have you noticed that is different about what Curtis does when you are able to control your temper now?" Eva replies, "Well, I don't know, nothing much," describes how little contact she and Curtis have had since she started her new job, and then raises a possible new problem. The problem emerges over the course of a lengthy statement about her relationship with Curtis, and involves her suspicion that Curtis wants to return to his ex-wife. Eva explains that she intends to talk with Curtis about this issue, and is prepared "to set him free" and support their children by herself.

Eva's therapist does not follow up on this topic. Rather, she returns to the lack of communication issue. But Eva persists by first agreeing that she and Curtis have not talked much over the last week and then stating, "I feel the relationship was, um, used to be like one hundred percent, I would say that it's fallen in the thirty range now, between thirty and thirty five." At this point, the therapist turns her questions to the future of the marriage and pursues this topic for the rest of the session, thus constructing a new problem on which she and Eva might work in the future. The therapist first raises this issue by asking Eva to discuss the practical significance of the numbers for her relationship with Curtis, and then asking,

What kind of changes would you have to see to think that, to think that it's going to work out? What would have to be different in your relationship for you to say, "Yes, its working," or "It is working out, it has worked or is working?" What would have to be different? What would you be doing differently?

Yet another turn sometimes taken in second and subsequent interviews involves ecosystemic therapists raising the possibility that the positive changes reported by clients might not last. The therapists raise this issue with clients who report extraordinary improvements in their lives and, from the therapists' point of view, express unrealistic expectations about the future. The move is designed to encourage clients to adopt more realistic expectations about past and future changes, thus countering the possibility that they might overreact to problems that might emerge in the future and return to their previous complaint patterns. Ecosystemic therapists might raise the issue at any point in the interview. In one session, for example, a Northland Clinic therapist questioned two clients about the "astounding" improvements that they reported for about thirty minutes and then asked, "OK, is there anything that you can imagine at this point that would, if you will, accidentally push you back into the old pattern?"

Another Northland Clinic therapist employed a slightly different strategy in responding to parents who, based on past improvements in their son's behavior, stated that they were thinking about giving him the weekly allowance that they had previously terminated as punishment for his unacceptable behavior. The therapist recommended against this change, stating, "Uh huh [. . .], OK, [. . .] OK, is, I wonder if it's time or you want to wait with that for a while yet. [. . .] Till he, till you find out whether its gonna hold." The therapist justified the recommendation by telling the parents that they might "have to pick the pieces up once more," and noting that meaningful change often involves "three steps forward and two steps back."

Thus, while client reports of positive changes in their lives is the response most preferred by ecosystemic brief therapists, this claim is not sufficient in itself. Ecosystemic therapists treat it as a beginning for developing cycles of positive change that will get clients "unstuck" from their problems. The changes include encouraging clients to see how the changes that they report are related to other changes in their social systems, developing hopeful (but not unrealistic) attitudes toward the future, and initiating further changes to better manage other circumstances that clients define as troublesome.

Choosing Change

Clients who state that their lives are partly improved present ecosystemic brief therapists with a choice. The therapists might respond by inquiring about the improvements or they might focus on clients' troubles. Consistent with the philosophy of ecosystemic brief therapy, Northland Clinic therapists usually respond to clients who describe their lives as partly improved by asking about the positive changes in clients' lives. How they ask these questions and pursue this issue, however, varies from interview to interview, based on clients' responses to their opening and subsequent questions. Consider, for example, the following therapist-client exchange:

Client: Between the last time I talked to you, and now, uh, [. . .]
some things are better, some things have stayed the same.
Therapist: Uh, huh.
Client: Uh [. . .]
Therapist: What's better?

Here, the client presents the therapist with a clear-cut choice by stating, "Some things are better, some things have stayed the same." When the client does not respond to the therapist's minimal response of "Uh, huh" by elaborating on his claim, the therapist then expresses an interest in change by asking, "What's better?" Other times, clients present ecosystemic brief therapists with less clear-cut choices, including responses that might be taken as indicating positive change or as no improvement in clients' lives. One way in which ecosystemic therapists respond to these "ambiguous" client claims is by inviting clients to elaborate on their circumstances, and then stating that the clients' descriptions are signs of positive change. Consider the following exchange involving a married couple who are having trouble getting along with each other:

Wife: Not really too bad over all.
Therapist: OK.
Wife: The holiday season and so forth is very hectic pace, you don't have much time for anything else.
Therapist: OK, so it's been real hectic in terms of planning for the holidays.
Husband: Oh, yeah, we've just been going, going, gone. There's always something.
Wife: Doesn't seem to be much free time for anything.
Therapist: Uh huh [. . .] OK, and that's good.
Husband: Sure.
Wife: I suppose.
Husband: Right.
Wife: Keeps us out of trouble.
Therapist: Sure, sure. OK, what are some of the things that you are noticing at this point or things that you know are pleasant and uh [. . .]

The wife begins this exchange by offering a generally positive assessment of the couple's relationship over the past week ("Not really too bad over all") to which the therapist offers a minimal response, "OK." The wife then elaborates by noting the hectic pace of the holiday season and that "you don't have much time for anything else." She and her husband further extend this claim as the interaction proceeds. These statements might be interpreted in several different ways, including as complaints about the couple's inability to deal with their problems over the past week. But the Northland Clinic therapist treats them as signs of positive change, stating "OK, and that's good." The clients agree with this depiction of their circumstances without offering much elaboration, and then the therapist asks the clients to discuss pleasant developments that they have recently noticed. This question initiated a shift in the interaction to mapping the positive change reported by the clients. In other interviews, Northland Clinic therapists initiate this topical shift by asking, "Well, what have you done differently then?"

A related strategy used by ecosystemic brief therapists in responding to clients who report improvement in some aspects of their lives but problems in other areas involves discounting client concerns about the problematic circumstances. Sometimes ecosystemic brief therapists do so by noting that change takes time and that the clients should be patient with achieving all of their goals. Ecosystemic therapists often combine this claim with expressions of how impressed they are with the substantial changes already achieved by clients, suggesting that clients should feel pride in their accomplishments and anticipate future positive changes.

An alternative ecosystemic strategy involves portraying the unimproved circumstances as unsurprising developments and therefore matters about which clients should not worry. In an interview at Northland Clinic involving a mother who was concerned about her son's (David's) behavior at home and in school, for example, the client began by describing the past week as having gone "very well," and describing the techniques that she had successfully used to better manage David. She concluded this description, however, by stating, "He did get his report card and it was abysmal." The Northland Clinic therapist discounted her concern by replying, "Well, that's what you expected," and "That wasn't surprising." The client agreed with the therapist and then began to talk about the new study rules that she had established to encourage David to improve his grades. The therapist briefly questioned the client about the rules and whether they were working, but then shifted to other positive changes by asking, "So, you're not, um, as far as David feeling moody or down or having the, just the glazed look in his eyes, you don't see that so much any more?"

In sum, ecosystemic brief therapists usually choose to talk about positive changes even when clients respond to their questions by talking about their problems. Sometimes they do so by continually asking clients, "So, what is different, what is better?" until the clients cease talking about their troubles and begin to speak of change. Other times, ecosystemic therapists employ more indirect strategies, such as asking clients about positive changes, then shifting to their problems, only to return to the positive changes a little later. Consider, for example, the following sequence involving a Northland Clinic therapist and a mother who is concerned with her child's (Jeremy's) problems in school. The client reports that she has had some modest success with the therapist's prior recommendation to reward Jeremy for good behavior, but that his behavior has taken a turn for the worse in the last two weeks. The therapist first asks the client to describe how Jeremy's behavior has improved and then asks her for a detailed description of the circumstances associated with the sudden and undesired change in his behavior. Shortly thereafter, however, he returns to the initial issue:

Therapist: Getting back to the start of, you said, up to that point things were going pretty well.

Client: Fairly well.

Therapist: And then?

Client: Not great because there are still some things, we'll talk about that.

Therapist: So, then things kind of were getting better. Have they, have they gotten better since then?

Client: Well I don't know. Today's incident just happened not too long ago, so he [. . .]

Therapist: [Interrupting] But he must have gotten better in school for a while.

Client: Yeah, he did, he did. The last of, Friday, Thursday, Friday, and Monday he had some really good days. OK, 'cause he wasn't in school Wednesday, he was out of school Wednesday. 'Cause Monday he was suspended from the bus, Tuesday he was suspended from school.

Therapist: What do you think, what do you think makes it a good day, I mean, do you have any idea what it takes for him to have a good day?

Notice here that the client offers the therapist several opportunities to further pursue the discussion of Jeremy's troublesome behavior but he doesn't follow up on any of them. First, she describes the improvements in his behavior as going "fairly well" and "not great." She also states that there are some problems to talk about, mentions a very recent troublesome episode, and notes that mixed in with Jeremy's recent "good" days were three "bad" days. The Northland Clinic therapist, on the other hand, continues to pursue his interest in positive change, once hedging his question by stating that "things kind of were getting better" but later phrasing his question in a way that might be heard as disbelief that Jeremy's behavior had not improved at some time since the last session ("But he must have gotten better in school for a while?"). Finally, the therapist asks the client to focus on Jeremy's "good" days by asking "what it takes for him to have a good day."

Through the interactional procedures discussed here, ecosystemic brief therapists and clients enter the ecosystemic discourse of change. Once in it, they elaborate on changes in clients' lives by using the same interactional and interpretive methods discussed in the previous section. That is, the therapists assign positive identities to clients and hold them responsible for the changes to clients. Ecosystemic brief therapists and clients may also map the changes within clients' social systems and construct new problems on which they might work in the future.

Negotiating Change

Ecosystemic therapists treat clients' statements that their lives have not improved as the opening moves in negotiations that might move in several different directions within a single session or across several interviews. The negotiations might focus on whether change is discernible in clients' lives, how clients' problems might be solved, and—in a few cases—the terms of the therapist-client relationship. From ecosystemic therapists' standpoint, these negotiations are designed to get clients moving in the direction of change by pointing out how their lives have already changed, constructing observable goals toward which they and clients might work in solving clients' problems, and specifying to clients the therapists' expectations about their relationships.

I discuss how the therapists and clients negotiate these issues in the next three sections. It should be noted, however, that while I analyze them as distinct negotiations, these interactions frequently involve negotiations about several different issues. In particular, most second and subsequent sessions include negotiations about whether signs of change are evident in clients' lives and about constructing solutions to clients' problems.

Negotiating Improvement

Ecosystemic brief therapists are taught that they should accept clients' claims that their lives have not improved since their last therapy sessions, but that the therapists should not believe the claims. The logic of the instruction is that clients who are "stuck" in cycles of complaint often cannot see positive changes when they happen. The practical significance of this instruction is that the ecosystemic therapists should not directly refute clients' claims, but that they should pursue lines of questioning designed to identify positive changes that are unrecognized by clients. The most confrontational therapist response that I observed at Northland Clinic was the following question, "So, nothing has really changed for you since the last time?" Northland Clinic therapists sometimes stressed the word *nothing,* thus conveying a greater degree of skepticism about clients' claims.

Ecosystemic brief therapists usually respond to clients who report no improvements in their lives by restating their opening questions, this time being more specific in indicating their interest in change, or they ask clients to elaborate on their perspectives and circumstances. The responses are designed to allow clients to express their concerns about their lives and problems while also providing the therapists with information that the therapists might use to cast clients' lives as changed. If clients do not provide such information, ecosystemic therapists return to the issue of change, as in the following Northland Clinic therapist's question asked after the client and therapist had spent approximately twenty minutes discussing the client's troubles:

> Well, what, uh, kind of [. . .] good things happened? [. . .] You know, [. . .] things that you're concerned about, that you're telling me, but can you tell me a little bit about what happened since I saw you that, the good things you saw for that time and the good things that you remember.

In another case, a Northland Clinic therapist responded to a client's statement that the task given during the previous session had not worked by revising her initial question. This time the therapist specified the details of the task, which involved having the client pay attention to what happens just prior to his deciding to go drinking. When the client again stated that he did not notice anything special about these times, the therapist replied, "Well let's see if we can come up with something together then. What must, let's say, for example, what time of day does this happen?" In this way, the therapist orchestrated the interview to hold the client accountable to their prior agreement, and initiated a questioning process designed to elicit information that might be used to construct positive change in the client's life.

Clients sometimes respond to ecosystemic brief therapists' questions with information that is useful in casting their lives as positively changed. The therapists use the information to note and congratulate clients on the changes, to begin mapping the changes within clients' social systems, and/or to inquire about how clients might construct further changes in their lives and social systems. Consider an interaction involving a Northland Clinic client who reported at the outset of the session that she was not improved and was very angry with some of her friends who were not supporting her in her time of need. The therapist asked the client to elaborate on her concerns, to which the client responded by portraying herself as a "giving" and "nurturant" person who had surrounded herself with needy people who could not help her with her problems.

The Northland Clinic therapist replied that the client's statement was "amazing" and a "great insight" about herself and friends, to which the client responded by describing her plans for spending more time with her more supportive friends, a topic shift that the therapist's subsequent questions encouraged. After about fifteen minutes, the therapist summarized the discussion by casting it as about positive change. The therapist did so by first stating, "So, you've been doing some really good things for yourself, constructive things for yourself," and then suggesting that these changes were the beginning of a new life for the client. This aspect of the interaction unfolded in the following way:

Therapist: It almost seems as though you're being [. . .] forced to, you know, if people sort of hover and protect and support, uh, it almost would seem that it would take a lot more to get on your feet by yourself, like that, than you're doing. I'm so impressed with how [. . .] efficiently you're handling all this and how independently. And this is all new and yet you're, [. . .] you know, almost catapulting yourself into this life in a very, uh, constructive manner.

Client: Well, it might. Well, I suppose, I mean, 'cause what I was gonna say is that I have to, and it isn't that, I don't think it's so much that people aren't around me, as it is that it's real apparent to me that I have to be the one who does it. I have these children.

Here we see how ecosystemic brief therapy interactions that begin with clients reporting that their lives have not improved may be orchestrated to construct the alternative visions of clients' lives as dramatically and positively changing. In the above case, the Northland Clinic therapist offers the client an image of herself as a person who is almost "catapulting" herself into a new life. The therapist then asks the client about her relationships with her children, and how they are positively affected by her recent insights. These questions are designed to extend the newly constructed changes by mapping their influences within the client's social system. The questions also invite information that the therapist and her team might use in constructing new intervention messages, and provide the client with reasons for adopting an optimistic orientation to her present and future life.

A different, but related questioning strategy was displayed in another session at Northland Clinic, in which the therapist responded to a married couple's claim that their lives were "not any better" by stating "I didn't figure they would be," and then asking, "How far are you?" The therapist's initial response discounted the possible negative implications of the clients' claim that their lives had not improved and signaled his lack of interest in the issue. Indeed, neither the therapist nor the clients returned to this issue in the rest of the interview. The therapist's subsequent question focused the interaction on the couple's ability to work together as a team in dealing with their troublesome children, and on the problem on which the therapist and clients had previously agreed that they would work. The clients responded to the therapist's new question by describing how they had effectively worked together during the week, although they were not fully satisfied with their efforts. The therapist asked the clients to describe in detail how they had succeeded in cooperatively managing problems with their children. He then highlighted the change and initiated discussion of how it might be extended by stating, "OK, so you're on the right track. [. . .] OK, but how do you make sure that you two work together quick enough?"

Negotiating Solutions

When clients do not provide information that ecosystemic brief therapists can use to construct positive changes and/or they persist in talking about their troubles, the therapists refocus the interviews on negotiating solutions to clients' troubles. This sometimes occurs within ongoing interactions, but ecosystemic therapists also sometimes begin interviews by focusing on this issue. In both cases, the focus signals the therapists' orientations to prior and ongoing interviews as not having produced solvable problems on which they and their clients might collaboratively work. The therapists' shift to negotiating solutions, then, is a strategy for moving clients beyond their complaints and toward developing acceptable problem definitions.

Ecosystemic brief therapists' strategies for negotiating solutions with clients in second and subsequent interviews are similar to those they employ in first sessions with new clients. Ecosystemic therapists use these questions to return to the issues and concerns associated with first sessions. An example of how this is done is the third interview with a Northland Clinic client who, in describing the prior week, reported a positive change in her relationship with her daughter. After the therapist and team congratulated the client on her strength and courage, the client discounted the change and returned to discussing her concerns about her daughter. The therapist then asked, "Deirdre, what, clarify for me, what are you wanting some help with tonight?"

Depending on clients' responses, ecosystemic brief therapists employ a variety of rhetorical moves in focusing interviews on problems and solutions. In the above case, for example, Deirdre explained that her concern was that the positive changes of the last week were illusory, and that her daughter was really on course for a "serious breakdown." Deirdre's therapist then asked, "Suppose that was true, that she was heading in that direction, what would you do then?" The question redirected the interaction away from the client's vague concerns and interpretations of her daughter's behavior as signs of trouble and toward the concrete options available to the client in responding to this possible problem. Further, the therapist initiated this shift without agreeing or disagreeing with Deirdre's portrayal of her daughter's seemingly positive behavior as really a sign of impending, serious trouble.

Related ecosystemic brief therapist responses involve asking clients to specify the signs that would convince them that their lives are beginning to really change for the better (the therapists then treat the signs as goals toward which they and clients can collaboratively work) and to decide which of their competing problems are most serious or pressing (thereby identifying an initial problem on which they might work). Then they reframe the clients' complaints. Sometimes ecosystemic therapists do this by describing the complaints as possible signs of positive developments in clients' lives and by asking clients to consider how they might be so interpreted. Another way in which ecosystemic brief therapists reframe clients' complaints is by asking clients to think about the matters at hand within new vocabularies. Consider, for example, the following Northland Clinic therapist-client interaction, which began with a call from the team and involves a client who is concerned about her granddaughter, who has been diagnosed as suffering from paranoid schizophrenia:

> Therapist: The team wants to know if you never heard this diagnosis. You didn't know that she has been labeled a paranoid schizophrenic and had done some reading, and some understanding of what that meant. [. . .] What would you think about a granddaughter who behaved this way?
>
> Client: I would still say that there is something wrong with her, but I would also call her a brat. That's just exactly what she's acting like.
>
> Therapist: Uh, uhm.
>
> Client: A big sassy, disrespectful brat.
>
> Therapist: And if that's what you were thinking, what would you do about it, this big, sassy disrespectful brat?

Three aspects of this exchange merit further discussion. First, notice that the Northland Clinic therapist invites the client to reframe the issues at hand in her own words. The therapist does not offer an alternative professional vocabulary, nor does she suggest that the granddaughter's behavior might be understood as bratlike. Second, the client's reframing of her granddaughter's behavior casts the problem as a matter that she might handle on her own, using the personal resources already available to her. Dealing with paranoid schizophrenics is the business of professional psychotherapists, not grandmothers. But, as the client notes later in this interaction, she knows how to deal with "a big, sassy, disrespectful brat." Thus, the new definition of the trouble prefigures a solution.

Third, this exchange displays one way in which ecosystemic brief therapists ask clients to use their imaginations in defining and solving their problems. In this case, the Northland Clinic therapist asks the client to imagine a circumstance in which she has never heard of the concept of paranoid schizophrenia. At other times, ecosystemic brief therapists ask clients to imagine and describe what might happen if they change their attitudes and/or behavior toward troublesome others in their social systems. The question invites clients to imagine how they might interrupt and alter the patterns. As shown in the following exchange involving two parents who have come to Northland Clinic seeking help in managing an incorrigible child, ecosystemic brief therapists sometimes use this question to initiate discussion of the pattern interruption solution. Also note that the therapist allows the clients to decide how they might concretely alter the ongoing, troublesome patterns.

> Therapist: OK, so what, let's say that you decided you weren't going to do that anymore. You're going to do something different, OK? I'm not sure what that is but just something. Uh, [. . .] do you think [. . .] you could really surprise him?
> Wife: Sure maybe [. . .]
> Therapist: See, he knows that you're talking to him or just anybody, he can predict with probably one hundred percent accuracy, well ninety nine, exactly what reaction he's gonna get out of both of you. [. . .] Do you agree? Do you think he could come close to 100% accuracy.
> Wife: Probably.
> Therapist: OK, now, what you do now is upset the apple cart in this game—you need to become unpredictable. Both of you.

A related ecosystemic strategy involves asking clients if they might consider doing wild or strange tasks in order to solve their problems. The question is often initiated by team members, and signals their interest in developing intervention messages designed to radically interrupt the troublesome patterns in which clients are stuck. Ecosystemic brief therapists also use the question to assess clients' commitments to solving their problems.

They assume that clients who state that they will do wild or strange tasks really want to solve their problems. Ecosystemic therapists often describe these clients as "not coming to therapy to just complain."

A final and less frequently employed ecosystemic strategy involves making suggestions to clients about how they might change their activities, relationships, and/or attitudes. Ecosystemic brief therapists usually reserve this strategy for clients who persist over several sessions in describing their lives as troubled. Consider the following exchange involving a Northland Clinic client who discounts his successes by insisting that the changes will not last:

Therapist: Well it's been my experience that one of the ways to keep success going is to [. . .] acknowledge it, and congratulate ourselves, and reward ourselves sometimes for successes. Have you ever tried that?

Client: I've heard the theory before. I've read a number of positive thinking books in my time. [. . .] Um, [. . .] I don't know that I've ever implemented something [. . .] on a consistent basis so, [. . .] so I'm not really sure how I'd do it.

Therapist: Uh, huh. [. . .] Well, it's kind of what you were saying earlier about success breeds success. The way that happens is [. . .] by building on the good times rather than focusing on failures.

Notice that the therapist in this interaction still maintains a nondirective orientation to the interview by describing her advice as "my experience," casting aspects of it as a question, and noting that her advice is similar to the client's earlier statement.

Negotiating Therapist-Client Relationships

Occasionally, clients persist across several sessions in offering what ecosystemic brief therapists consider to be complaints, and reporting that their troubles are not improving. The clients often justify their claims by describing changes that might be called positive as insignificant or as only temporary improvements that will disappear in the future. These clients also sometimes redefine the issues of greatest concern to them across sessions, thus making agreements developed in prior sessions irrelevant to subsequent therapist-client meetings. These cases are troublesome for ecosystemic brief therapists because they are not moving toward solutions.

These cases may be compared to first sessions in which clients state that they have no problems. Ecosystemic brief therapists respond to these clients by questioning them about the circumstances of their lives, and suggesting how others might interpret some of these circumstances as problematic. If clients continue to report that they have no problems, the therapists state that they can no longer meet with the clients, since the therapists' jobs involve working on problems. In this way, ecosystemic brief therapists define for clients the minimal professional conditions for establishing ecosystemic therapist–client relationships. In second and subsequent sessions, ecosystemic therapists also respond to clients who emphasize complaints by focusing the interactions on the therapist-client relationship. With these clients, however, the therapists are more willing to negotiate the terms of the relationship than with clients who insist that they have no problems in first sessions.

Given the small number of cases in which this happened at Northland Clinic, it is difficult to identify a typical pattern of response by the therapists and team members. Once, for example, a therapist suggested to a married couple that their troubles weren't going to get any better, but that they could occasionally return to the clinic to complain about them if they wished. At other times, Northland Clinic therapists confronted clients with their concerns and asked them to clarify the issues at hand. This therapist move also provides clients with new opportunities to define problems and/or construct solutions. Consider, for example, the following Northland Clinic therapist statement made to a client near the outset of their fourth meeting, and in response to the client's opening of the interview with a new set of concerns and complaints about her son:

> Well, uh, I am concerned if there are specific things that he is doing or saying, and those kinds of things that lead you to conclude that he has low self-esteem, or what kinds of specific things do you, or he, think he is to be doing differently, or saying differently, or what have you, which are expressions of self-esteem or what have you. Um, so that's the kind of thing I'm interested in. What you've been telling us, and in detail last time, was that by and large by his days were better. I just take that at face value. If his days aren't better, and I assume that better was that he seemed to be less depressed and his self-esteem was better, and that suggests to me that things are getting better, and you're feeling that maybe that's not really true.

Here, the Northland Clinic therapist asks for a concrete problem from the client (what the "specific things" are that have led the client to conclude that her son suffers from low self-esteem), stating that these details are "the kind of thing I'm interested in." She then summarizes the client's statements in prior interviews as indicating that the client's son is getting better, and states that she takes these statements at face value. The latter move might be

analyzed as an expression of the therapist's "good faith" in the therapist-
client relationship. That is, the therapist is fulfilling her role by uncritically
accepting the client's prior claims and taking them as signs of progress.
Finally, all of this might be viewed as the preface for the therapist's final
move, which involves contrasting her sense of progress with the client's
opening remarks in the interaction.

The therapist elaborated on these themes and provided the client with
opportunities to redefine her complaints as a problem in the rest of the
interview. She followed the above statement, for example, by summarizing
the major themes of prior interviews and asking the client to respond to her
summaries. The therapist started by noting that the client reported dramatic
improvement that "was too much to be believed" at the second session, and
that the changes had become more "normal" after that. She then offered the
client a problem on which they might work, stating

> OK, um, what were, so the changes have now gone back to normal. And I take
> that to mean, kind of like, you would expect him to be. What would it take for
> you to be convinced that, um, he needs to work through, and that he's still OK?

Through these interactional moves then, the Northland Clinic therapist
suggests to the client that their relationship is not proceeding satisfactorily
and provides the client with an opportunity to reconstruct the relationship
by focusing on a problem. The new problem does not involve the son's
behavior and feelings, so much as the client's orientation to her son.

Finally, one unusual incident should be noted. It involved the intercession
of a Northland Clinic team member in an ongoing interview with a married
couple who could not decide whether to stay together or get a divorce. The
clients were unable to specify problems in prior interviews, focusing instead
on their concerns about each of their options. They also responded to the
therapist's moves designed to construct problems and solutions by emphasizing their feelings of ambivalence and reasons for their indecisiveness. The
former team member replaced the previous therapist at the start of the fourth
session, explaining her actions in the following way:

> It's that it seems that this problem just keeps coming up over and over and over.
> And, somehow we don't seem to be getting anywhere. The same issue keeps
> coming up over and over, until last week. That was the first time we really
> heard, got a very good picture of how much this headache plays a part in the
> problem. And it was really startling for us to hear. And so, I was getting
> frustrated with, that things were not really happening, and we will hash over
> the same ground over and over. Same issue coming up over and over. So I think
> that perhaps, changing the therapist might do something to trigger, enough of a
> trigger to maybe do something. OK? That was the reason. [. . .] But anyway,
> so I think that this time you need to have some clear sense of when will you

know that you don't have to come here anymore? I need to know that. What will be the, sort of, sign to you down the road that you can go on your own. [. . .] So, maybe we need to be clear about that.

The new therapist's remarks to the clients suggest something of the unusualness of this case. She describes the team as frustrated with prior sessions, hopeful that the change might "trigger" a change, and specifies some new issues on which she wishes the interview to focus. Each of these aspects of the therapist's statement may be analyzed as rhetorical moves designed to cast the prior therapist-client relationship as unacceptable, to hold clients accountable to the conditions of ecosystemic therapy, and to provide clients with opportunities to redefine the relationship.

The opportunities provided by the Northland Clinic therapist, however, are less open-ended than in most sessions. Indeed, the therapist further focuses the discussion on her preferred issues as the interaction proceeds by stressing to clients that they have to make a decision about their marriage and therapy. She asks, for example, "so, how are you going to be able to make up your mind, or you know, shit or get off the pot?" And later, she asks, "Right, so, what will help you decide, one way or the other? Do it or don't do it?" The therapist uses these questions to orchestrate the interview away from clients' ambivalences and vague concerns and toward a new problem that she constructs as a dichotomous choice. The questions are, in other words, procedures for initiating entrance into the ecosystemic language of problems and change.

Ending Ecosystemic Brief Therapy

The vast majority of therapist-client relationships at Northland Clinic end without note because the clients cancel their scheduled appointments (explaining to the therapists that they do not need or want more therapy) or they do not appear for their scheduled appointments. The therapists sometimes contact the latter clients, requesting information about their circumstances and plans. Based on their actions in interviews and reactions to intervention messages, the therapists and team members sometimes make predictions about whether new clients will return for their second interviews. The therapists accept clients' assessments that they do not need more of the clinic's services, and portray clients who fail to keep their appointments as not needing their services any longer or likely to be happier with a different therapy approach.

While less frequent, it is not unusual for Northland Clinic therapists to anticipate and facilitate the ending of therapist-client relationships. For example, the therapists sometimes suggest to clients that they might think about when they will not need to come to the clinic any longer, thus making the termination of therapy the clients' choice. Less often, the therapists simply tell clients that they don't think more meetings are needed, or they tell them that their next session will be the last one. Another way in which Northland Clinic therapists anticipate the termination of the therapist-client relationship is by refocusing their questions on matters that might justify decisions to end the relationship.

One such shift involves asking clients to elaborate on the many positive changes that have occurred since the start of therapy and to explain why they think that they have occurred. The therapists then congratulate clients on the changes, and stress how the changes display clients' problem-solving insights and skills. The latter moves are designed to suggest to clients how they might generalize on their past problem-solving successes to more effectively deal with future troublesome circumstances. A related ecosystemic move involves asking clients first to anticipate problems in the near future and then to describe how they might deal with the problems. Again, the therapists note skills and understandings that the clients might use in responding to diverse troubles, thereby informally instructing clients on the ecosystemic concept of skeleton keys (see Chapter 3).

Ecosystemic brief therapists also respond to clients' discussions of their problem-solving successes and concerns about future problems by providing them with a practical philosophy for orienting to their future lives and troubles. The philosophy emphasizes the unevenness of life, how good times are followed by not so good times, which are then replaced by good times again. The following Northland therapist statement made to a client during her scheduled last interview illustrates how ecosystemic therapists instruct clients on this orientation to life and troubles:

> Now, as you know, uh, and I guess, as you anticipated, that there will be ups and downs, that things will go up for a while and then you are going to have some setbacks. . . . That's one of those two steps forward, one step backwards patterns. You are going to do a lot of that.

Thus, the therapists' final instructions to clients further elaborate on their prior focus on clients' problem-solving skills. The instructions emphasize that troubles and setbacks are an expected part of life, and that clients need not get stuck on them again.

CHAPTER 7

TEAMWORK IN ECOSYSTEMIC BRIEF THERAPY

This chapter is concerned with the activities that take place in the observation room during ecosystemic brief interviews. It deals with the ways in which team members orient to and participate in ongoing interviews. Team members do so in three major ways. First, they assess and comment on the interviews, particularly on the meaning of clients' statements and behavior. They also formulate questions that they wish clients to answer, and convey them to interviewing therapists. Team members might be described as a support staff for interviewing therapists. Second, they monitor the content and flow of interviews and suggest new directions to therapists whose interviews are, in the team's views, "going no where" or "off track." Finally, team members discuss intervention strategies that might be used to get clients "unstuck" from their troubled circumstances. Each of these activities is potentially relevant to therapist-team meetings that take place near the end of interviews, and during which intervention messages are constructed for clients. We take up therapist-team meetings in the next chapter.

Team members' participation in the ecosystemic brief therapy process is also defined by their distinctive positions as reactors to events taking place in the interviews and by the invisibility of their activities for clients and interviewing therapists. Team members' activities only become known to interviewing therapists and clients if team members choose to inform them. This circumstance may account for part of the "free-wheeling" and "playful" quality of team members' discussions, a quality that is less evident in ecosystemic brief therapy interviews. Team members regularly try out a variety of ideas on one another as they respond to aspects of the interviews.

Also, the teams' activities are not guided by a coordinator or dominant member. This may be contrasted with ecosystemic brief therapy interviews, which are orchestrated by the interviewing therapists. Any team member can offer an observation or suggestion, and the topics of discussion quickly change as team members introduce new issues into their conversations. Establishing closure or consensus on issues is not given high priority by team members, who often leave significant issues unresolved until they are joined by interviewing therapists and confronted with the task of developing intervention messages for clients. Team activities take on a clearer focus at these times.

We consider the four major ecosystemic brief team activities in the rest of this chapter: constructing problems, assessing interviews and clients' perspectives, proposing intervention strategies, and assessing the progress of ongoing cases. The latter team member activity takes place in second and subsequent sessions, whereas the others might occur in any session. It should also be noted that all intervention proposals developed by ecosystemic team members are provisional. They are contingent on the interviewing therapists' reactions and recommendations, a circumstance that team members frequently note as they discuss possible intervention strategies. As one team member stated at the conclusion of a lengthy negotiation about a proposed intervention, "I agree, it makes perfect sense to me. I don't know if [the interviewing therapist] will go along with it though." We begin by briefly considering a more general issue involving the vocabularies of solutions and cases used by team members and therapists in orienting to clients' problems and how they might be solved.

Solutions and Cases as Vocabularies

Much of ecosystemic brief therapy team members' work involves categorizing clients' social systems, perspectives, and troubles. Team members use the categories to assess the issues at stake in ongoing interviews and their options in responding to the issues. The categories, then, might be treated as practical vocabularies for organizing team members' interpretations of and negotiations about ongoing interviews. Thus, one way in which the Northland Clinic team members enter into and operate within the ecosystemic discourse is by applying ecosystemic categories to the details of the interviews that they observe.

The categories used by team members at Northland Clinic are related both to the formal literature and teachings of ecosystemic brief therapy and to the local history of Northland Clinic. While different in some ways, these categories are similar in their indifference to defining clients as disordered and to finding the causes of clients' putative disorders. This indifference is evident in the Northland Clinic therapists' typical response to clients referred by other human service agencies. The referring documents often include formal diagnoses of clients' problems made by officials of the referring agencies. Northland Clinic therapists inform their teams of the diagnoses prior to their meetings with the clients, but usually devote little or no time to discussing the referring officials' assessments.

More important for Northland Clinic therapists is whether clients have previously been in therapy and—sometimes—information about the remedies that the referring officials have tried. The therapists state that clients who have prior experience with other therapy approaches are distinctive because they often assume that all therapies emphasize identifying the causes of clients' troubles and stress psychoanalytic introspection as an important part of solving their troubles. Northland Clinic therapists explain that these clients are sometimes less able or willing to follow their lead in moving interviews away from complaints and toward problems. Consider, for example, the following comment made by a team member while watching an interview with a client who had previously been in a different form of therapy:

> This is a perfect example of how people get trapped, and they don't know where to go. They just don't see anyway out, she's trapped. . . . She is a classic case of a person who has been in therapy, too. You know, she could go on with this for twelve years, if we let her. She comes here to cry and that's all.

In place of disorder categories, Northland Clinic staff members emphasize solution categories and case names. Together, they form two different, but related vocabularies that ecosystemic brief therapists use to describe and respond to clients' troubles in ways that fit with clients' distinctive perspectives and circumstances. The solution categories used by ecosystemic team members and therapists are largely derived from the formal literature of ecosystemic brief therapy, including those associated with Eriksonian, strategic, and related family therapies. The categories are also topics of discussion in seminars and workshops conducted by the Northland Clinic staff members, who describe them as skeleton keys—that is, as intervention strategies that are effective with diverse clients and troubles.

It should also be emphasized that ecosystemic brief therapists and team members' selection and use of general solution categories in any particular case require that they take account of clients' potentially distinctive problems, perspectives, and social systems. Ecosystemic brief therapists and team members fit these solutions to clients by describing clients' motives and life circumstances in ways that justify using one of the skeleton keys. Of course, others sometimes disagree by arguing that the proposed solution categories are inappropriate and/or by offering alternative solutions. In both cases, however, the application of a solution category to a particular case involves describing clients, their social systems, and troubles as particular kinds of persons, systems, and troubles.

The therapists also take account of the uniquenesses and similarities of their clients' lives and troubles by naming cases. All of the videotaped interviews conducted by Northland Clinic staff members are given names that characterize salient aspects of the interviews for the therapists. Most are descriptions either of clients' concerns and problems (such as "The Gambler," "Dilemma," and "Don't Blame Me") or of the interventions recommended by the therapists. For example, the case named "Bed Switch" involved the suggestion that a couple switch the sides of the bed on which they slept as one way of breaking up their ongoing, troubled behavior patterns. Less frequently, the therapists name their cases based on other client characteristics (such as "Nice Pants," a case involving an affluent client who wore expensive clothes to his therapy sessions). In one case, the therapists decided that they could not identify an appropriate name for a case, so they called it "No Name."

This approach to naming cases serves at least two of the therapists' interests. First, the names protect the confidentiality of clients, whose videotapes are labeled and stored under their new names. Anyone who wishes to see a videotape of a particular case must be well enough acquainted with it to know its name. The names also provide the therapists with a vocabulary for comparing, contrasting, and categorizing cases. That is, the therapists do not speak of clients as being schizophrenic, anorexic, or learning disabled so much as they say that one case reminds them of another, even though the latter case often involves very different client complaints, or might be classified by other therapists as a very different kind of problem.

The vocabulary that has emerged through this process is practical, evolving, and not well suited to formal abstraction into universal categories. Rather, it is a vernacular vocabulary that is locally produced and articulated. Ecosystemic brief therapy team members use aspects of the vocabulary to construct family resemblances between cases. The vocabulary both complements and is an alternative to the general solution categories that they also use. While "Bed Switch," for example, might be described as just another way of describing the pattern interruption strategy, Northland Clinic therapists' may also use this case name to establish other resemblances between this and other cases, such as similarities in the ways in which clients' describe their lives and troubles. The vernacular vocabulary of cases is, in other words, a metaphoric language that is available for elaboration in many different ways.

In the abstract, at least, every case name is potentially available to ecosystemic brief therapists and team members in making sense of any particular case. Therapists and team members make them available by suggesting that the case at hand is similar to another case or, less frequently, by contrasting the two cases. Consider the following exchange, which occurred behind the mirror at Northland Clinic. Notice, in particular, that while the team member (TM) discusses how the case at hand is like "a fog" and "the piano," he never mentions the details of the ongoing interview or of the cases that were the sources for these categories. The focus is on the clients' abilities to describe their troubles and circumstances.

> TM: We have half a fog here and if we brought his wife in, we'd probably have a whole fog. Ya know, they just don't know what's going on?
>
> Miller: A fog?
>
> TM: Yeah, a fog is when both parties of a couple don't know what's happening. Everything is unclear, fuzzy, a fog. It's not that rare either. There's a subtype of it that's called the piano.
>
> Miller: The piano?
>
> TM: Yeah, that's when they think they know what's going on, but they don't. They have the mistaken notion that they know what's happening to each other, but they really don't know what the other is thinking. We have to get through that before we can do anything with 'em.
>
> Miller: So, they don't understand each other?
>
> TM: Yeah, they just go right past each other, but they really don't think so. Sort of like an Englishman and an American trying to communicate, ya know, it can be real difficult. The words sound the same but there are real cultural differences in how they're used. Ya hafta listen carefully to see.
>
> Miller: Why piano?
>
> TM: Oh, because it started with a guy who worked on pianos and his wife.

The vocabularies of solutions and cases, then, are practical resources that ecosystemic brief therapists and team members use to describe aspects of interviews with clients and to justify ecosystemic responses to them. They are related, but different aspects of the discourse of ecosystemic brief therapy. Ecosystemic team members apply the vocabularies to particular cases as they go about the practical work of monitoring, interpreting, and sometimes intervening in ongoing interviews. We turn to these aspects of ecosystemic teamwork in the rest of the chapter, beginning with the circumstances associated with team members' intervention into ongoing interviews.

Assessing and Intervening in Interviews

Ecosystemic brief therapy team members' interest in how interviews are conducted is practical. They cannot construct problems or solutions that fit with clients' perspectives and other aspects of clients' social systems unless clients provide them with professionally useful information. Eliciting that information is a major responsibility of interviewing therapists who are expected to ask appropriate questions and to guide the interactions toward therapeutically preferred topics. One setting in which team members aid this process is in presession meetings where therapists sometimes ask for advice on how to orient to upcoming interviews. Consider, for example, the following interaction involving a Northland Clinic therapist and two team members about the therapist's upcoming second interview with a married couple. The therapist states that she and the clients were unable to construct a problem in the first session, although several possibilities were discussed. She also states that the previous intervention message given to the clients was to "pay attention to what is good in the relationship."

> Therapist: So, should I start with that [the intervention message], with what has happened this week?
> TM1: Uh, huh.
> Therapist: Unless they bring up something else and then I go with that, right?
> TM1: No, hit them hard with that [the question about the intervention message], try to take control right away.
> TM2: Otherwise, you may get a lot of complaints with them going back and forth again, without anything getting accomplished.

A major interest shared by ecosystemic brief therapists and their teams, then, is in orchestrating interviews toward discussions of problems and solutions. Team members express this interest in preinterview meetings with therapists and in their comments made to each other while observing ongoing interviews. They note, for example, when interviewing therapists orchestrate interviews in professionally approved ways, such as by asking creative questions and/or persisting in asking clients to specify workable problems. When clients are unable or unwilling to follow the interviewing therapists' lead in moving from complaints to problems, on the other hand, team members discuss how the interviewing therapists' actions might have contributed to this circumstance. Consider, for example, the following comment made by a team member during a session that she described as "off track":

> Don't let her [the client] do that. She's controlling the session, and you can't let her do that. She's wallowing in her problem, we don't have a problem yet.

Ecosystemic team members usually attempt to get such interviews back "on track" by calling the interviewing therapists and suggesting alternative lines of questioning. Occasionally, however, they are more directive, telling the therapists to be more assertive in asking questions and/or insisting that clients answer their questions. In either case, the teams' telephone calls halt the ongoing interactional pattern and introduce new concerns into the interviews. The calls remind ecosystemic brief therapists and clients of the teams' presence behind the mirror and call for some measure of accountability to the teams' concerns. Thus, the orchestration of ecosystemic interviews is a collaborative process involving both therapists and team members.

One example of this collaboration is an interview with a mother and her two teenage children at Northland Clinic. As the session proceeds, the interviewer begins to direct most of her questions to the mother, a shift that is noted by a team member who states,

> She's too focused on the mother, she's gotta do more with the kids. Ask them what they think. It's important that she give 'em a sense of fairness, or she'll lose 'em. Look at 'em, they look like they're tuning the whole thing out. We don't want to alienate 'em, or we won't get anywhere. [The team member picks up the telephone and states to the interviewing therapist,] What we seem to have here are three people with three different agendas. We need to acknowledge that, and say that they have three situations, and ask 'em what or, er, uh, how we can help them. Ask each one of them how their agenda can be met. OK?

Notice, here, that the team member precedes her telephoning of the therapist with a description of how the interview has gone off track: it is "too focused on the mother." She then notes how the interview needs to be changed (ask the kids "what they think"), and precedes her telephone call by giving reasons for why it was warranted, including, "It's important that she give 'em a sense of fairness, or she'll lose 'em." These prefatory comments might also be seen as invitations for comments from other team members. When no responses are forthcoming, she telephones the therapist with her suggestions. On other occasions, however, such team member comments initiate discussions among team members about ongoing interviews, including discussions of whether they are going off track and how they might be repaired.

Ecosystemic team members assess the usefulness of their telephone calls by closely attending to clients' responses to their questions. They pay attention to both the content of clients' answers and how their bodily positionings and gazes change in response to the questions. When team members assess clients as having misunderstood their questions, they quickly call the therapists again, offering new versions of their questions. Team members also sometimes call therapists back when they assess clients as evading their questions, this time asking therapists to press the issues of interest to the teams. At other times, ecosystemic team members treat the clients' "evasive" responses as useful information in itself, and not necessitating further queries.

Finally, ecosystemic team members assess some of their questions as having gotten the interviews back on track. As in the following Northland Clinic team member statement, they often note and elaborate on this assessment by emphasizing the significance of asking "good" questions in achieving the goals of ecosystemic therapy goals. The interview involved a married couple who report that they "fight all the time." The team member's call stressed the importance of the therapist moving the husband away from talking about the couple's fights and toward discussing the "good times, when things work." The team member assessed and elaborated on the husband's description of the "good times" by stating,

> See what useful kinds of information you can get with a question like that? He'd talk about the fights all night if she [the therapist] let him, but when you focus on the positive you get all kinds of good information. She [the wife] wants him to fulfill her needs, not just sex, but when he's happy, she's happy. That explains the [her] anger.

Team members elicit three major types of information through their telephone calls to therapists: clients' problems, perspectives, and social systems. We consider these issues in the next three sections.

Constructing Problems

Ecosystemic brief therapy team members express an interest in constructing problems from the outset of interviews. They pay special attention to clients' reasons for coming to therapy, treating them either as possible bases for defining solvable problems or as complaints. Team members cast clients' answers as complaints by describing them as vague or unreasonable. As in the following exchange, their comments often stress how life is filled with troubles with which we must learn to cope. Clients who express concerns about these matters, then, are complaining:

TM1:   She doesn't have a problem. We have to find something to work with here.

TM2:   Yeah, I know, she jumps at the opportunity to do things and she does them, but she gets scared 'cause they're hard or something. You know, she gets upset.

TM1:   Yup, she overreacts, if you will.
       [Client states that she wants a solution to being self-conscious.]

TM1: Die, that's the only way that you'll solve it. Just die. [Other team members laugh.]

TM2: She doesn't have a problem

TM1: She wants us to tell her how to not be aware of herself without being self-conscious and without dying. That's what life is about.

TM2: She wants to be tranquilized.

TM1: It's enough to drive her to drink.

While such Northland Clinic team member responses to clients' concerns might be interpreted as dismissive of clients, an alternative view treats them as expressions of the ecosystemic assumption that the construction of problems cannot proceed in desired ways so long as clients remain "stuck" in their complaints. The character of clients is not so much at issue as the professional usefulness of their responses to interviewing therapists' questions. Even as team members portray clients' statements as complaints, they continue to observe and react to the interviews as sources for problems. Indeed, a discussion of a client's vague or unreasonable complaints might suddenly end when one or more team members proclaims that the client has just offered a problem or at least the beginnings of a problem. Such a proclamation occurred in the above case. Very shortly after the above exchange, the client stated that she didn't know what she wanted to do with the rest of her life, and the following interaction ensued:

TM1: Ah, we now have a problem that we can work with. All these problems are signs of confusion. She doesn't know what she wants to do.

TM2: She's going through a midlife crisis.

TM1: It's interesting how people go through them at different times. Some people go through them at ten and some go through them a thousand times. You know, what we have here is a female version of "Dilemma" [another case involving a man who was confused about how to deal with his future after the dissolution of his marriage].

Two features of this interaction warrant further discussion. First, notice that in portraying the clients' concerns about what to do with the rest of her life as a problem (i.e., she's confused), TM1 recasts her prior complaints as aspects of the problem. They are now matters on which the client and therapists might work in finding solutions to her confusion. The practical significance of complaints, then, is potentially subject to redefinition as ecosystemic team members construct clients' problems. TM2 further transforms the complaints into aspects of a recognizable and solvable problem by portraying it as a "midlife crisis," a characterization that TM1 generalizes to other people. In these ways, the team members construct not just a problem, but one that is mundane and shared with others, further suggesting that it is solvable.

The second notable feature of this exchange is TM1's linking of this case to another case—"Dilemma"—by declaring that the present client's trouble is a "female version" of the other case. In this way, TM1 categorizes the case within the clinic's distinctive vocabulary of cases. He also initiates a discussion of how this case is like "Dilemma," and whether the intervention strategy used in the prior case might work in this one. The comparison moves the discussion away from the question of "what is the client's problem," and toward consideration of solutions that might fit with a client who is a female version of "Dilemma."

Ecosystemic team members are not always able to construct such clearcut problem definitions from clients' statements, however. One way in which they signal their uncertainty is by proposing possible problems and inviting other team members to respond. Sometimes other team members elaborate on the proposals, thus transforming them into workable problems. The proposed problems are rejected when team members describe them as inappropriate (they don't fit with clients) or do not respond to them (such as by changing the subject of the discussions). At other times, ecosystemic team members state that clients' answers are so vague or unresponsive to therapists' questions that they cannot formulate even provisional problems.

Ecosystemic team members respond to both of these situations by telephoning the interviewing therapists, giving them questions that the teams want answered or suggesting that the therapists might explore alternative issues. The following exchange is an example. It involves a woman whose children have been removed from the home by a local court and placed with her mother. The children accompanied the client to the session at Northland Clinic. The exchange occurred when the client temporarily halted the session to take her children to the bathroom.

> [TM1 joins the team after the start of the interview]
> TM1: This is one of those amorphous cases, boy.
> TM2: Yeah, we're trying to figure out what's going on here. We think maybe she's here because of a court order. We need to get to why she's here. [She goes to the telephone, picks it up, and speaks to the interviewing therapist.] When they come back in, you wanna ask 'em questions about, it's very difficult to ask with the kids and all, ask her about how this situation came to be, why she lost the, uh, lost the kids and her relationship with her mother. You know, how her mother got the kids in the first place and what she wants from us, 'cause it sounds like she's just here 'cause the court said so.

This exchange illustrates two major aspects of ecosystemic team members' decisions to intervene in ongoing interviews. First, the call took place well into the interview, after the interviewing therapist had asked several times about the client's reasons for coming to therapy. Second, team members verbally noted their difficulties in constructing the client's problem. They were noted by team members prior to TM1 joining the group, and raised again by TM1 who described the case as "amorphous." These statements might be interpreted as invitations to other team members to propose possible problems, but none were forthcoming. Rather, TM2 agreed with TM1's characterization of the case and added, "We need to get to why she's here" just prior to telephoning the interviewing therapist.

The Northland Clinic team's decision to intervene in the interview, then, was an interactional event that developed over the course of the interview. The interactional processes through which these decisions emerge are often more complex and shifting than in this case, however. The decision might, for example, be preceded by team member attempts to construct problems, by the posing of alternative lines of questioning, and/or by discussions of what to communicate to interviewing therapists. Consider the following exchange that began when TM4 joined the team after the session had begun and asked what the case was about:

> TM1: This is a couple where things aren't going the way they used to, but it's kind of vague and they don't really know what's wrong? I think I see the problem. Boy he is stone faced, geez.
>
> TM2: I get the sense that it's like he's not here.
>
> TM3: Does anyone know what the problem is? I don't know what the problem is.
>
> TM2: I don't really know what the problem is, it's too vague.
>
> TM1: How is this gonna be different in two years, three years, whatever?
>
> TM4: Yeah, how will they be different when they don't have the problem?
>
> TM1: This is what we would call intellectualizing.
>
> TM3: Yeah, it's uh [. . .]
>
> TM1: It's mind-fucking, [looks at TM3 and smiling] that's what we call this in group. You get the feeling that this could just go on and on for hours, not get anywhere.
> [TM4 goes to the telephone and turns to the group]
>
> TM4: Okay, what should I say? [begins to talk to the therapist] Uh, the team is wondering how things would be different in the situation with the kid the other night if things were better between them?

> TM3:   And if he was more trusting.
> Therapist: Anything else?
> TM4:   Uh, yeah, TM3 wants to add if he was more trusting. [jok-
>   ingly] I don't know what that has to do with anything, but, ya
>   know. Go ahead and ask it, I guess. [other team members
>   laugh]

This interaction may be analyzed by dividing it into four parts. The first phase begins with TM1's description of the case to TM4, which includes the suggestion that the problem at hand is the husband because he is so "stone faced." TM1 signals that it is a proposed problem or suggestion by hedging his statement, stating that he "thinks" that he sees the problem. This approach to problem construction may be contrasted with the prior exchange in which a team member proclaimed, "We now have a problem." TM2 elaborates on the proposed problem by stating that the husband seems to be elsewhere. At this point, however, TM3 redirects the interaction back to the initial question by asking if anyone sees a problem, and declaring that she doesn't. The proposed problem definition is thus set aside to—perhaps—be reconsidered at a later time.

The interaction takes a very different turn when TM1 asks, "How is this gonna be different in two years, three years, whatever?" This question initiates the second part of the interaction and process. Team members often ask such questions while watching interviews. The questions raise issues that team members wish interviewing therapists to explore in moving clients away from complaints and toward problems. As in this interaction, however, these questions are not always immediately conveyed to interviewing therapists. Although it did not happen in this case, the alternative questions voiced by team members sometimes become topics of extended discussion and even disagreement.

Next, TM1 refocuses the team's attention on the client's answers. He casts them as not useful by describing them as "intellectualizing," "mindfucking," and likely to "just go on and on." This third phase of the interaction ends when TM4 gets up from his chair, picks up the telephone, and invites others' advice on what to say. Notice also that the questions conveyed to the interviewing therapist are not the same as those asked during the second part of the interaction. The questions that are eventually conveyed to the interviewing therapist, then, do not emerge in a straightforward, linear fashion, such as from a predetermined script. Rather, the questions evolve as ecosystemic team members react to aspects of ongoing interviews, and to one another.

In sum, the construction of client problems by ecosystemic team members is sometimes a complex process, and the definitions that they propose are always contingent. Team members might reconsider their definitions based on new information offered by clients later in the interviews, the ideas of other therapists who join the teams later in the sessions, and—particularly—in light of the interpretations expressed by interviewing therapists during the therapist-team meeting.

Assessing Clients' Perspectives and Social Systems

Ecosystemic brief therapy team members' interest in assessing clients' perspectives focuses on how clients' orientations to social reality might be part of their problems. The assessments involve both the content of and ways in which clients respond to the therapists' questions. Ecosystemic brief therapists state that clients' ways of describing their concerns and circumstances as well as their demeanor are expressions of clients' perspectives and are relevant to understanding their troubles. A major topic of ecosystemic team members' discussions during sessions, then, is their assessments of clients' perspectives, and how the perspectives are related to clients' problems. They use the assessments to construct coherent and professionally useful understandings of the issues at hand.

One assessment procedure used by Northland Clinic therapists and team members involves classifying clients' self-presentation styles, such as by describing some clients as boring. They state that this is not a pejorative term because it is not a description of clients' character or even a problem on which the therapists have any interest in working. Rather, it is a classification of the way in which clients present their troubles in interviews, particularly their lack of energy and emotional involvement in the issues that they describe as troublesome. Ecosystemic team members also assume that clients' "boringness" is the usual way in which they conduct themselves in life. Thus, ecosystemic team members often treat clients' "boringness" as a relevant aspect of the clients' social systems, within which their troubles are embedded.

We can see each of these aspects of assessing clients' perspectives in the following interaction, which is concerned with a Northland Clinic client whose wife has left him for another man. First, the team members describe the client's style of answering questions as "part of his problem," reflecting "his reality," and involving "too much information." They then elaborate on his perspective and problem with a computer metaphor, and by comparing him with the prior client, who was also unable "to do anything." Finally, they characterize the client's demeanor as "boring."

TM1:   Doesn't he ever have a simple answer to a question?

TM2:   That's right.

TM1:   That's part of his problem.

TM2:   Yup, that's right. He, uh, doesn't know, it reflects his reality, uh, forgive the expression, but he can't talk straight and so he can't think straight. That's his problem.

TM1:   Too much information.

TM2:   Yup.

TM1:   His computer's broke.

TM2:   That's right, his disk is full.

TM1:   I'm surprised he gets anything done. He imagines all these bizarre contingencies for everything. How does he get anything done?

TM2:   Yeah, like the case just before, her problems all come from her being so self-critical and not able to do anything. This guy's problem is all these contingencies.

TM1:   That's right, it's all in his head.
       [Discussion turns to how well the therapist is handling the interview.]

TM1:   Boy is he [the client] boring or what?

TM2:   Yeah, I know, I'm having trouble following it, he's so boring.

Through these interpretive procedures, ecosystemic team members construct professionally useful understandings of the clients' orientations to life, and relations with others in their social systems. Later in the above interaction, for example, the team members elaborated on their portrayal of the client and his problems by describing his wife's departure as a response to the client's confused perspective and "boringness."

Ecosystemic team members' assessments of clients' perspectives and social systems are more complex in interviews involving more than one client. In these cases, team members not only take account of each client's answers and demeanor, but also treat clients' responses to one another as meaningful. Consider, for example, the following interaction concerned with a married couple. The exchange followed several team members' portrayal of the husband as "strange," and another team member's statement that the interview seemed to be going "off track."

TM1:   Well, maybe it's the way his mind works. He goes off on things. He almost sounds retarded.

TM2:   Yeah, he does, but she doesn't seem to think he is.

TM3:   Yeah, you know, she was real concerned with the mirror, maybe it's because of him, ya know, she's protecting him.

TM4:   Yeah, I know, but she doesn't say he's dense, she doesn't seem to see it.

TM1:   Maybe he's on drugs.
       [They discuss the possibility that he is on drugs or retarded.]
TM2:   Maybe he's just thinking in a new way that he hasn't thought before?
TM1:   Yeah, he's talking too abstract to be retarded.
TM2:   He's a poet, maybe he's a poet. He's offering us different metaphors. He's offered us two "M*A*S*H" metaphors and one Republican party one.

Notice how the Northland Clinic team members link their assessments of the husband's state of mind to his wife's behavior. While he "almost sounds retarded," she doesn't respond to him as retarded. Still, the issue isn't settled. The team members also consider the wife's prior uneasiness about being observed by the team (her concern "with the mirror") as related to the husband's possible retardedness, suggesting that maybe "she's protecting him." At this point, TM4 notes that the wife has never stated that she believes her husband is "dense." The statement might be understood as suggesting that if the wife doesn't "see it," then the husband's seeming denseness may not be related to their problems or family system. This and other possible understandings are left undeveloped, however, because TM1 changes the subject by raising the possibility that the husband is "on drugs."

Eventually, TM2 raises the possibility that the husband's behavior reflects a new way of thinking for him. TM2 characterizes the client as a "poet" who is thinking metaphorically, describing the client's prior references to a television show ("M*A*S*H") and the Republican party as signs of the client's poetic state of mind. This turn in the interaction is significant for several reasons. First, the portrayal of the client as a poet recasts his behavior. It is no longer a possible sign of retardation or drug use, but reasonable for a person who is "thinking in a new way." The turn also moves the discussion away from the wife's concern for the mirror and the possibility that she is protecting him. Rather, the team members use the poet characterization to construct an alternative social system for the couple. They eventually construct an intervention message that fits with this system by portraying aspects of the couple's problem as similar to aspects of "M*A*S*H" and the Republican party.

The above instruction is an example of a major theme in many ecosystemic team member discussions about clients' social systems and troubles. While they often consider a variety of possible categorizations and portrayals of clients' perspectives, team members usually prefer accounts that emphasize the reasonableness and normality of clients' concerns and points of view. This is consistent with the philosophy of ecosystemic brief therapy, which stresses the systemic contexts of clients' troubles (not clients' personal pathologies) and clients' problem-solving abilities. As in the above interaction, ecosystemic team members sometimes apply these ecosystemic emphases by considering several possible understandings of clients' troubles and perspectives, eventually selecting one that casts clients as reasonable persons whose troubles might be remedied through ecosystemic intervention.

Proposing Interventions

Ecosystemic brief therapy team members' discussions of possible responses to clients' problems are inextricably linked to the other activities discussed above. At Northland Clinic, team members' discussions usually start with constructions of problems, but then often quickly move to other topics. Team members might, for example, discuss the interviewing therapist's style of questioning, then consider a possible intervention strategy, only to return to the question of what the client's problem is. Consider, for example, the following interaction, which occurred behind the mirror at Northland Clinic. It begins with a proposed problem definition (the client doesn't want to be blamed for her husband's decision to leave her), and then moves to the client's perspective (whether she is feeling guilt or anger), and finally to how the team should respond to the client's concerns (validate her anger.)

TM1:   It just keeps coming up, over and over again. She doesn't want to be blamed.
TM2:   Um huh.
TM1:   Do you think she's feeling guilty?
TM2:   I think she's just pissed.
TM3:   Yeah, she's pissed. [TM3 describes the circumstances of the husband's leaving.] She has a right to be pissed, you'd be pissed too.
TM1:   [laughs] I'd clobber him. [. . .] Well, we have to tell her that she has been dumped on, and has a right to be angry. You know, validate her anger. [Others nod in agreement]

Ecosystemic team members' problem constructions and assessments of clients' perspectives, social systems, and intervention proposals are interrelated. For example, team members' concern for developing appropriate interventions is prefigured in their prior constructions of client problems and assessments of clients' perspectives. They are the conditions with which the interventions need to fit in order to be ecosystemically appropriate. And all possible responses to clients' problems are not equally likely to be defined by team members as appropriate for the problems and perspectives at hand.

In the above exchange, for example, TM1's statement that the intervention message should address and validate the client's anger is responsive to the team's prior depiction of the client as being "pissed." Had the team assessed the client's perspective as feeling guilt, however, the proposed intervention might not have been offered and, if made, it is unlikely that it would have been so readily accepted by other team members. Another example of this pattern is the following Northland Clinic team member exchange concerned with a married couple who state that they are on the verge of getting a divorce:

TM1: It sounds like he's trying to see how far he can go with her without, ya know, anything happening.

TM2: So, you're saying that we should give him an ultimatum?

TM1: No, uh, ya know, give her something else, like "Dick's Jane."

This interaction illustrates how an assessment of a client's perspective sometimes initiates a discussion of an intervention strategy. That is, TM2 responds to TM1's description of the husband's attitude toward the marriage by asking about an intervention strategy that might be seen as fitting with TM1's assessment. TM1 rejects this possibility, suggesting instead that they consider another approach, one that is known in the clinic's vocabulary of cases as "Dick's Jane." The interaction also illustrates one of the potential complexities of fitting interventions with problem constructions and assessments of clients' perspectives and social systems. Not only are there several appropriate ecosystemic intervention strategies available to team members in responding to clients who test the limits of their marriages, but the strategies have different implications for understanding the problem at hand.

In the above case, giving the client an ultimatum response would assume that the husband needs to have the limits of acceptable behavior clearly specified. For example, his wife might tell him that if he stays out all night again, she will divorce him. The response makes saving the marriage a choice that is within the husband's purview. The "Dick's Jane" response, on the other hand, involves the assumption that inattentive husbands take their wives for granted, partly, because the wives are always available and that their loyalty is never doubted. This ecosystemic intervention is given as a suggestion to wives that they create mystery in their marriages by seeming to be involved with other men. The strategy may be implemented in a variety of ways, including asking a friend to call the house and hang up when the husband answers, sending one's self flowers, and staying out late at night while offering no (or minimal) explanations.

The ultimatum and "Dick's Jane" intervention strategies, then, involve different understandings of the husband's perspective, the couple's social system, and the problem of saving their marriage. However, both strategies might be said to fit with clients' perspectives and family systems. Which of the available responses is to be defined by ecosystemic team members as the most appropriate is an open question, and therefore potentially open to continuing negotiation as team members observe and participate in ecosystemic brief therapy interviews. Indeed, the negotiations might even consider the temporal appropriateness of these possible responses, such as whether it might be too early in the therapy process to try the more direct, ultimatum response.

While prior definitions prefigure later moves by ecosystemic team members, they do not determine subsequent developments. The linking of problems, perspectives, systems, and interventions might be done in a variety of ways. Sometimes, for example, ecosystemic team members respond to proposed interventions by reconsidering their definitions of clients' problems, relationships, and perspectives. Indeed, as the following interaction concerned with a mother and her son shows, team members do not always need a problem definition prior to proposing an intervention strategy:

TM1:   I wonder what it is that he isn't willing to talk about?
TM2:   He probably won't ever say.
TM1:   Yeah, but a clue is what he said, is that she's not such a hot lady.
TM3:   And she agrees
       [They watch in silence for several minutes.]
TM1:   It's one of those cases where we're not gonna get anywhere, get any information until we compliment them. You know, they're not gonna relax until they hear that. They're gonna be real surprised by the intervention.

Notice here that not only have the Northland Clinic team members not proposed a problem on which they might work, but they assume that all pertinent information is not being provided by, at least, the son. Yet, they don't call the interviewing therapist to suggest questions that might elicit problem statements from the clients. Rather, TM1 shifts the interaction to the clients' family system by stating that it is the kind of family that won't relax until they have been complimented, thereby negating the value of any questions that might be asked by the team. The construction of a problem, then, is set aside in anticipation of the family's response to the intervention message, which TM1 assumes will include compliments, a safe assumption for virtually all ecosystemic intervention messages.

Ecosystemic team members' discussions about possible intervention strategies also address the practical complexity of initiating change in clients' social systems. The discussions emphasize giving clients intervention messages that are both feasible within their lives and make sense within their perspectives. This is the nub of ecosystemic brief therapists' concern for fitting therapy to clients and, according to the Northland Clinic staff, their most important ethical responsibility to clients. The concern is evident in the following intervention proposal made by a team member as a part of a conversation about how a client wants all aspects of her life to be perfect, and blames herself when they aren't:

> She's hurting but she's afraid to change. So we need to change her thinking away from all her problems being her fault. Maybe we could make them bad luck 'cause that can be changed? Whatta ya think?

While less complex than others, this proposal illustrates two major aspects of many ecosystemic intervention strategies. First, the proposal is indirect, it does not involve confronting the client by suggesting that her perspective is the "real" problem or even that it is wrong. Rather, the proposal implicitly accepts the client's concerns about her life, but "reframes" them by suggesting that they reflect her "bad luck," not her culpability. The second and related instructive feature of this proposal is that the new framing of the client's troubles offers hope for change and a better future for the client. Bad luck is a condition that comes and goes in persons' lives; thus it is reasonable to expect that it will eventually go away, to be replaced by happier times.

Ecosystemic team members also express an interest in identifying signs of change in clients' lives and social systems in second and subsequent interviews. We turn to this aspect of ecosystemic brief therapy teamwork next.

Assessing Change

Northland Clinic team members' assessments of change begin with clients' entry into the interview room. They treat clients' dress, grooming, and demeanor as signs of clients' states of mind and success in remedying clients' problems. The signs of positive change noted by team members are sometimes subtle and/or limited to only one aspect of clients' appearances, such as their hair or carriage. As in the following interaction concerned with a client who has arrived for her last session, ecosystemic team members sometimes note multiple signs of positive change in clients' appearances:

TM1:   My god, she does look better. My god, she looks better, so much better.

TM2:   She looks so different, even attractive.

TM1:   Well, she always was attractive, she's just more, uh, feminine or whatever. She's changed her hair too, that helped a lot.

TM2:   She must have lost weight or something, she looks good in pants,
       and before she looked so dumpy.
TM3:   She really does look better.

Ecosystemic team members continue to attend to clients' appearances
and demeanor as the interviews proceed. They treat their initial assessments
as confirmed by clients' reports of positive changes in their lives. Even when
clients report little or no change, however, team members may still treat
their initial assessments as relevant and possibly signifying changes that are
not yet recognized by clients. Consider, for example, the following interaction concerned with a married couple who report no change in their marriage since their first session, including no change in their primary reason for
remaining married—they are doing it for the good of their child. Nonethe-
less, based on his assessment of the couple's demeanor toward one another,
TM1 suggests that change has occurred since the first session.

TM1:   They seem different than last week.
TM2:   Really.
TM1:   Yeah, they seem different. [. . .] Don't seem so pissed at each
       other.
TM2:   Oh really, they're staying together for the kid.
TM1:   Yeah, but they're not so pissed either.

Ecosystemic team members' general assessments of their clients' lives
and troubles may be classified within three major categories, each of which
has implications for team members' orientations to their prior understandings of and responses to clients' troubles. The responses may be summarized
as (1) "The problem is solved," (2) "We're on the right track," and (3) "It's not
working." The first two responses are most frequently expressed by the team
members, particularly the "We're on the right track" conclusion. They are
part of the team members' recommendations that therapeutic relationships
be terminated, or that existing courses of action be continued. The "It's not
working" conclusion, on the other hand, is central to team members' recommendations that existing courses of action be ceased, and that new understandings of and responses to clients' problems be developed. We consider
each of these recommendations in turn.

Elaborating on Prior Understandings

Ecosystemic brief therapy team members' portrayals of previous interventions as working are associated with explanations of why and how they are

successful. The accounts are generally expressed as confirmations of the usefulness of ecosystemic brief therapy for producing change in clients' lives. More specifically, they involve client reports of change as confirming the accuracy of team members' prior understandings of and responses to clients' problems and social systems. Consider the following team member exchange concerning a couple who originally reported that the husband was depressed and felt left out of the family. One part of the intervention message previously given to the clients was the recommendation that the husband assume more home maintenance tasks. The husband reported in the next interview that he was no longer feeling so depressed.

TM1: Of course he feels better, she isn't doing everything, she's not carrying the whole load. She was doing everything and he was feeling useless, uh, unneeded . . .

TM2: Was it during the last session that you got the idea that his problem was that she was doing everything?

TM1: Uh, no, I think at the end of the first session. It was what she said, you know, she kept the kids away from him and does everything so that he could be depressed. What else was he doing to do? It was her whole demeanor and her anger, she got angry at some point in that session. . . . I'll bet her behavior changed [taking over the running of the household] six years ago [when he was seriously ill], I'll bet it's been going on a long time.

Of special interest to ecosystemic team members are occasions when clients report faster or more extensive changes in their lives than anticipated. Team members treat these client reports as extraordinary confirmations of the ecosystemic approach to brief therapy and signs of the clients' willingness and abilities to apply the approach to their lives. Team members also offer explanations about why the unanticipated improvement occurred, including how clients might have intentionally or unintentionally changed their behavior to alter their social systems and solve their problems.

Whether described as extraordinary or in a less dramatic language, ecosystemic team members' assessments of clients' lives as improved are justifications for continuing the change strategies developed in prior interviews. This response is consistent with a major tenet of ecosystemic brief therapy, which may be stated as "once change has started, keep doing whatever is working." Team members may also propose possible new interventions that might be implemented to further encourage change in clients' lives and/or raise the possibility that clients no longer need therapy. An example of the latter discussion is the following Northland Clinic team member interaction that took place during the third interview with a woman who sought counseling in separating from her husband:

TM1:   Boy, she's really doing well.
TM2:   Yeah, maybe we should start thinking about a last session. She's
       not gonna need us much longer.
TM1:   All that's left is for her to find a job. She needs to be [financially]
       independent [from her husband]. When she's done that, she'll be
       on her own.

This exchange also illustrates the emphasis on concrete problems and
solutions in ecosystemic brief therapy. That is, while TM1 argues that the
client should remain in therapy, he justifies his position by offering a final,
concrete solution (financial independence) to the client's problem.

Constructing New Understandings

Ecosystemic brief therapy team members justify their assessments of prior
intervention strategies as not working by portraying clients as showing no
signs of positive change. Team members use the assessment to raise questions about their previous understandings of clients' problems and social
systems, and about strategies for solving clients' problems. This assessment
is also part of team members' recommendations that existing courses of
action be ceased and new ones be developed. Specifically, ecosystemic
team members often recommend that interviewing therapists return to questions associated with first-session interviews, including questions designed
to elicit problems from clients. The following interaction illustrates how
Northland Clinic team members sometimes intervene in ongoing interviews
with clients whom they assess as not changing because they were unable to
get beyond complaints:

TM1:   OK, so, what can we do with these people?
TM2:   I don't know yet. It's confusing.
TM3:   Maybe the team should suggest an intervention that asks them
       what they want?
TM1:   Maybe we should just ask it now?
TM2:   Go ahead [gestures toward the telephone], do it now.
       [TM1 calls with the team's question, which the therapist improp-
       erly conveys to the clients. TM2 immediately goes to the
       telephone]
TM2:   No, no, no, we don't care if they have a relationship or not, but
       we need to find out what they want from us. You know, they may
       have to keep things like this for a while, ya know, be pissed at

each other for a while. That's fine, we don't care. What we need to know is what we can do with them when they're here. He can't say that he has to be here, that won't do, he has to tell us what we can do for him. He can't cop out with that other stuff. We don't do that. He has to tell us what he wants. They have to tell us what we can do for them. OK?

Ecosystemic team members also often assume that the reason that clients' lives are not improving is because prior interventions have not produced sufficiently concrete problem definitions. Their questions, then, are designed to rectify this circumstance. Indeed, Northland Clinic team members are sometimes willing to terminate the therapist-client relationship if clients do not provide them with the requested information.

On other occasions, however, ecosystemic team members portray the lack of improvement in clients' lives as evidence that their prior assessments of clients' perspectives and/or social systems are wrong. They describe past intervention strategies as ineffective because the strategies did not fit with clients' perspectives and social systems. Team members' reconsideration of these issues may take place over several sessions as they and the therapists with whom they work try several different remedies to clients' problems, seeking one that clients will report as producing positive changes in their lives. An example of this process involves a client who came to Northland Clinic seeking help in ending his long-standing reliance on prostitutes as a major sexual outlet. His therapist and team members made several suggestions to the client over the first several sessions, none of which produced positive results according to the client.

Prior to the fifth session with the client, a team member suggests that they consider reframing the client's behavior as an addiction. She explains that her recommendation is based on an article that she recently read about addictive behavior, and that the client's behavior generally fits with that described in the article. The client's therapist and other team members agree to consider this definition of the client's problem in constructing a new intervention message for him. The team further elaborates on this possibility as they observe the ensuing interview. Consider, for example, the following interaction, which begins as a response to the client's statement that he will not be convinced that he has overcome the urge to visit prostitutes until he has not seen one for a year:

TM1:   Even a year wouldn't be enough. He needs another kind of indicator. Even a year isn't enough.

TM2:   If it's an addiction, he's gonna have to keep at it. It'll never go away. It's like alcoholism, he'll always be tempted and he'll have to keep fighting it, one day at a time.

TM1:   That's right, one day at a time.
TM2:   Yes, it's not gonna go away.
       [Discussion turns to other aspects of the interview.]
TM2:   You see, he wants this to go away, and he has to learn that this will
       never go away.
TM1:   That's right. We can assure him that it will diminish.
TM2:   But it'll never go away.
       [Discussion turns to intervention strategies that might be effective
       in responding to the client's addiction.]

This interaction displays how ecosystemic team members construct new understandings of clients' perspectives, social systems, and/or problems by reframing them. It also shows how they use the new understandings to interpret and respond to clients' concerns about their troubles, sometimes developing intervention proposals in the process. It might even be said that this interaction illustrates how ecosystemic team members persuade themselves and each other that new proposed definitions of reality are credible. Further, because their interest in these issues is practical (to get clients unstuck from their problems as quickly as possible), ecosystemic team members are willing to consider a wide variety of possible understandings of clients' problems and circumstances. The critical tests of any proposed definition of reality are whether clients will treat the definition as a sensible depiction of their lives and troubles, and whether it might be useful in designing effective intervention messages for clients.

CHAPTER 8

CONSTRUCTING AND DELIVERING ECOSYSTEMIC INTERVENTIONS

Ecosystemic team members' activities change significantly when interviewing therapists join them behind the mirror to construct intervention messages for clients. A major change is that these discussions are not provisional. The question at hand is no longer about what intervention strategies might fit with clients' perspectives and social systems, but which of the available strategies is most appropriate. Ecosystemic therapist-team meetings are also about constructing intervention messages for which the therapists will be accountable to clients. They are held accountable through clients' immediate responses to their messages, and in subsequent sessions when clients return to report on changes in their lives and troubles. Thus, therapists and team members pay considerable attention to the wording, delivery, and reception of their intervention messages.

Another major change is the centrality of the therapist's role in the deliberations. The Northland Clinic staff assume that interviewing therapists' face-to-face experiences with clients provide them with distinctive understandings of clients and their troubles and that these understandings need to be considered in developing intervention messages that fit with clients' perspectives and social systems. They also state that interviewing therapists should not be asked to deliver intervention messages with which they disagree. Thus, team members act as consultants to the therapists in therapist-team meetings. Team members may, for example, suggest possible intervention strategies, raise problems about proposed strategies, and suggest refinements to the messages once a general intervention strategy has been selected.

Therapist-team meetings also signal a shift in therapist-client relationships. Up to this point, most interviews consist of question-and-answer sequences orchestrated by the therapists. Ecosystemic brief therapists usually limit their comments to expressing sympathy for clients' concerns (joining), approving clients' efforts to change their lives, and pointing out how clients' circumstances might be positively interpreted. During meetings with their

teams, however, ecosystemic brief therapists assess the practical significance of clients' statements and demeanor in interviews, and sometimes
offer critical appraisals of clients' perspectives and life-styles. Indeed, ecosystemic therapists sometimes begin meetings with their teams by noting
their (previously unvoiced) disagreements and/or frustrations with clients.
Most of the therapists' interest in evaluating clients, however, is related to
their professional responsibility for developing appropriate intervention
messages for clients. The following exchange is typical of how ecosystemic
therapist–team meetings move from discussions of therapists' feelings about
their clients to developing professionally appropriate responses to clients'
troubles:

	[Immediately upon entering the observation room, the thera-pist says that she is frustrated by the client, stating that the client "is always looking for problems and not solutions." The therapist describes her prior meetings with the client and her assessment of the client's attitude toward life as unrealis-tic. The therapist also reviews her failed attempts to get the client to talk about her life in different ways.]
Therapist:	I'm real frustrated with this one. Nothing ever gets better with her. I think she's looking for problems, not solutions. What I'd really like to say to her is, "Look, lady, this is life." I'd also like to get rid of her.
TM:	Okay, stop and think for a minute, don't use your gut, use your head. What do you do with a person who always finds something new, ya know, adds on? What is the logic here [. . .] or illogic for that matter, ya know, whatever makes sense.
Therapist:	Uh, today, I got the sense that she thought we were trying to get her to say, ya know, that things are getting better. And she just wouldn't say that. She won't say that 'cause [. . .] her goals are just unrealistic.
TM:	I don't think it's her goals so much as her way of looking at things. She always sees problems, more and more problems.
Therapist:	Yeah, right.
	[Discussion moves to the need for the client to "break the therapy habit," and the strategies that the therapist might take in ending the client's "therapy dependence."]

Ecosystemic therapists negotiate the terms of intervention messages with
team members, sometimes taking as long as fifteen minutes to construct
them. The messages are written down (later to be read to clients) in a style
that suggests that they are summaries of the therapist-client discussions,

although they do not mention all (or even most) of what was said during these meetings. A shift in ecosystemic therapist–client relations is also evident in the therapists' delivery of the intervention messages to clients. Only in exceptional cases do interviewing therapists invite clients to add more information to the prior interview or clarify their previously expressed views. Occasionally, clients insist on offering new information or restating their orientations toward previously discussed issues. Northland Clinic therapists often tell these clients that they might need to consider the new information in the future, that clients should bring it up in subsequent sessions if they still think it is important at that time, and by stating, "But right now, the team and I have a message for you that I'd like to read to you."

On those rare occasions when clients object to parts of the intervention message, ecosystemic brief therapists tell the clients not to do anything that they find objectionable. The therapists might also apologize for making the recommendations, stating that they and their teams need to rethink their assumptions about clients' perspectives and circumstances. A more typical client response, however, is to ask questions about aspects of the intervention messages. Ecosystemic therapists usually respond to these questions by clarifying detailed aspects of the messages, such as by redefining and rephrasing key words or phrases.

But ecosystemic therapists evade client questions that might open their intervention messages for extended discussion and interpretation. The therapists respond to the latter questions by telling clients to go home and think about what the messages mean, and perhaps report on their thoughts at their next sessions. According to Northland Clinic therapists, extended negotiations about the meaning or appropriateness of intervention messages undermines the effectiveness of the messages. To accentuate their unwillingness to negotiate such issues, Northland therapists usually rise from their chairs and began walking to the door of the interviewing room when they have completed reading the intervention messages, thus signaling that the session is over. We begin by considering how ecosystemic brief therapists use compliments to encourage positive changes in clients' lives.

Compliments in Ecosystemic Brief Therapy

The most pervasive element of ecosystemic brief therapy intervention messages is compliments for clients. While they are sometimes the last issue discussed in ecosystemic therapists' meetings with their teams, compliments are the first issue addressed when intervention messages are read to clients. The compliments stress how therapists and team members are impressed with clients' concerns for others, strength in dealing with their troubles, and/or honesty in answering therapists' questions. When possible, ecosystemic therapists and team members fit compliments to clients by agreeing with positive comments made by clients about themselves and others in their social systems. The following is an example of how Northland Clinic therapists begin their intervention messages with compliments. The message was given to a mother (Freda) and her two daughters (Jane and Naomi). They have come to therapy seeking advice on how Jane might increase her weight, and develop better eating habits.

Therapist: One thing, we were all pretty well pleased with, how well the family could describe the problem. We were able to get a much better picture than we usually do. We know exactly what's going on, and that doesn't mean that we completely understand. [Clients and therapist laugh.]

Freda: We don't either.

Therapist: At least we have a pretty good description. Um, we were also impressed by, um, the effort that has already been done to make some changes, or even trying to eat more compared to what you are eating now, and thinking of ways you can eat higher calorie foods, getting a malt or shake for lunch, and trying to eat less sugary foods.

Jane: That's what I was wondering about 'cause the only high-calorie foods I can think of are things with sugar in them.

Therapist: Well, it sounds like you're thinking in terms of adding calories, which may mean added sugar, but also

Jane: [interrupting] Yeah, like adding a shake is adding so much chocolate, and not so good things.

Therapist: Sure, but it sounds like you're tackling the problem from different directions. One is by eating more at some meals by adding higher calorie foods, another certainly would be non-sugary foods with protein, that sort of thing. And, Naomi sounds like she really is, really been good at observing the changes Jane does try to make. Or even noticing how it is when she goes to the babysitter that she loosens up and that she has fun.

This exchange illustrates several general features of how ecosystemic compliments are used in ecosystemic brief therapy. First, notice that the therapist complimented all of the participants in the interview, even though most of the prior interview focused on Freda's concerns about Jane's problems, and Jane's efforts to remedy them. This is the usual practice of ecosystemic therapists and their teams who use compliments to express empathy with all clients' concerns and problems. When clients disagree about their problems, therapists use multiple compliments to indicate to clients that they are not taking sides in clients' disagreements. This is not to say, however, that ecosystemic brief therapists divide their compliments equally among clients. When they assess one or more clients as more committed to solving the problems at hand than others, ecosystemic therapists focus more of their compliments (and other aspects of their intervention messages) on the "committed" clients.

A second notable feature of this interaction is how the compliments focus on aspects of the interview that might be treated as mundane and/or insignificant by clients. In this case, the therapist complimented the clients on the clarity of their descriptions of the problem, their efforts to remedy it, and she singles out Naomi's positive contribution by complimenting her on having noticed changes in Jane's behavior. Emphasizing the mundane is a pervasive aspect of ecosystemic compliments, particularly those given to new clients. It is designed to convey to clients that the therapists consider them to be competent and caring persons, and to encourage the development of optimistic attitudes by noting positive aspects of clients' lives.

Where possible, the therapists use compliments to suggest to clients that "since positive change is already happening, you should assume that it will continue into the future." To this end, ecosystemic brief therapists and team members might interpret virtually any aspect of clients' statements and behavior during interviews as positive signs. They tell married couples who can't get along, for example, that their strong feelings demonstrate how much they really care about one another, and contrast the clients' situation with other couples who care so little that they cannot muster enough emotion to fight with one another about their differences. Another compliment frequently given to new clients treats the clients' decisions to seek therapy as positive signs. Ecosystemic brief therapists state, for example, that this decision demonstrates the clients' great concern about their problems, commitment to solving them, and the positive inner resources (such as courage, maturity, and honesty) that they might draw upon in solving the problems.

Finally, notice in the above exchange that the clients (like many others who come to Northland Clinic) are not passive recipients of the intervention message. First, the clients laughed in response to the therapist's caveat that the clients' detailed description of their circumstances did not mean that she or her team fully understood their problems, and Freda states, "We don't either." More instructive, however, are Jane's later comments and the therapist's responses to them. Each of Jane's comments—which emphasize her concerns about finding high-calorie, but nutritionally rich foods—might be interpreted as interruptions of the therapist's orchestration of the session. The therapist manages these potential difficulties by reasserting the positive emphasis of the prior compliments, stating, "It sounds like you're tackling the problem from different directions." Upon completing this response, the therapist then returns to the planned intervention message by directing attention to Naomi and her positive contributions to the interview.

Constructing Compliments

Constructing compliments is seldom a matter of disagreement or extended negotiation among Northland Clinic therapists and team members, perhaps because they assume that more compliments are better than fewer. This assumption is especially prominent in ecosystemic brief therapists' and team members' responses to new clients. When extended discussions about compliments occur, they are usually about the best choice of words for clients, not whether they are being complimented too much. Consider, for example, the following Northland Clinic therapist-team interaction concerned with how to most appropriately compliment a client whose husband has left her for another woman:

TM1: It seems to me she sees herself as being mistreated, abused.
TM2: Oh, yeah.
Therapist: Dumped, and she's pissed.
TM2: Absolutely, dumped.
Therapist: Yeah, absolutely angry [. . .]
TM1: We're impressed that she hasn't, uh, [. . .] what?
TM2: Clobbered, clobbered him.
TM1: Yeah, yeah, whatever [. . .]
TM2: She hasn't, she hasn't jumped on his back or [. . .] something to that effect. I think it has to be more, um [. . .]
TM3: She didn't tear him down to the kids, she didn't do that.
TM2: Now there you go.
Therapist: Uh huh. When, you know, it would be perfectly reasonable. [. . .] Yeah, to have done that. [. . .] Well, should we [. . .] say then that, you know, its certainly understandable how angry she is and must feel and [. . .]
TM2: Uh huh.
Therapist: [writing] We're

> TM2:   impressed
>
> Therapist: [continuing to write] impressed with the fact that she has not let this anger [. . .] loose and not attacked him or
>
> TM1:   Yeah, OK [. . .]
>
> Therapist: [finishes writing] OK [. . .]
>
> TM2:   I think maybe something could, in fact, there's certainly a lot of things you coulda done to make his life more miserable for him. [. . .] We're impressed that you managed to [. . .] to control yourself.
>
> Therapist: [writing] Uh, huh.
>
> TM1:   It must be a, a tremendous urge to try and get even.
>
> Therapist: [writing] Uh, huh.
>
> TM2:   Yeah [. . .]
>
> TM1:   OK, [. . .] OK, and then [. . .] I guess maybe we need to say something about [. . .] what she's come up with this past hour to say to the kids.

The first notable feature of this interaction is the therapist's and team members' interest in assessing the client's feelings about her problem. TM1 begins the discussion by stating, "It seems to me she sees herself as being mistreated, abused." This assessment—which is elaborated on by TM2 and the interviewing therapist—is related to the client's emphasis in the interview that her primary concern was with the well-being of her children. The therapist and team then turn to the construction of compliments that address both their assessment of the client's feelings and the client's expressed concern for her children. Notice that TM1 initiates the discussion of compliments by asking what issues they should tell the client are impressive, not by asking if they might want to compliment her. Ecosystemic brief therapists and team members assume that compliments will be included in the vast majority of their intervention messages.

This interaction also illustrates how ecosystemic brief therapists use compliments to simultaneously address multiple issues, not all of which have been emphasized by clients during their interviews. In this case, they did so by stating that it would be expected that the client would be angry at her husband, yet she has not let her anger "loose." The compliment addresses what the therapist and team assess as the clients' feelings, and casts the client's control of her anger as impressive and an appropriate response to her problem. Thus, the response might be interpreted by the client as normalizing feelings that she might not want to discuss and emphasizing her strength and maturity in controlling her anger.

Finally, this case illustrates how ecosystemic brief therapists sometimes justify other aspects of their intervention messages with compliments. In this case, the Northland Clinic therapist uses compliments to cast the client as already competently dealing with her problem, and then states that she should trust her own—good—judgment in dealing with her husband and children. Notice also in the following exchange (which took place as the therapist read the intervention message to the client) how the therapist ignores the client's initial comments by continuing to read the message, and later responds to her question about how to deal with her husband by continuing to stress that the client use her own judgment. Further, while the intervention message emphasizes the client's ability to manage her problems, it also suggests that "this is just going to be a tough period of time."

Therapist: [reading] Well, everybody agrees, of course, that [. . .] this is a real tough situation [. . .] very upsetting [. . .] and we were impressed with [. . .] the amount of control which you've shown in not, you know, overreacting to this, you know there must be a tremendous urge to get even or try to get even.

Client: Not any more. I just feel sad.

Therapist: [reading] We were impressed with how well you control that urge.

Client: [interrupting] Control, you'd be surprised.

Therapist: [reading] You certainly have come up with some good ideas with what to tell the kids and what not to tell them [. . .] and to tell them in an honest and straightforward manner. [. . .] And we agree with what you've come up with so far [. . .] and we agree that there's no need to tell them anything more than they can understand [. . .] but we don't know when you should tell the kids.

Client: Uh, huh

Therapist: [reading] You have to be the judge of that.

Client: Uh, huh.

Therapist: [reading] And we don't know if telling them is going to make it any easier for anybody. [. . .] This is just going to be a tough period of time.

Client: Do you think that I should ask him to come with me, or to come over when I tell them?

Therapist: I would say you be the judge of that too, we are not sure.

Client: Yeah.

Therapist: But we'd be glad to work with you and to help you cope with this, if you want us to? [. . .] We can see you next week, OK?

On other occasions, however, ecosystemic brief therapists suggest to clients how they might deal with their problems. We turn to these therapist—

team members intervention messages in the next several sections, beginning with therapists' responses to new clients.

Initial Interventions

The first-session task is the preferred response of Northland Clinic therapists and teams in dealing with new clients' problems. They explain that compliments combined with the first-session task is all that is often needed to get clients "unstuck" from their complaints and problems, even if other—more complicated—intervention strategies might also be effective. In its simplest form, this intervention strategy asks clients to pay attention to the "good things" in their lives that they would like to have continue, and to report on them at the next session. The task encourages the development of optimistic client attitudes by focusing on positive aspects of clients' lives. The following intervention message is an example of how ecosystemic therapists combine compliments with the first-session task:

> OK. Now, the team was impressed with the things that you have done to help yourself. And the fact that you felt so much better about yourself, and that you kind of talk more freely now to other people. And, uh, also, mother, they were very impressed about the fact that you are supporting your daughter. And that, uh, how dedicated you have been really to her, to help your daughter achieve her health and happiness. . . . Um, in order to get some information, we would like you, between now and the next time when we see you again, we want each of you to notice what happens in your life that you want to continue to have happen.

All intervention messages given by ecosystemic brief therapists are not so simple or straightforward as this one, however. Therapists and their teams often modify this strategy to take account of clients' unique perspectives and social systems, that is, to make them better fit with clients and their problems. For example, Northland Clinic therapists sometimes assess clients as more likely to do the first-session task if they are told to write down what they notice, and at other times they ask clients to keep their observations secret from others in their social systems until their next meetings at the clinic. As the following interaction shows, these modifications in typical practice are preceded by therapist-team discussions of the problems at hand, clients' perspectives and social systems, and the several possible intervention strategies available to them in responding to clients' problems. It was through this interaction that the therapist and her team developed the intervention message given to Jane, Freda, and Naomi discussed above. The exchange begins just after the therapist and team have constructed compliments for the clients:

TM1:   Well, [. . .] I think, what can I say, that we are very puzzled by someone who is so perfectionistic [. . .] is so imperfect, so imperfect [. . .] in her ability to take care of herself.

TM2:   Well, that might be the last thing, further down, our punch line here [pointing to the bottom of the therapist's paper on which she is writing the intervention message].

Therapist: That's fine 'cause I was thinking the way to go was, it's an achievement thing. Just, just say that, it that way, yeah.

TM3:   Well, I, uh, that doesn't mesh with what we were saying earlier though about, that now she's taking care of herself. [. . .] She's getting more proteins, uh, more. I think you might want to use that later with her, individually, you know, when you see her alone. [. . .] You're already complimenting her on the changes she's already made, taking better care of herself.

TM1:   Well, we can say that we're puzzled by the changes.

Therapist: We can say that we're puzzled by why she's already making the changes, that's one way around that. [. . .] I'm impressed with the changes.
[A telephone call for TM1 interrupts the discussion, which begins again when she rejoins the group.]

TM2:   OK, what was the phrase, [looking at TM1] you had a nice phrase.

TM1:   OK, [to the therapist who is writing] the team is wondering why [. . .] why someone like [. . .] Jane, who is so perfectionistic, is so imperfect [. . .] in her ability to take care of herself. [. . .] And we don't quite understand that.

Therapist: So, no task?

TM2:   Well, I'd sure like to give a task.
[Discussion turns to several ideas for tasks, which are rejected as good ideas that might be useful in later sessions (such as displaying Jane's imperfection for her by flushing the food that she doesn't eat down the toilet) or as inappropriate because they are too obvious (such as having Jane's parents' keep track of her calorie intake).]

TM1:   Listen, why don't you just give a normal task around, uh, her doing what's good for herself, that they'd like to see, keep, you know, happening.

TM2:   OK, right on.

Therapist: That they see what she does that's good for her?

TM1:   Uh, huh.

Therapist: [writing] OK, and then everybody keeps track of it.

TM1:   Everybody keeps track of it.

TM2:   Secretly, all three of 'em, independently and secretly keep track of what she does [. . .] that's good for her.

TM1:   That they like, they'd like to see, keep on, keep on, see her continue to do.

Therapist: [finishes writing] OK, sounds good. [She rises and leaves the observation room to return to the interview room.]

While lengthy, this interaction conveys the give-and-take through which ecosystemic brief therapists and team members negotiate and construct intervention messages. It includes two possible framings of the problem at hand (a perfectionist who is being imperfect about her health and a problem of achievement), a discussion of how to structure the message to achieve maximum effect on the clients (TM2's suggestion that TM1's initial recommendation be put at the end and treated as the "punch line"), a concern for making later aspects of the message consistent with the prior compliments, and evaluation of several possible tasks for the clients. Each of these aspects of the interaction might be analyzed as candidate concerns to be taken into account as the therapist and her team construct the message. But they also might be discarded or simply ignored as the interactants turn their attention to new matters or return to previously raised issues.

In this interaction, for example, the possible framing of the client's problem as an achievement issue, the suggestion that TM1's framing be saved for the end of the message, and TM3's interest in being consistent disappear from the conversation once the interactants focus on TM1's suggested framing of the problem. Notice also how this conversational shift occurs. It is not preceded by extended debates about the merits of each suggestion. Rather, TM2 begins the second part of the conversation (after the telephone call) by asking TM1 to repeat her earlier phrase, calling it "a nice phrase." The therapist collaborates by beginning to write it down as TM1 repeats her suggestion and by asking, "So, no task?" The question moves the interaction to a new issue.

The construction of ecosystemic interventions, then, involves more than applying a predetermined format to clients' problems. The process is an interactional accomplishment that varies across situations, as therapists and team members consider relevant aspects of clients' problems and circumstances and respond to the practical contingencies of their mutual interactions. A major practical contingency is the requirement that they formulate a message for clients within a relatively brief time period. Thus, extended negotiations about the issues at hand are precluded by the practical contexts within which the therapists and team members fulfill their professional responsibilities.

A final significant aspect of this interaction involves the therapist's and team members' recourse to the first-session task after discussing several alternatives. Indeed, TM1 refers to it as the "normal task." This move in the interaction displays the ever-present availability of the first-session task to ecosystemic brief therapists and their teams in responding to new clients' problems, even when it is not explicitly noted early in their deliberations. The priority given to this response by ecosystemic therapists is also indicated by the lack of discussion that followed TM1's suggestion. Unlike others' critical responses to the less typical tasks suggested earlier in the interaction, TM2 responds to the suggestion of the first-session task by stating, "OK, right on." And the therapist responds by first clarifying the suggestion, and then writing it down.

The Northland Clinic staff also modify the first-session task and fit their intervention messages with clients by sometimes adding other concerns with the first-session task. The messages might include, for example, statements that "the team is wondering about" some aspects of clients' circumstances and might suggest that clients "might want to" think about the issues. Occasionally, Northland Clinic therapists and team members also provide clients with relevant information about their troubles and/or recommend particular actions to them. Often included in intervention messages for clients whom the therapists and team members determine to be in need of medical, legal, or social services, for example, is information about where clients can obtain the services and recommendations that they obtain them.

Ecosystemic brief therapists and team members justify other responses to new clients' problems by describing clients' problems, perspectives, and/or social systems as inappropriate for the first-session task. For example, they sometimes describe some clients as unlikely to positively respond to the first-session task, but willing do something else. Other times, however, ecosystemic therapists and their teams describe clients as unlikely to do any type of task suggested to them, in which case they turn to other intervention strategies, such as combining compliments with positive reframings of clients' problems and circumstances.

Northland Clinic therapists also sometimes suggest to families in which there is consensus that one member is causing trouble for everyone, for example, that while the "troublemaker" might not consciously know why he or she is disrupting the household, the therapist and/or team believe that the "troublemaker" is intuitively making a positive contribution to the family by signaling to others that all is not right in the family. The therapists then suggest that family members might wish to think about this possibility prior to their next session. A variation on this intervention strategy is the "split-team technique." It involves telling clients that half of the team believes that the "troublesome" family member is making a positive contribution to the family and that the other half disagrees. The clients are then asked to consider both sides of the disagreements and to report on their thoughts at the next session.

Finally, Northland Clinic therapists and team members sometimes describe aspects of new clients' perspectives and/or social systems as justifying recourse to atypical responses. An example of this circumstance involved a married couple who came to therapy complaining of their incorrigible son. The therapist and one of his team members described the wife as very devoted to her son and deeply concerned with his behavioral problems. They described the husband, on the other hand, as feeling that the counseling that their son was already receiving in another setting was quite adequate. A team member also stated that she thought the husband was uninterested in participating in therapy, to which the therapist responded, "Maybe. But I think we can hook him." The discussion then turned to how that might be done:

> TM: Why don't we tell him that we don't think that she could do it alone without his helping. That they have to band together as a team, and that's the only way we're gonna do it. And if they want to go home and think about [. . .]
>
> Therapist: [interrupting] how far they are willing to go.
>
> TM: How far they are willing to go. And then come back and tell us about it.
>
> Therapist: [writing] Uh, huh.
>
> TM: Do you want to do it that way? We have an idea that might work but [. . .] it takes teamwork [. . .]
>
> Therapist: [writing] But uh [. . .] we [. . .] want to wait with seeing [the son] until [. . .]
>
> TM: Uh, huh. OK.
>
> Therapist: [writing] Um, [. . .] OK, let's see, until they have [. . .] until things have just inched in the right direction? [. . .] How's that?

The intervention message that emerged from this interaction (asking the clients to think about "how far they were willing to go" to solve their problem) might be understood as a request that the clients (particularly the husband) specify the extent of their commitment to participating in therapy. More generally, the interaction displays how ecosystemic therapists' and team members' constructions of intervention strategies involve linking their descriptions of clients' problems, perspectives, and social systems with available skeleton keys.

Later Interventions

Ecosystemic brief therapists and team members orient to second and subsequent sessions with clients as opportunities to assess their prior understandings of and responses to clients' problems. The therapists' preferred assessment is that they are succeeding in achieving their professional goals. They make this assessment when clients report that they are making satisfactory progress in managing their problems. Northland Clinic therapists and team members initially respond to these client reports by "celebrating" the good news. They note, for example, how clients' reports confirm their earlier assessments of clients' problems and/or social systems. Other times, however, clients' reports of significant positive change come as unexpected good news to ecosystemic brief therapists and teams. The following interaction displays how they react to these cases:

> TM: It's a miracle.
> Therapist: Jesus, yes.
> TM: Cure [. . .]
> Therapist: Well, next best thing to one certainly.
> TM: Oh, yeah.
>   [Discussion turns to the anticipated difficulties with the clients that the therapists mentioned during the prior sessions, the dramatic ways in which family members have changed in the course of only one month, and that the clients should be told to go slow in making further changes because relapses are likely to happen. Throughout these discussions, the therapist and team members restate their surprise at the changes reported by the clients. The therapist states, for example, "That's nice. It's a relief. I was, [. . .] I don't know, I was really feeling kind of shaky about these guys." In the end, the discussion turned to the content of the intervention message to be given to the clients.]
> Therapist: [writing] Well, yeah, that they need to keep doing what they are doing, doing. Expect him to, expect something to goof up.
> TM: Yeah.
> Therapist: [writing] Uh, [. . .] and uh, [. . .] basically continue doing what they are doing.
> TM: And when, uh, he goofs up they just start over. [. . .] Or, if he goofs up, goofs up.
> Therapist: [writing] Right, right, glad to see, got a miracle going, [. . .] miracle going, and we're [. . .]

TM: Do you want to say something like "glad to see that you created a miracle"?

Therapist: That's where I'm going, right. [writing] Really impressed that miracle is your fault. [. . .] Your fault, uh, you guys doing something right [. . .] [looking at TM] How about that, accusing them of doing things right? It's just terrible. [pause as he writes] It's your fault, you are doing something right, [. . .] doing something right . . .

This exchange displays two general aspects of Northland Clinic therapists' and teams' usual responses to clients' reports of improvement. First, they note the significance of the changes reported by clients. In this case, they do so by describing the changes as a "miracle" and "cure." Most of the time, however, they mark positive change with a less dramatic language. Whatever the language used by them to characterize clients' reports, ecosystemic therapists and team members treat clients' statements as confirming the effectiveness of their approach to therapy. Indeed, a Northland Clinic therapist stated in response to a similar case of unanticipated change, "This is the kind of case that gives you the delusion that your theory works." Northland Clinic therapists also frequently save the videotapes of these cases so that they might later review them in order to identify aspects of the interview and/or intervention strategies that were most effective and might be useful with other clients.

The second notable aspect of the above interaction involves the therapist's and team members' advice for the clients. Note, in particular, how they assign responsibility for the "miracle" to the clients. The response affirms clients' abilities to competently manage their lives and problems, assigns positive identities to the clients (they are effective parents), and encourages them to be optimistic about the future. Combined with this response, however, is the caution that while clients should continue to do what is working, they should be prepared for possible future problems. Indeed, TM offers two possible formulations of the caution, first suggesting that a relapse will happen ("And when, uh, he goofs up"), and later revising it to say, "if he goofs up."

Ecosystemic brief therapists may respond in either way to clients who report significant improvements in their lives. They use the first formulation— relapse *will* happen—to predict the emergence of problems in clients' lives, and the second—relapse *might* happen—to remind clients of the possibility of relapse. The specific wording used by ecosystemic brief therapists and teams in conveying these messages to clients varies based on their assessments of clients' perspectives and social systems. That is, some clients' circumstances warrant more positive framings of the caution.

At Northland Clinic, at least, clients do not usually provide therapists and teams with reports that might be cast as miracles. More typical are client reports that the therapists describe as expected and/or hopeful. Northland Clinic therapists and teams respond to these client reports by considering how they might modify their prior assessments and intervention strategies in light of clients' latest descriptions of their lives. So long as clients report positive change, ecosystemic brief therapists and team members continue to modify and elaborate on their prior intervention messages across the next several sessions with clients, until the therapists and/or clients determine that further meetings are unnecessary.

Modifying Ecosystemic Interventions

Ecosystemic brief therapists and teams justify the modification of ongoing intervention strategies by describing the strategies as "on the right track." Indeed, they sometimes interpret client reports both of modest positive change and of no change at all as confirming their assessments. Clients' reports of modest change suggest that the therapists are on the right track, because the reports are consistent with the ecosystemic focus on creating far-reaching changes in clients' social systems by first creating small changes. Ecosystemic therapists and team members treat client reports of no change as unsurprising news when clients are unable to formulate ecosystemic problems in prior sessions and/or when their lives are in great flux.

An example of how Northland Clinic therapists and teams respond to clients who report no positive change follows. The client in question is a woman who is separated from her husband, and neither one can decide whether to get back together or to get a divorce. The therapist and client have focused much of their prior interactions on the development of a problem that is mutually acceptable to them, a goal that has yet to be met. The following interaction begins at the outset of the therapist-team meeting:

Therapist: Well, what do you make of it? [. . .]
     TM: Very confused [. . .]
Therapist: I think that's all we need to do [. . .] is, uh, uh, [. . .] I don't know what I'll start with yet, but I think the main body of the message should be something like [pause and starting to write] that we can understand [. . .]
     TM: Uh, huh.
Therapist: how confused, his, how confusing. I'm sorry, his, his confusion is to her. [. . .] Uh, [. . .] maybe how confusing her confusion is to him. [. . .] Uh, so, we wouldn't expect things

to just settle very quickly. [. . .] Uh, [. . .] and suggest that she not try and settle things because [. . .] decisions made out of confusion, [. . .] uh, are the kind of things, frequently the kind of things we live to second guess and regret. [. . .] Yeah, yeah, in a way we realize how painful waiting around for the confusion to clear up can be [. . .] , uh, [. . .] and suggest that she might want to take a vacation from it all by herself, go to a motel away from the kids, away from him, um, [. . .] relax in a whirlpool, a sauna. [. . .] But not bother to try and solve this, not try to think about it just enjoy herself [. . .]

TM: Do we want to give her a task? [others nod affirmatively] OK. [. . .] How about, you know, keeping notes about her confusion [. . .] or we'd like her to, OK, another possibility, a better one maybe, is to, we'd want, we'd like her to [. . .] note [. . .] what she does when she overcomes the temptation [. . .] to rashly [. . .] unilaterally, if you can say that word, solve this for herself.

This exchange displays the ad hoc ways in which ecosystemic brief thera-pists and teams construct intervention messages. They evaluate and revise the messages as they formulate and voice them to one another. Note in the above exchange, for example, how the therapist revises his initial framing of the confusion issue from how confusing "his confusion is to her" to "how confusing her confusion is to him." The therapist also positively evaluates his advice about decisions made out of confusion ("the kind of things we live to second guess and regret") by saying, "yeah, yeah." Finally, notice how TM revises the proposed task as he formulates it, initially suggesting that the client keep "notes about her confusion" and then quickly offering "another possibility, a better one maybe." Each of these moves might also be under-stood as invitations for others to disagree with or to elaborate on the emer-gent intervention message. The other team members tacitly assent to the emergent message by not responding to the invitations.

This exchange also illustrates one way in which ecosystemic brief thera-pists pursue their professional interest in constructing problems by modify-ing and fitting their intervention messages with clients' perspectives and concerns. In this and similar cases, they respond to clients whom they describe as confused by mirroring the clients' confusion back to them. Sometimes ecosystemic brief therapists and teams do so by describing them-selves as confused, noting the issues about which they are confused, and asking clients to think about the therapists' and/or teams' confusion. The logic of this request is that clients might clarify their own confusion by making sense of the therapists' dilemmas.

In the above case, the proposed intervention assumes that part of the client's confusion is related to her primary focus on her troubles and her desire to remedy them as soon as possible. The intervention message is designed to interrupt this pattern by asking the client to "take a vacation" from her troubles, and to note how she "overcomes the temptation" to solve them. Even if the client does not comply with the therapist's request, the message suggests that the client's focus on her troubles is a choice, and that she might choose otherwise. It might also be understood by the client as suggesting that her past choice to focus on her troubles hasn't worked, and that a different choice might be warranted.

Finally, the exchange illustrates a general feature of how ecosystemic brief therapists and teams modify prior intervention messages. The modifications are expressions of therapists' and teams' ecosystemic reasoning about clients' problems, perspectives, and social systems. Through their interactions, ecosystemic therapists and teams link aspects of clients' lives into coherent wholes, thus making clients' newly constructed lives therapeutically understandable. Ecosystemic therapists and teams use these constructions to evaluate proposed intervention strategies and to predict how clients might respond to their messages. Consider, for example, the following exchange about a married couple whom the Northland therapist and team members have previously described as typical of family systems in which the husband acts like a child and the wife acts like his mother. A team member suggests that the intervention be organized as a game in which the husband gives signs to his wife of his desires and needs.

TM1:   Yeah, he'd like that. He's at about age three, so he should love it. [others laugh]
TM2:   We've got to give her a game back though.
TM1:   Well, mothers let their children play games, don't you think? A good mother goes along with it and we have to let her still be the good mother as long as he can feel more in control, because I don't think she's gonna give up her control. Do you?
TM2:   No, but we have to do something with her response, though. Um. Maybe, just have it that he can't tell her what the code is, that she has to figure it out. That might be enough.
TM1:   OK. Yeah.

Here we see how ecosystemic brief therapists' and team members' reality construction sometimes turns on treating clients' perspectives and relationships as typical of a family system type. Further, this categorization of the clients' relationship provides the therapist and team members with an interpretive framework for assessing the significance of the clients' behaviors and motives in interviews, and for evaluating the appropriateness of proposed intervention messages. The evaluations turn on the question, Does this strategy fit with clients and/or social systems of this type? This interaction also shows how ecosystemic therapists' and teams' depictions of clients emerge as they make sense of clients' circumstances and their options in responding to the circumstances. Specifically, the Northland Clinic therapist and team first construct an account of the couple's relationship, and then develop an intervention strategy that is consistent with their emerging story.

It should also be noted that this interaction—like other ecosystemic brief therapist–team meetings—did not produce a fully developed account of the clients' problems, perspectives, and social system. Rather, the details of this story emerge piece by piece as the therapist and team members go about the practical process of fitting their intervention strategies to clients' circumstances. It is significant that—as in most ecosystemic therapist–team interactions—they cease this line of talk and reasoning when the intervention message is finally agreed upon and written down.

Finally, ecosystemic brief therapists' and team members' assessments of clients and their social systems are seldom directly conveyed to clients in ecosystemic intervention messages. The therapists and their teams usually assume that these assessments are not useful to clients in understanding or solving their problems. This assumption is evident in the above case, where the Northland Clinic therapist delivered the following message to the clients. It begins after the therapist has complimented the husband (Stuart) and wife (Amanda) about how much they care about one another:

> [To Stuart,] So, uh, it also struck us, you know, how thinking and talking about how much you care for each other and how good it is that you are aware that a career is one thing, but a relationship is hard to come by, it struck us that Amanda loves you so much . . . that she actually wants to take your hurts away, you know, her questioning is her way of . . . wanting you not to hurt and trying to alleviate anything bothering you. And, it struck us that you, that you love her so much that you want to spare her some of your frustrations and not upset her. . . . Uh, now we have a task for you, . . . What we'd like you to do . . . , you sound like a really creative person, so we'd like you to figure out some creative signal for Amanda to know when you want to talk about work, and when you don't. [To Amanda,] And we want you to guess what those signals are. [To Stuart,] We'd like you to . . . predict for yourself beforehand whether she'll guess them or not.

As with other constructions of social reality, however, ecosystemic therapists' and team members' assessments sometimes become matters of disagreement and negotiation. The negotiations usually turn on the meaning of clients' behavior and statements made during interviews, and the implications of the competing meanings for proposed responses to clients' problems. Different accounts might be used to justify different intervention strategies. The disagreements may raise the possibility that the therapists' prior assessments of and responses to clients' problems might be "off track."

Reconsidering Intervention Strategies

Two major circumstances are associated with ecosystemic brief therapists' and teams' reconsideration of prior intervention strategies. The first involves significant changes in clients' life circumstances and/or the therapeutic relationship. When, for example, clients who are uncertain about whether to stay married finally make firm decisions about this issue, ecosystemic therapists and teams treat the decisions as new goals that require new intervention strategies. They also sometimes reconsider prior understandings and intervention strategies when one or more members of client groups cease participation in therapy, and when new persons join client groups. Both changes have potentially significant implications for ongoing therapeutic relationships and strategies.

A decrease in the number of clients involved in therapy sessions provides ecosystemic brief therapists and their teams with opportunities to focus on the concerns and perspectives of the client or clients still participating in therapy. For example, in one case at Northland Clinic, a therapist and her team used the wife's decision to stop coming to therapy as an opportunity to focus on what the husband had to do to satisfy his angry wife, not on what the two of them had to do to satisfy one another. They also developed a new intervention strategy designed to encourage the husband to decide—on his own—what changes he wished to make in order to save his marriage. The addition of new clients provides ecosystemic therapists and their teams with new information about clients' problems and social systems. At the least, the new clients provide therapists and teams with new perspectives on the issues under discussion and increases the number of persons whom they take into account in formulating their intervention messages. Adding clients also sometimes signals dramatic changes in clients' lives and/or orientations to their problems, which may require significant adjustments by ecosystemic therapists and team members.

Consider, for example, a case involving a wife who came to Northland Clinic seeking counseling on whether to remain married or to divorce her husband. After several meetings and with no advance notice from them, the client and her husband came to a session together, stating that they wished to work out their differences in order to salvage their marriage. These changes redefined the therapeutic relationship, including the therapist's and team's responsibilities to the clients. No longer were the therapist and team responsible for helping a single client develop a problem; rather they were accountable to two clients who wished help in solving their shared problem of salvaging their marriage. This shift in focus was evident in the therapist-team meeting, in which no mention was made of the prior interviews with the wife. The Northland Clinic therapist and team members started the meeting instead by briefly discussing their surprise at the husband's appearance and demeanor (they had imagined him to be quite different), and then quickly moved to intervention strategies when a team member asked, "Well, what do you think, are they going to do what we tell them?" When others responded that they believed that the clients were likely to do tasks, the team member proposed a task that was designed to address the clients' new concerns.

The second circumstance associated with ecosystemic therapists' and teams' reconsideration of their prior intervention strategies involves clients who report no positive change across several sessions. These cases present a distinctive challenge to ecosystemic brief therapists, who stress the importance of creating change in clients' lives as quickly as possible. Equally important, such client reports might be understood as signs that therapists and team members have misunderstood clients' problems, perspectives, and/or social systems. This issue might arise at any point in ecosystemic therapists' interactions with one another. Northland Clinic therapists often raise it in presession meetings with their teams, and team members sometimes broach the topic while watching interviews. The issue also sometimes emerges in Northland Clinic therapist-team interactions concerned with developing intervention messages for clients.

These discussions provide ecosystemic therapists and team members with opportunities both to reconsider their past assumptions about clients' problems and to construct new understandings of clients' circumstances. The discussions also display the practical importance of ecosystemic brief therapists' assessments of clients' perspectives and social systems. Without the assessments, developing intervention strategies that fit with clients' circumstances becomes nothing more than a trial-and-error process. Consider the following exchange occurring in a team meeting at Northland Clinic that concerns a married couple who—previous to the session—were portrayed by the interviewing therapist as frustrating because they had been in therapy for a long time and had shown no signs of change:

TM1: I think we've misunderstood this couple all along. What I'm wondering about here is if they're really suffering from this or not. They don't seem to really be suffering here, they seem to be getting along. Are they really suffering as much as they say, you know, I wonder? They say that they want to change, but I don't think they do.

TM2:   Yeah, I agree. Maybe what we have here is a couple that fits the stereotype of the Irish couple, you know, they just love to fight. They don't want to split up or to murder each other, they just fight. They must love to fight.

TM1:   Do you suppose they have any good times together? You know, do you think they have any good times when they aren't fighting?

TM2:   Oh yeah. I'll bet they have lots of good times together, between fights. Just look at how they get along here [points to the couple quietly chatting in the interviewing room while the team and therapist are meeting], that's not a couple that never has any fun together. . . . Is there an Irish saying or custom that would fit here? You know, some Irish tradition that we could use to give them the message?

TM1:   Well, I don't know, why don't we just say that the team has decided in their case the Irish stereotype is correct and that they just love to fight. You know, that the team has decided that they are both committed to the marriage and that they love to fight and that they're just Irish and that's the way it is and that we can't do anything for them. Wouldn't it be OK to just tell them that, and then tell them that they're just going to have to accept this as part of their marriage. Then we can tell them that the team doesn't think that we can do anything more for them and thank them for coming.

TM2:   It won't work. They take their fights seriously. . . . They're not going to like that message because they're serious about their fighting. They're concerned that it is a problem.

TM1:   What if we blame it on the unconscious? You know, that unconsciously they don't believe that they can have a peaceful relationship.

TM2:   [We've] done that. It didn't work.

TM1:   It didn't work? Well, how about if we say that it won't work, that there's no way to work it out?

TM2:   That's the only way. We don't have any other choice.

TM1:   No, what if we say that it won't change, but they are welcome to come and, uh, . . . bitch at each other and get things off their chests every once in a while. You know, they're welcome to keep coming. . . . What else are we gonna do? They don't wanna split up. They don't wanna do anything about this.

TM2:   They don't do tasks.

TM1:   They don't do tasks, that's right. So, let's just do that. What do you think?

TM2:   Course, if we tell them that there's no hope for change, then they

> may change. [Discussion turns to a similar case involving the therapist in which a couple responded to a similar message by changing.]

This exchange is notable for several reasons. First, it displays—once again—how ecosystemic therapists' and team members understandings of and responses to clients' circumstances emerge within the give-and-take of their mutual interactions. The intervention message that emerged in this negotiation cannot be predicted by simply considering the early exchanges in the interaction. Notice also that TM1 initiates the discussion by casting the therapist's and team members' prior orientations to the clients' troubles as a misunderstanding, suggesting that more needs to be done with them than simply modifying the prior intervention strategy. She justifies her claim by describing the clients as not suffering from their disagreements. That is, their actions in the interview are incongruent with that associated with couples (family systems) of this type.

TM2 agrees with TM1's assessment, and begins to develop an account that casts the couple as like a stereotypical Irish couple who "just love to fight." The intervention message emerges slowly as the interaction proceeds. The Northland Clinic therapist and team consider, for example, whether the clients ever have any fun together, if there might be an appropriate Irish saying for the couple, how the clients will receive the message (since they "take their fights seriously"), and if blaming the fights on the unconscious might be more effective. Each of these interactional moves also illustrates the practical focus of ecosystemic therapists' and teams' reality construction. The account emerges as a way of identifying and evaluating possible intervention strategies, and they elaborate on it only so long as it serves their practical ends. Notice, in this regard, how quickly TM1 shifts to a new framing of the issue (blaming the fights on the unconscious) when TM2 states that the proposed intervention won't work.

Finally, the interaction ends with an example of ecosystemic irony. While ecosystemic brief therapists and team members devote considerable energy to assessing clients' circumstances and developing intervention strategies that fit with their assessments, they also state that clients often respond to their messages in unpredictable ways. Northland Clinic therapists sometimes explain this development by noting that little changes are often transformed as they move through clients' social systems. At other times, however, they simply state that some changes cannot be explained, and that they don't need to be explained so long as they are positive. As the above interaction shows, ecosystemic brief therapists and teams sometimes consider the ironic possibilities of their intervention messages even before they deliver them to clients.

Direction and Indirection in Ecosystemic Brief Therapy

All of the intervention strategies that we have considered to his point have been indirect, because they do not involve telling clients how to properly orient to their problems or how their problems must be remedied. Indirection is pervasive in ecosystemic intervention messages. It is perhaps most evident in therapists' reliance on compliments and the first-session task in responding to new clients. But the other intervention strategies frequently used by ecosystemic therapists and teams—such as reframings, the confusion technique, and various pattern interruption strategies—are also indirectly given to clients. They are offered as suggestions or as matters of concern to the therapists and teams, not as commands.

As the following example shows, Northland Clinic therapists sometimes cast their advice as feelings, thoughts, and as "something that we've noticed." This advice is further relativized by the therapist's use of such terms and phrases as "I guess," "probably," and "something . . . that sometimes works." The message excerpted below was given to a mother who was seeking guidance on how to deal with her daughter, Samantha, and begins with the team's feelings about the client's circumstances:

Therapist: They [referring to her team] feel that, um, that you are really on the right track, when you, uh, don't wait to get, um, angry about something that Samantha has done. Um, or that she is doing. You, right away, take a firm stand, and say, "I want you to do this," and "I want you to do that, I want you to stop, I want you to," um, "do whatever," and that you say it in one sentence, and that you don't offer any explanation, and then you just walk away as if you just fully expected her to do whatever it is that you told her to do. Um, we think that this is probably going to get the best results, and that Samantha is going to know that you mean business. Um, we're also pleased that you recognize that your attempts to reassure her anxiety don't work, and aren't gonna work. Um, something that we've noticed that sometimes does work with people like Samantha is instead of trying to give explanations, and to reassure you, simply make a statement, something like, "Samantha, that doesn't make sense," and then just walk away.

There are times, however, when ecosystemic therapists and teams take more directive approaches to the definition and remedying of clients' problems. One such circumstance involves cases of physical abuse in which one or more clients are still at risk. The therapists use aspects of their intervention messages to tell—not just suggest to—clients how they must deal with the most threatening aspects of their circumstances. Northland Clinic therapists explain this response as related to their legal and ethical responsibilities in these cases. That is, the therapists are obligated to give priority to the physical well-being of these clients, after which they can turn to other issues and intervention methods.

While morally and legally consequential, these cases are not typical of the circumstances faced by most of Northland Clinic's clients. Thus, Northland Clinic therapists and teams take a different tack in giving directives to most clients. Their usual strategy involves embedding commands in the intervention messages given to some clients. According to ecosystemic brief therapists, it is possible to construct intervention messages that appear—on paper—to be indirect and only suggestive, but that are delivered in ways that make them directive. Constructing such directives is part of the rhetorical artfulness of ecosystemic brief therapy practice.

Consider, for example, the following suggestion made by a Northland Clinic team member to add a pause to an intervention message that partly states "it would be important for you to, Karin, maintain your health. OK?" The pause sets off the second part of the phrase from the first part, thus making it possible for the client to hear the later part as a command from the therapist. Notice, also, that the team member's suggestion involves moving the word *to* forward, thus producing the more commandlike statement of "Karin, maintain your health":

> OK. You know, you could kind of pause, "it would be important for you to, [. . .] Karin, maintain your health. OK?" It's just like you, kind of stop and think a moment [. . .] when you get to that point.

The changes made in the above intervention message in order to command Karin are typical of how embedded commands are constructed by ecosystemic therapists and teams. This example suggests how readily available this intervention technique is to ecosystemic brief therapists and teams. Embedded commands might be included in virtually any intervention message and used to convey a variety of messages to clients, such as to stop a troublesome activity, to alter one's attitudes toward others, and to do tasks that therapists and team members believe will be helpful to clients. Northland Clinic therapists also sometimes use embedded commands to achieve multiple ends.

In Karin's case, for example, the therapist and her team combined the embedded command that she maintain her health with a prior message specifying the conditions under which they were willing to continue to work with her. These aspects of the emerging intervention message became linked as the therapist and team members constructed the various pieces of their message and then arranged them into a coherent whole. Specifically, they began by developing the embedded command, then shifted to how Karin and her mother might be complimented, and finally to this exchange:

> TM: [to therapist] Next, uh, we would be willing to work with you.
> Therapist: [writing] Uh huh.
> TM: Towards some of the goals that you each have mentioned [. . .]
> Therapist: [continuing to write] Uh huh.
> TM: However, only on condition that [. . .] , we can be assured that your health and energy [. . .] is sufficient.
> Therapist: [continuing to write] OK [. . .] OK.
> TM: That it's real nice for you to work with us on this. [. . .] Um, maybe we get in the command here? [suggests how the therapist might incorporate the above command that the client maintain her health]

Through these procedures then, ecosystemic brief therapists and teams construct intervention messages that direct clients in therapeutically preferred directions, while not telling clients to do so. We next consider how the ecosystemic strategies and practices discussed in the previous four chapters are transformed and displaced in solution-focused therapy.

CHAPTER 9

CONSTRUCTING SOLUTIONS IN
SOLUTION-FOCUSED BRIEF THERAPY

Ecosystemic and solution-focused brief therapy discourses provide therapists and clients with differing practical concerns and vocabularies for constructing social realities. While solution-focused brief therapists sometimes
ask questions that are similar to those asked by ecosystemic brief therapists,
they are not the same questions. Such terms as detective, constructive, and
systemic questions, for example, make sense only if we consider the ecosystemic assumptions associated with them. Solution-focused therapists, on the
other hand, use their questions to construct mutually satisfactory conversations with clients. The questions are not designed to elicit information about
worlds outside ongoing therapy conversations, but to elicit information in
building new stories about clients' lives.

Within solution-focused brief therapy discourse then, all questions are
constructive. They are designed to define goals and to construct solutions
that solution-focused therapists assume are already present in clients' lives.
As one Northland Clinic therapist stated in comparing the solution-focused
approach to other therapy approaches:

> The thing about this model that's different for me is that it's, uh, this negotiated
> thing. This is the first model I ever worked with where I don't tell them what to
> do. Except for child abuse cases, then I tell 'em what to do. But that's the law, I
> have to. You know, I work with them in this model. I hafta react to what they're
> doing, not tell 'em what to do. It's so cooperative. That's real different. I don't
> assume that they don't know what to do. I hafta work with 'em to find out what
> they've been doing and get 'em to do it again. They are the solution. It's so
> cooperative, that's what's different about this and what I like about it.

"Restorying" clients' lives is a practical project for solution-focused brief
therapists. It involves taking account of clients' preferences and the other
unique circumstances of any single session, while focusing the interaction
on the future. Solution-focused therapists express their interest in the future
by asking solution-focused questions very early in their interactions with

clients, repeatedly asking them as the interactions proceed, and complimenting clients when they report improvements in and exceptions to their
troubled circumstances. Indeed, during a workshop, one solution-focused
therapist (only somewhat flippantly) described this approach as "boring therapy," because it involves "asking the same questions over and over."

The emphasis on the future is also evident in solution-focused brief therapists' other interactional practices. Solution-focused therapists, for example,
express less interest in "joining" with new clients at the outset of their first
session than do ecosystemic brief therapists. While solution-focused therapists ask new clients about their families, jobs, and related aspects of their
lives, this information is not so useful to them as to ecosystemic therapists.
Much more interesting to solution-focused brief therapists are clients' descriptions of their postmiracle lives. Moving to the miracle and related
solution-focused questions is a priority in solution-focused therapy.

This emphasis is also evident in solution-focused brief therapists' "blend-
ing" of ecosystemic therapists' differing orientations to first and subsequent
sessions. This shift is related to the solution-focused emphasis on constructing solutions as early as possible. When clients are able and willing to
provide solution-focused therapists with useful descriptions of exceptions to
their troubles, miracles, and/or positive presessions changes, the therapists
congratulate clients on the changes, and ask clients to elaborate on their
descriptions. These "first-session" questions are also the focus of subsequent
solution-focused therapist-client encounters.

Finally, the involvement of therapy teams is different in solution-focused
brief therapy conversations and ecosystemic interviews. These teams are
more actively involved in ecosystemic than in solution-focused therapy.
While solution-focused teams might telephone suggestions to therapists during interviews, for example, the practical circumstances of the solution-
focused approach reduce the chances that team members will do so. These
practical circumstances include the minimalist questioning strategy of
solution-focused therapy, which involves emphasizing a few carefully developed and interrelated questions throughout the interactions. This strategy
provides solution-focused therapists with a general structure for orchestrating their conversations with clients, and reduces the possibilities that team
members will assess the therapists' questions as "off track."

The role of team member is also affected by the stress in solution-focused
brief therapy on having clients define the solutions to their problems. Clients
may do so by noting existing exceptions to their problems, describing presession changes, and imagining how their lives might be miraculously
changed. When clients provide this information to solution-focused therapists and team members, there is little basis for therapist-team negotiations
about how to properly respond to clients' circumstances. They compliment
clients on the positive changes reported by clients, or on clients' success in

specifying new—postmiracle—lives. They also recommend that clients do more of whatever is working. These responses restate and affirm the compliments and "do more" questions already expressed by solution-focused therapists during their conversations with clients.

Opening Moves

Solution-focused brief therapists use a variety of opening moves in their interactions with clients. With new clients, for example, Northland Clinic therapists usually begin by asking clients about their jobs, families, neighborhoods, or whatever topics clients indicate are important to them. They also explain the general structure of the therapy process to clients, including noting that there is a support team behind the mirror, and that the therapist will take a consultative break to meet with them later in the session. Northland Clinic therapists often conclude this conversational line by asking clients, "So, what brings you here today?" or "How might we be of service to you today?"

Most clients respond to these questions by describing their concerns and/or reasons for coming to therapy. Solution-focused therapists respond in several different ways. Sometimes the therapists ask clients to provide more detail about their circumstances and worries, much as ecosystemic therapists ask questions designed to transform clients' complaints into problems. Much more quickly than ecosystemic therapists, however, solution-focused therapists shift to asking clients about the future. They often initiate this shift by asking clients to describe what they wish to get from therapy. As the following Northland Clinic therapist's statement shows, this might involve asking clients to project themselves into the future. The exchange follows the clients' discussion of their marital problems:

> Therapist: Let's say, imagine for a moment that we're now in August [. . .] three months from now, [. . .] And, uh, you're looking back at this three months, you both would do it, [. . .] , you're looking at this three months, [. . .] what needs to happen between now and August twenty-seventh [. . .] to tell you that [. . .] coming here was useful, wasn't a waste of your time?

Clients' responses to solution-focused brief therapists' opening moves are also variable, both in the content of their answers and the amount of time that clients need to adequately describe their lives, concerns, and desires for therapy. Some Northland Clinic clients and therapists move through these opening exchanges very quickly, sometimes taking no more than five minutes. At other times, they take more time. In the above exchange, for example, the clients and therapist devoted thirty minutes—roughly half of a typical session—in describing clients' problems and hopes for the future. To the extent that the discussion was concerned with the future, however, it might be seen as moving in a solution-focused direction. Describing what one hopes to get from therapy is one way of specifying goals toward which clients and therapists might work.

Clear entrance into solution-focused brief therapy discourse does not occur, however, until therapists pose solution-focused questions for clients. Solution-focused therapists might initiate this process by asking any of several solution-focused questions, particularly asking exceptions, scaling, or miracle questions. Consider, for example, the following solution-focused brief therapy conversation involving a Northland Clinic client who reported that he wished help in dealing with several interrelated problems. The client added that his participation in therapy was part of an arrangement that he had made with his creditors, concluding with, "So, I'm sorta half here on my own and half here because I have to be." The client's therapist pursued these issues by asking, "How would you know that you no longer hafta be here?" and "Is there somebody else who's, you know, judging whether you hafta be or not, or just your judgment?" The client responded to the latter question by further explaining his agreement with his creditors, and concluded by stating:

> Client: I guess it's, [. . .] well, worth my while, [. . .]
> Therapist: Right.
> Client: And I'd like to, uh, I just, uh, I've been doing [. . .] the same thing for the last ten, fifteen years, you know, uh, [. . .] it's the same pattern, up and down, up and down.
> Therapist: Right, so how, suppose you go home and go to bed tonight, [. . .] um, and go to sleep.
> Client: OK.
> Therapist: And while you're asleep a miracle happens. [pause, client laughs] OK, and the problems that bring you here today are gone, [therapist snaps his fingers] just like that, [. . .] now, [. . .] you can't know it happened 'cause it happened while you're sleeping [. . .]
> Client: OK.
> Therapist: How do you discover that, once you wake up tomorrow?

This interaction illustrates several significant aspects of solution-focused therapy. First, notice that the therapist simultaneously shifted the conversation toward better future times and elicited goal statements from the client by asking him to describe the conditions under which the therapy could be terminated ("How would you know that you no longer hafta be here?"). We also see how the therapist immediately responded to the client's statement of personal commitment to participating in therapy by asking the miracle question. This move shifted the discussion away from the client's focus on his problems ("it's the same pattern, up and down, up and down") and toward the specification of how the client wished his life to change. Notice that the therapist's question is worded to ask for details of the client's postmiracle life ("How do you discover that?"). It took slightly less than five minutes for the therapist and client to move from their initial exchanges to the miracle question.

This example is not unique in solution-focused brief therapy. These therapists look for any client statement that they might use to justify asking solution-focused questions. An unusual but instructive opening exchange involved a mother who had been referred to Northland Clinic by a local court. The judge had previously found her to be neglectful of her children and had removed them from the home. The judge stated that one condition for getting the children back was that the client had to participate in therapy. The client's Northland Clinic therapist began the interaction by asking several questions reviewing the clients' circumstances. The questions dealt with how long the children had been gone, whether the client wished to participate in therapy or was just going along with the judge's order, and the client's involvement with a man who had physically abused her and possibly her children.

These opening moves by the therapist might be interpreted as information gathering, problem defining, or even joining questions, but any such interpretations became irrelevant when the client stated that she had gotten out of the abusive relationship. The therapist immediately asked a solution-focused question: "I wonder how you did that?" This question shifted the focus of the rest of the session, which was now about the client's personal strengths and good judgment. The Northland Clinic therapist first developed these themes by asking about the client's success in dealing with the abusive relationship and later with other aspects of her life. She then asked the client how the client might learn from these experiences to better raise her children in the future. The time period beginning with the therapist's first question for the client to her "I wonder how you did that" question was less than three minutes.

Solution-focused brief therapists modify these opening moves in dealing with clients who are already in therapy. The therapists open these sessions by focusing on positive changes in clients' lives. They often ask, for example, "So, what's better?" Depending on the clients' answers, these interactions might move to questions about what the clients did to create the recent positive changes and how they might do more of it. Solution-focused therapists might also ask the clients to rate how much better their lives are on a scale of zero to ten and then ask what needs to be done to move closer to their target rating (which isn't ten for all clients). A variation in this technique involves asking clients to rate how close the recent positive changes in their lives have moved them toward their miracles.

Solution-focused brief therapists pursue a similar, change-oriented strategy in responding to clients who report no change since the inception of therapy. In these interactions, the therapists' questions focus on imagining better futures, rather than on describing past changes. The following Northland Clinic therapist-client exchange is an example of how solution-focused therapists pursue this strategy. It also shows how they sometimes modify their usual scaling question by treating zero as the therapy goal:

Therapist: OK, uh huh, [. . .] first question, [. . .] it's like this, [draws on a piece of paper] it's a scale from minus ten to zero, huh? [. . .] OK [. . .] And zero stands for things are better enough that you don't need anymore therapy. OK? [. . .] And minus ten is how things were when you started therapy, [. . .] this time. Where would you say you are today?

Client: The situation hasn't changed, it's, uh, it's as bad as when it started.

Therapist: Uh huh, [. . .] so, you're still at minus ten?

Client: Yeah, I think so, 'cause the problem hasn't, there is no solution.

Therapist: OK, OK. And, uh, [. . .] so, [. . .] how long has it been at minus ten?

Client: In April it has lasted over a year, eighteen months.

Therapist: That's a long time.

Client: Yes.

Therapist: So, [. . .] well, [. . .] I guess, [. . .] my next question then is how would you know if things, that things had gotten a little bit better, [. . .] and you had gotten up to minus nine? What would need to be different for you to say, [. . .] "Oh, yes, I've made progress, its now minus nine?"

This exchange includes several notable solution-focused therapist moves. First, notice that the therapist responds to the client's initial statement that her situation has not improved by asking for an affirmation of her claim ("So, you're still at minus ten?"). In his next interactional turn, the therapist accepts the client's assessment ("OK, OK"), and then asks, "How long has it been at minus ten?" The therapist then expresses sympathy for the client's difficulties, stating, "That's a long time." Each of these moves illustrates how solution-focused therapists cooperate with their clients by expressing concern and sympathy for their problems. Finally, notice how quickly the

Northland Clinic therapist moves back to his initial interest in change by asking the client how she would know if her life improved to minus nine.

Solution-focused brief therapists elaborate on their opening exchanges with clients by asking solution-focused questions designed to identify exceptions to clients' problems, develop progressive stories of clients' lives, and make clients responsible for the positive aspects of their lives. While we begin with scaling questions, a major theme in the following discussions involves the ways in which these solution-focused questions are interrelated in solution-focused brief therapy.

Scaling Problems and Solutions

Solution-focused therapists frequently follow their opening interactional exchanges with clients by asking scaling questions. We have already seen, for example, how solution-focused therapists use scaling questions in responding to clients who state that their problems are not getting better. That is, when the Northland Clinic client reported that "the situation hasn't changed" and "there is no solution," the therapist expressed sympathy for her situation, and asked how her life would be different if it improved only one point on the ten-point scale. The therapist used this question to move the interaction toward the specification of one or more goals on which he and the client might work. The process took several interactional turns in which the client stated that she would know that her life was improving when she was clearer about her problems and felt better. The therapist persisted in this line of questioning, and eventually the client specified a goal that was mutually agreeable to both of them. The client stated that she would know that her life was getting better when she was able to go dancing. The goal emerged out of the following exchange:

Therapist: So, at minus nine, how will it be different? You will be feeling better and, therefore, what will you do?
Client: I'd be healthier, move a little bit more. Uh, so much of my strength goes to work.
Therapist: You mean more active at doing things?
Client: Uh, I'd go out, for example, dancing.
Therapist: Dancing.
Client: Now I don't have the strength to go dancing.
Therapist: Uh, huh, So, you'd go dancing. What else might you do?

Here we see how solution-focused brief therapists use scaling questions to focus interactions on the future. In this case, the therapist asked the client to imagine how her life might be improved by only 10 percent, and to concretely describe how she should know that this change had happened. Imagining and constructing such goals is fundamental to developing progressive stories in solution-focused therapy. These stories are, by definition, about moving toward a desired end or goal. One way in which solution-focused therapists extend clients' initial goal statements is by asking them to scale their progress toward their goals. These questions might be asked at any point in the therapy process, but they are especially prominent in second and subsequent sessions. Finally, notice how the Northland Clinic therapist in the above interaction responds to the client's goal of going dancing by asking for more signs of improvement, and that his question assumes that the client can identify other signs. He asks "What else might you do?" and not "Can you think of anything else?" or "Is there anything else?"

Solution-focused brief therapists use scaling questions to invite a wide variety of possible client responses. As we have seen, some clients respond that their problems are as bad as they have ever been, perhaps even getting worse. Other clients (including new clients), however, report that their lives are getting better, sometimes dramatically better. An example is a first session at Northland Clinic involving a married couple, in which the therapist asked:

> On a scale of zero to ten, with zero being how things were the day you called for your appointment and ten being everything is perfect between the two of you, at what point will you not need to come here any more?

The wife responded by stating, "I disagree with the premise of the question," and explained that the decision to make the appointment was a major positive development in their relationship. She further stated that when her husband finally agreed to her long-standing request to seek therapy, their problems moved from zero to five. In this case then, the therapist's asking of a scaling question provided the wife with an opportunity to report on a presession change, even though this response was not explicitly invited by the question. Her response also opened new questioning opportunities for the therapist, such as asking how the wife's rating compared with her husband's and what the couple needed to do to build on the presession change.

Clients also sometimes report exceptions to their problems in responding to solution-focused brief therapists' scaling questions. Like reports of presession changes, these client responses provide therapists with opportunities to move the interactions in therapeutically preferred directions, particularly toward discussion of how clients are responsible for the exceptions and how they might make them happen more often. Solution-focused therapists' interest in using scaling questions to build progressive stories is also evident in the following exchange, which begins with the Northland Clinic therapist asking the client to rate how her problems have changed since she started therapy (the zero point on the scale). An interesting feature of this interaction is that while the client eventually states that her positive answer is an exception to most days, this information did not emerge until later in the interaction:

> Client: It depends.
> Therapist: Uh huh, right now, today.
> Client: Six.
> Therapist: Uh huh, OK, and what's the difference between six and zero, what are the differences?
> Client: My tiredness.
> Therapist: Uh huh, tell me some more about that.

Notice that the therapist did not ask whether six was better or worse than most days for the client, but shifted the discussion to the differences between days that are six and the client's circumstances when she started therapy. The therapist's response might be analyzed as the first step in constructing a progressive story of the client's life: she is progressing toward a goal that has not yet been specified. Notice also that the therapist asks for more details when the client states that the difference between six and zero is her tiredness. These details might be useful in identifying other signs of positive change in the client's life and/or in identifying therapy goals. The therapist periodically returned to these issues as the conversation proceeded, asking, for example, "So, uh, where, how high between six and ten does it have to be before you feel that you can go to work?" and "So, how come some days you are at, like you were saying, four days in the last two weeks, some days you are at six, seven, eight, and some days you are not?"

Solution-focused brief therapists frequently elaborate on clients' answers to scaling questions by asking clients to describe how they or others will notice that their lives are getting better. The question is designed to elicit concrete, behavioral descriptions from clients. This technique also illustrates how clients' ability to imagine change is often as useful to solution-focused therapists as their direct observation of it. Both contribute to the development of progressive stories. As the following exchange shows, solution-focused brief therapists may even elicit therapeutically useful client responses to this question when clients have limited contact with others:

> Therapist: When you're at eight or seven or six, how do you think people at work [. . .] see you differently, compared to when you're at zero?

Client: I work a lot alone . . .
Therapist: Uh huh, uh huh, [. . .] but if they could see it, what would
            they see?
Client: The looks on my face would change.

Scaling questions are the workhorses of solution-focused therapy. They are pervasive in these conversations, partly because they might be asked about virtually any aspect of clients' lives and orientations. Indeed, as the above exchange shows, scaling questions might even be effectively asked about hypothetical situations that clients describe as improbable. Thus, solution-focused brief therapists treat scaling questions as an ever-present resource that they use to pursue diverse practical ends, depending on the issues and opportunities that emerge in their interactions with clients. For example, Northland Clinic therapists often use scaling questions to ask clients to assess their chances of achieving their therapy goals or the amount of effort required to achieve them. Solution-focused therapists use clients' answers to this scaling question to assess clients' confidence and optimism about the future. One therapist asked, for example:

> OK. Well, [. . .] um, [. . .] what do you think, [. . .] on a scale from one to ten [. . .] ten would be [. . .] a sure thing, [. . .] OK? And zero would be, [. . .] uh, not a snowball's chance in hell [. . .] OK? Where do you think, [. . .] that the odds are, where would you put it on that of, uh, you [. . .] getting rid of these, you know, these, uh, destructive actions again?

Two related uses of the scaling question involve asking clients to rate how willing they are to follow whatever suggestions the therapists' might make about solving their problems, and asking clients if they would be willing to live with a rating that is less than their preferred goal. Solution-focused brief therapist sometimes use the first question in conversations with client groups, and then use clients' responses to it in assessing each members' concerns about their problems. The therapists use the second version of the scaling question to suggest what they consider to be more realistic goals for clients.

Solution-focused brief therapists also use scaling questions to elicit comparative information from clients. For example, they might ask other clients involved in the session to state their rankings and ask about the differences between them or why they are so similar. Whether similar or different, clients' ratings provide solution-focused therapists with opportunities for focusing the interactions in preferred directions. Clients who report similar ratings might, for example, be complimented on their reasonable assessments and like-mindedness. The ratings might even be described as signs of their sensitivity to and concern for one another. With clients who report different ratings, the therapists might inquire about the reasons for optimism associated with the higher scores, and ask less optimistic clients, "What would be a sign that things are getting better?"

Solution-focused therapists also construct comparisons by first asking clients to rate their past and present levels of optimism about solving their problems, and then asking them to account for the differences between the scores. The preferred response, of course, is when clients report that they are more optimistic than in the past. This ranking provides solution-focused therapists with several possibilities in responding to clients, including complimenting them on their positive attitudes and asking them to explain their optimism. Even when clients report that they are less optimistic, however, solution-focused brief therapists can ask, "What will have to change in order for you to be more optimistic?" thereby inviting clients to specify therapy goals. As the following interaction shows, solution-focused therapists use virtually every possible opportunity to compliment their clients, even when the clients report no change in their lives:

Client: As far as trust is concerned it would still be a nine [. . .]
Therapist: So, it's the same?
Client: Yes.
Therapist: I see [. . .] OK [. . .] How come that trust is as high as nine? What, what are the signs? How do you know?

Solution-focused therapists also use scaling questions to set up other lines of questioning that they intend to pursue later in the sessions. Thus, solution-focused therapists might ask scaling questions at any point in a therapy session.

Imagining the Future

While solution-focused brief therapists do not ask their clients to gaze into imaginary crystal balls, as ecosystemic brief therapists sometimes do, they use similar techniques to encourage their clients to specify concrete goals on which they might collaboratively work. We have already considered, for example, a session in which a Northland Clinic therapist asked a married couple to project themselves forward three months and then to describe "what needs to happen between now and August twenty seventh [. . .] to tell you that [. . .] coming here was useful, wasn't a waste of time?" Thus, solution-focused therapists are similar to their ecosystemic brief therapy counterparts in emphasizing that clients visualize and describe their future lives, and in their frequent use of the language of pictures and picturing in their conversations with clients.

Sometimes, for example, solution-focused therapists tell their clients that they are unclear about where the conversation is going and ask the clients to describe how the clients picture the future. A related technique involves treating clients' hopes and ideas for the future as pictures that might be described for the therapists. One Northland Clinic therapist, for example, sometimes follows her request that clients describe how their lives will be different after their problems are solved by asking, "Do you have any ideas what that, are there some pictures coming up of what that would be like?" This imagery is useful to solution-focused brief therapists in encouraging clients to develop concrete goals for the future and formulating strategies for achieving the goals.

The miracle question is the most recent development of this emphasis in solution-focused brief therapy. But it also includes some distinctive elements that make it more than just another version of previous questions. The miracle question does not, for example, ask clients to project themselves several weeks or months forward in time and then to describe how their lives have changed. Rather, the miracle question asks clients to image that a miracle happens when clients are asleep tonight or sometime soon. The clients' task, then, is to discover signs that change has happened without their knowing about it. This phrasing of the question casts the change as something that just happens (it is beyond the clients' control), and suggests that clients must work at recognizing that it has happened. Each of these aspects of the miracle question is evident in the following example in which the phrases that were stressed by the Northland Clinic therapist are italicized:

OK, uh, you said, uh, you don't want to be depressed any more and you don't want to be stressed any more, [. . .] let me [. . .] come back to this, OK? I'm going to ask you a very strange question [. . .] I have a lot of these strange questions, maybe you never heard of before. OK [. . .] Uh, let's say [. . .] after you and I talk [. . .] and uh, uh, whatever you do, you, uh, you're gonna do the rest of the day, all right? And uh, uh, you're going to go to bed tonight [. . .] And, uh, [. . .] when you are sleeping, [. . .] uh, *a miracle happens,* [. . .] *the miracle is* [. . .] that the problem that brought you here today, to talk to me about [. . .] about how you want your children back, and how, [. . .] you, uh, want to be, uh, uh, stronger and all these things [. . .] *happened* [. . .] because of this miracle, [. . .] all of the problems that are related to your children, related to Daniel, anything that's, uh, you know, uh, that's in your life is solved, it's all taken care of. [. . .] Uh, but, [. . .] this happens when you're sleeping, [. . .] tonight, so you don't know [. . .] the miracle actually happened [. . .] and the problem that [. . .] brought you here [. . .] is gone, it's solved. [. . .] It's all taken care of. [. . .] So, [. . .] when you wake up [. . .] tomorrow morning, [. . .] how will you find out, what will make you say, [. . .] *"Wow, maybe something happened in the middle of the night, when I was sleeping,* [. . .] *maybe there was a miracle."* [. . .] How will you be able to say, *tell* that tomorrow morning?

This example displays two additional aspects of the miracle question as a solution-focused strategy. First, notice how often the therapist pauses during the course of asking the question. This practice is partly related to solution-focused therapists' interests in emphasizing aspects of their questions, making certain that clients understand what is being asked of them, and keeping clients' attention focused on their questions. Solution-focused therapists also orient to these concerns in asking scaling questions, which often include several pauses, especially around the phrases that the therapists wish to stress. The therapist's use of pauses in the above statement is distinctive, however, because several of the pauses surround phrases that might be experienced by the client as embedded commands.

Embedded commands are declarative phrases that tell clients how the therapists wish them to think about or to change their lives. Solution-focused therapists mark their commands by placing them in longer statements that usually end as questions. In the above example, the therapist pauses prior to several phrases that might be taken by the client as commands. They include four times in which the therapist states that a miracle has happened (once she states "maybe there was a miracle"), and two times she uses pauses prior to stating that the client's problems are gone. The therapist accentuates her message for the client by slightly emphasizing (the italicized words) some words and phrases, mostly those that declare that the miracle has happened.

The second significant aspect of this example is its length and redundancy. It took the Northland Clinic therapist two minutes to complete the question, which includes a preface that takes the interaction back to the client's prior statements of concern about being depressed and stressed, and an announcement that a "very strange" question is coming. The therapist also states that she has "a lot of these strange questions, maybe you never heard of before." At this point, the therapist begins to ask the question, which includes a description of the circumstances surrounding the miracle (it occurs after the client has completed her activities for the day and is sleeping) and a review of the problems that the client has previously mentioned in the interview. The therapist then repeats that the miracle will happen while the client is sleeping "tonight," adds that the client won't know that it has happened, and briefly returns to the client's problems. Just prior to completing the question, the therapist stresses that the client's problems will be solved "when you wake up tomorrow morning," provides the client with a question to ask upon rising in the morning, and finally completes the question by asking the client how she will be able to tell that a miracle has happened "tomorrow morning."

The therapist's use of pauses, measured pace, and redundant style illustrate the hypnotic potential of the miracle question. It may be asked in ways that lull clients into new orientations that increase their receptiveness to the therapists' message. Solution-focused therapists also use these techniques to blend two distinct ecosystemic brief therapy activities: problem definition and -solving. Indeed, they sometimes bypass problem definition altogether. When clients are able and willing to answer the miracle question very early in the session, solution-focused therapists do not need to ask about clients' problems. That did not happen in this case, but it is still significant that the Northland Clinic therapist posed the miracle question twelve minutes into the session, leaving the rest of the session to discuss how the client will recognize that the miracle has occurred and how aspects of her life might be interpreted as signs that at least parts of the miracle have already happened.

Solution-focused brief therapists use the miracle question to create opportunities for constructing new client orientations to life and to specify concrete plans for achieving clients' miracles. These opportunities may take many forms and come at any point in therapist-client interactions. Consider, for example, a Northland Clinic therapist-client conversation in which the client stated that one sign that her miracle had happened would be that she would smile more. Later in the session, and well after the discussion of the client's miracle, the client smiled in response to a question asked by the therapist. The therapist used his next conversational turn to ask, "So, when you just smiled like that now . . . is that what your face will look like at ten, after the miracle?" Notice that the therapist did not ask if this is what the client's face might or would look like but "*will* look like at ten, after the miracle."

Every asking of the miracle question is unique because, through their negotiations, solution-focused brief therapists and clients give distinctive and practical meaning to the question and its implications for clients' lives. Thus, the practical meaning of the miracle only becomes evident as therapists and clients pursue their conversations. In a session at Northland Clinic involving a married couple, for example, the wife stated that she would know that a miracle had happened when her husband's health improved. But, in responding to the therapist's subsequent question ("How will you know he's better?"), she and her husband began to talk about the husband's behavior and their relationship. They stated that two signs of improvement would be that the husband would "not be late" and that he would "be more independent."

The therapist then asked a series of questions about who would notice the changes first, what they would be doing after the changes that they were not presently doing, if part of the miracle was already evident in their lives, how they were going to take the next step in realizing the miracle, how each partner would see that the other one had taken a step toward the miracle, and how they would rate their confidence in "completing the job" of achieving the miracle. These questions might be interpreted as the beginning steps in developing a progressive story of the couple's relationship and future, a story that involves goals, strategies for achieving them, and the expectation that they will be achieved.

Notice also how these questions move the interaction toward preferred, solution-focused narrative themes. In particular, the questions invite clients to think of change as the beginning of new experiences (a presence, not an absence) and as a job to be completed. The Northland Clinic therapist combined these questions with others to raise the possibility that part of the miracle might already be evident in clients' lives and that they might discover that the miracle was happening by paying attention to their spouse's behavior.

Constructing Exceptions

Solution-focused brief therapists assume that exceptions to clients' troubles are always present in their lives. This assumption is related to another, that change is ever-present in our lives even though we often have difficulty seeing it. For solution-focused brief therapists then, constructing exceptions is not about making up fictional stories about clients' lives, but about creating stories that make it possible for clients to see and learn from what is already there. The new stories make it possible for clients to learn from their own successes and for therapists to better utilize clients' abilities and resources in helping them solve their problems. Thus in constructing exceptions, solution-focused therapists and clients create progressive stories that assert that clients have already begun to realize their miracles.

Solution-focused brief therapists use a variety of techniques in encouraging their clients to see and appreciate exceptions. One technique involves waiting for clients to mention pleasant or desired events and then asking if they have happened at other times. Therapists further pursue these issues by asking clients to describe the circumstances associated with these exceptions and asking how clients might increase their incidence. Solution-focused therapists also compliment clients on these events and ask clients how they made them happen. A related strategy for constructing exceptions involves beginning therapy sessions by asking clients what is better in their lives. This question, which is usually asked in second and later sessions, assumes that clients' lives have improved and that clients therefore have positive news to report to the therapists. Consider, for example, the following opening exchange of a second session at Northland Clinic:

Therapist: So, I'm wondering about, uh, [. . .] what you found yourself doing when you overcame the urge to withdraw from some situations?

        Client: What happened when it happened?
    Therapist: Uh, huh.
        Client: What did I do?
    Therapist: Yeah, what did you do instead of withdrawing?

This exchange shows how solution-focused brief therapists sometimes combine several potential questions into one. That is, the therapist asks a version of the "what is better" question and asks the client to explain the circumstances surrounding the assumed exception. The question also assumes that the client is responsible for the exceptions, an assumption that is noted by the client when she asks, "What did I do?" Notice also that the therapist persists in asking the client to answer his question by replying, "Uh, huh," and "Yeah, what did you do instead of withdrawing . . . ?" to her questions. The onus here is on the client to describe an exception to her problem, or else to explain why she was unable to overcome the urge to withdraw. Indeed, when clients report that nothing has improved in their lives, solution-focused therapists often express surprise, further emphasizing their assumption that exceptions are an expected part of life. They sometimes reply, for example, with "Really!" "Are you sure?" and "I am amazed, I can't believe that nothing has gotten better."

As they have become more solution-focused, the therapists at Northland Clinic have begun to combine their questions about exceptions with the miracle question and scaling questions. They ask, for example, if part of clients' miracles are already present in their lives. When clients answer affirmatively, the therapists may ask how clients might achieve more of their miracle or what signs would tell them that other parts of their miracles had come to pass. Northland Clinic therapists combine scaling with exception questions by asking clients to tell them about the differences between the exceptions and the times that clients rate as normal. We have already considered an example of this practice. It involves solution-focused therapists asking clients to rate their present circumstances by treating prior times— when the problems are at their worst or when clients started therapy—as zero. When clients report that their lives are presently better than zero, they provide therapists with the equivalent of exceptions. Solution-focused brief therapists respond by complimenting their clients, making them responsible for their successes, and asking how they might do more of what is working.

Negotiating How Clients "Get-By"

Related to the solution-focused brief therapy assumption that the solutions to clients' problems are already present in clients' lives is the assumption that clients already possess the resources needed to solve their problems. Identifying these resources is a major concern of solution-focused therapists, who often use client reports of exceptions to justify suggesting to clients that they are already "doing something right" and to ask how they might "do more" of what is working. The following exchange illustrates one way in which Northland Clinic therapists implement this strategy. In this case, the client reported earlier in the session that her life was improving, but later talks of her sense of frustration with the seeming intractability of her problems:

Therapist: So, [. . .] how do you manage to keep going, [. . .] when you're feeling so badly, much of the time, how do you manage to keep going?

Client: I force myself to keep going.

Therapist: Uh, huh, so where do you get the strength to do that?

Client: I always make up [. . .] some reason [. . .] why I have to get up and go to work.

Therapist: Uh, huh, for instance?

Client: I have to keep my job.

Therapist: And, uh, [. . .] OK. And, uh, [. . .] how long has it been this way, how long have you had this problem? [Client chronicles her problem.]

Therapist: Uh huh, uh huh, I see. OK, so, it's been a difficult year.

Client: Yes.

Therapist: But [. . .] in the last two weeks, you've had four days that were at six, seven, or eight [. . .] That's better than it was . . . before.

First, notice that the therapist does not challenge the client's portrayal of her life as troubled, even though she has already reported that her life is improving. He responds instead by asking, "How do you manage to keep going?" and "Where do you get the strength to do that?" Notice also that the client does not object to his characterization of her as competent and strong. Indeed, she provides information that supports this identity by stating that she forces herself "to keep going" and always makes up a reason to be strong. She then gives an example of her strength, that is, she tells herself, "I have to keep my job." The therapist follows this by asking about how long the client has suffered from her troubles and expresses sympathy for her plight by stating, "So, it's been a difficult year." Only at this point does he remind the client of her earlier statement that life has been substantially better in the last two weeks. He further develops this line of questioning by asking, "So, [. . .] what do you think needs to happen for, [. . .] oh, I don't know, let's say [. . .] what would it take for every day to be sort of six, seven, or eight?"

The above exchange shows how solution-focused therapists cooperate with and show respect for their clients by listening to the clients' problem-oriented stories and sympathizing with clients' frustrations. The therapists then use their conversational turns to move the interactions in desired directions. "Getting-by" questions and statements serve solution-focused therapists' interests in this process because they offer images of clients that clients are likely to find desirable, and often flattering. Put differently, in using "getting-by" questions and statements, solution-focused therapists invite their clients to use personal resources that were not available to them prior to their therapy sessions. This is one way in which solutions are talked into being within solution-focused brief therapy.

When clients report relapses of their problems, solution-focused therapists respond by treating this turn of events as normal, and ask clients what their past successes have taught them about dealing with their problems. The therapists often use these "getting-by " questions to elicit lists of concrete actions that have proven useful to clients in the past. The lists provide clients with detailed advice about how to respond to the relapses and how to contribute to the emerging progressive stories about their lives. A major theme in these stories is that, because clients already possess problem-solving knowledge and skills, they need not feel powerless in the face of life's problems. They have, in other words, a history of success in problem-solving from which to draw in the future.

A major "getting-by" question asked by solution-focused therapists is "How did you do (or think of) that?" The question compliments clients by making them responsible for their successes, and focuses the conversations on concrete developments in clients' lives. The question assumes that positive changes in clients' lives don't just happen, a theme that solution-focused therapists emphasize when clients respond by trivializing their accomplishments. As the following exchange shows, therapists are sometimes supported by other clients in their efforts to compliment clients. The exchange followed a Northland Clinic therapist's question about why the clients' marital problems have improved from zero to three or four:

Husband: There's a big difference between just talking about problems, [. . .] and talking about problems and what are solutions.
Therapist: Right.
Husband: Well, we can discuss the solutions. [. . .] I think that's a cure right there.
Therapist: That's right.
Wife: That's what I said too.
Therapist: How did you come up with this idea?
Wife: How did we come up with it?

Therapist: That's very unusual. [. . .] Actually, I've never heard that quite [. . .] what you just said, [. . .] I'd never heard that.
Husband: Read it somewhere.
Wife: No, you didn't.
Therapist: No, how did you come up with this?
Husband: Its the way I feel [. . .]
Therapist: That's good, really. [turns to scaling the improvement]

Notice how the husband initially responds by trivializing his observation that talking about solutions is a cure for the couple's problems, even though the therapist describes it as "very unusual" and something that she had never heard before. When the husband states that it is something that he read, his wife interjects, "No, you didn't." It is in response to this statement that the husband finally accepts credit for his insight, and provides the therapist with one more opportunity to compliment him. The therapist also uses this opportunity to ask both clients to rate the recent improvements in their relationship. Once again, we see how solution-focused brief therapists treat scaling questions as an ever-present resource for moving their conversations with clients in preferred directions.

Solution-Focused Interventions

Solution-focused brief therapy teams are little concerned with assessing clients' social systems. They focus instead on the emergent stories in therapist-client interactions and the opportunities that the stories offer for solving clients' problems. These opportunities include noting exceptions to clients' problems, improvements in clients' lives, and resources that clients might use in solving their problems. Each of these activities might be understood as expressions of the deconstructivist emphasis in solution-focused therapy, that is, an emphasis on misreading clients' problems and lives. A major way in which solution-focused therapists and teams misread clients' problems and lives is by treating them as normal. They use this misreading to achieve several different therapeutic ends.

For example, solution-focused therapists and team members use normalizing misreadings to counter client stories that assume that clients' circumstances are deeply troubled. These stories are, according to solution-focused therapists, expressions of a general cultural emphasis on the deficits and pathologies of individuals and families. They add that these structuralist stories are self-fulfilling prophecies that may be used to cast virtually any aspect of clients' lives as signs of deep-seated troubles that clients often experience as beyond their control. Solution-focused therapists' stress on the normality of clients' problems and lives, on the other hand, is a strategy for empowering clients. "You are normal" stories are designed to encourage hopeful attitudes in clients and emphasize clients' problem-solving abilities. Solution-focused therapists may combine this misreading of clients' lives with related professional interests, such as encouraging clients to take responsibility for their lives and problems.

Consider, for example the following interaction, which took place during the therapist-team meeting near the end of the client's second session. The discussion is about the client's report that her problems have greatly improved since her first meeting with her Northland Clinic therapist:

> TM: What did we do here, didn't we normalize it or somethin'?
> Therapist: Yeah, I asked her if it would be OK if she didn't have a problem, and didn't have to come to therapy anymore. She looked at me funny, and didn't say anything for a long time. Then she said that she thought that would be all right, except that then she'd have to admit that she was responsible for her mental illness.
> TM: That's right, we got her to take responsibility for her problems. Uh, she said that she created her mental illness, and then we normalized it. We told her that her feelings were normal and natural, and that she shouldn't worry about it.

Related to "you are normal" misreadings of clients' lives is solution-focused brief therapists' stress on compliments as a solution to clients' problems. Again, the therapists use compliments to focus clients' attention on positive aspects of their lives and to encourage clients to expect that their lives will continue to improve. Consider, for example, the following Northland Clinic therapist-team interaction concerned with how to compliment clients on their report that their relationship has improved to a three or four since their last session:

> TM1: I don't know what you were thinking, but I was thinking that we need to say something about how they have gotten this far, you know, to a three or four.
> Therapist: Compliment them on that?
> TM1: Yeah, they used a term, uh, resources or something like that. Say something like that, say that we're impressed with how they've used their resources to begin to solve their problems. Uh, say something about resources.
> TM2: Well, they're basically on the right track. They just need to keep doing what they're doing. Maybe they should watch

and see that they don't get off the track. You know, they don't want to fall back.

TM1:   How about if we say that they should watch how they stay on track, that's more positive.

TM2:   Yeah. OK. Tell 'em to keep track of how they stay on track. Then they'll know when they are getting off track.

This exchange also shows how solution-focused brief therapists and teams use aspects of clients' stories (in this case, the word *resources*) in developing their compliments. A major positive theme stressed by solution-focused therapists and teams is that clients already know how to adequately deal with their problems. Thus, they should keep doing whatever is already working for them. This intervention strategy is central to the following Northland Clinic therapist-team interaction about how to respond to a child's problems in school. Notice how the casting of the client as grown up is a compliment and makes adult abilities available to him in dealing with his teachers. Equally important, the teachers know that "he's very mature for his age":

TM1:   Also, tell him that there's somebody back here who hasn't seen him for a long time, and she thinks he's really grown up. You know, she's impressed with how grown up he looks and acts. He's very mature for his age.

Therapist: Yeah, and that's why he's getting along with the teachers better. He's more grown up and they know it.

TM2:   Also, if he has some problems with the teachers, he should remember that he's grown up. He should think about how a grown-up person would deal with 'em.

Therapist: Yeah, that's good. That'll answer his question about what to do with the teachers. He'll like that, that solves that problem.

Solution-focused therapists and teams also ask their clients to do tasks, although the tasks are usually less complicated and intrusive than those associated with ecosystemic brief therapy. The difference is related to solution-focused therapists' stress on restorying clients' lives, not interrupting troublesome systemic patterns. Part of restorying clients' lives involves constructing tasks that address issues and events raised by clients in their interactions with therapists. The issues and events of most interest to solution-focused therapists and teams are those which might be treated as signs of positive change, such as exceptions. We have already considered, for example, how these therapists and teams encourage progressive stories by asking clients who report improvements in their lives to pay attention to how "they stay on track."

Solution-focused therapists and teams often modify this strategy with clients who, on the one hand, report exceptions to their problems and, on the other hand, state that the expectations are random or otherwise beyond their control. They ask clients to predict when the exceptions will happen. From the solution-focused standpoint, this task increases clients' expectations that exceptions will take place, heightens their sensitivity to the occurrence of exceptions, and might help clients to better see the circumstances associated with the exceptions. Solution-focused brief therapists and teams also encourage progressive stories by asking clients to pretend that their miracles have happened or at least that their lives are improving. The second part of this task is to notice how clients' lives are changed by this experiment, including how others' behavior toward clients changes. When clients report that these and related solution-focused tasks have helped to improve their lives, they provide therapists and team members with new opportunities to compliment them and suggest that the solutions to their problems involve doing more of what is already working.

Solution-focused therapists deliver their intervention messages for clients in much the same way as ecosystemic brief therapists. That is, they usually read their messages to clients and discourage discussion about the details of the messages. Both types of messages also begin with compliments for clients and then move to other issues, including whatever tasks the therapists might have for clients. Solution-focused therapists also sometimes incorporate embedded commands in their intervention messages. Despite these similarities, however, solution-focused therapists' delivery of intervention messages is different than that of ecosystemic therapists.

Part of the difference involves solution-focused brief therapists' greater stress on finding change in clients' lives. Even with clients who state that their problems are getting no better, solution-focused therapists' messages stress that these circumstances are—or might be—positive signs. They are reasons for hope. Consider, for example, the following intervention message given to a client who has been referred to Northland Clinic by another therapist. The client stated during the interview that her long-standing problems are not getting any better (with the exception of her summer vacation in the country, when they got better) and that a sign that her miracle was happening would be that she would go dancing:

Therapist: I was, uh, impressed with how well you described things, and that, that [. . .] I was particularly struck with you telling us about this past summer when, uh, it was over zero. [. . .] Since it was over zero this past summer, that means you still know [. . .] how to be normal. [. . .] You haven't forgotten, [. . .] and this means the problem can be solved. [. . .] And, uh, another thing was that, you were saying that it's been minus ten for over a year, except for the summer, and it

hasn't gotten any worse and so, from what you've been saying, I would have expected it to be worse. [. . .] But since it
is not worse, that means that you must be doing something
very right. [. . .] So, I think you ought to really pay attention
to this, to what you are doing that prevents it from being
worse. [. . .] So, that's the first thing I suggest [. . .] I, uh,
have some ideas you might want to think about trying. I have
some experiments that you might want to think about trying.
Do you want me to start with the easiest one of them or the
hardest one of them?

Client: Easiest.

Therapist: Easiest one, OK. The easiest one first. Uh, it's sort of an
experiment. That is, the next time you sleep at home, when
you get up in the morning pretend that you are in the country
and not at home, [. . .] and see what difference that makes
for how things go that day [. . .] OK? The second one [. . .]
is pick one night in the next month and go dancing, one
night, even though you are not feeling much better. [. . .]
And see how that affects things. OK? Just as experiments, and
see what difference it makes. It's just an experiment. Now,
the other, last thing, and probably what I think is most important is for you, you should be observing what's going on
around you when you are feeling even a little bit better than
minus ten. [. . .] Watch for any signs that you are moving up
toward minus nine. [. . .] You can't expect to go from minus
ten to zero, but you can expect to go one step at a time from
minus ten to minus nine, to minus eight, and so on. [. . .] So,
maybe watch what you are doing, what's going on around
you when you're getting close to minus nine, maybe make
notes for yourself about this, so you can talk to your therapist
about that.

This message illustrates several major aspects of the solution-focused
approach to restorying clients' lives. First, notice that the message offers the
client several reasons for being hopeful about her future, all of which are
related to issues that she raised during the interview. The therapist begins by
emphasizing the significance of the client's experiences during the past
summer, noting that it was not only an improvement but evidence that the
client still knows "how to be normal" and "this means that the problem can
be solved." This is one way in which solution-focused brief therapists normalize their clients' problems and cast clients as already possessing the skills
needed to solve their problems. The therapist further states that the client has
not forgotten how to be normal. The therapist extends these themes by
treating the client's report that her problems are not getting any worse as a

good sign. He explains that "from what you've been saying, I would have expected it to be worse." He then compliments the client for this circumstance, and makes her responsible for it by stating, "That means you must be doing something very right."

At this point the therapist gives the client her first task, to pay attention to what she is doing that keeps her problems from getting worse. He elaborates on this recommendation by telling the client that he has some ideas that she "might want to think about trying," and later refers to them as experiments. This approach to giving tasks is common in solution-focused brief therapy. These therapists do not tell their clients how to solve their problems or give them direct assignments. Rather, they make suggestions and describe experiments that might be helpful to clients. This emphasis on experimentation and client choice is evident throughout the above intervention message, beginning with the first task and ending with the therapist's last suggestion that the client might want to take notes on what's going on when she gets close to minus nine.

The therapist describes three experiments that the client might try, pretending that she is in the country when she wakes up, going dancing even if she doesn't feel much better, and paying attention to what goes on around her when she's feeling a little better. The first two experiments are similar in asking the client to pretend that positive changes have happened and to notice their effects on her life. The experiments express the solution-focused assumption that—like problems—solutions are self-fulfilling prophecies. Part of being competent and happy involves believing and acting as if you are already competent and happy.

The therapist distinguishes the third experiment from the other two by describing it as the most important. It involves paying attention to "what's going on around you when you are feeling even a little better." He uses this experiment to provide the client with an alternative set of expectations about how her problems will likely improve and to emphasize that she should begin to look for signs of improvement, that is, moving from minus ten to minus nine. The therapist further states, "You can't expect to go from minus ten to zero, but you can expect to go one step at a time from minus ten to minus nine, to minus eight and so on."

This and previous chapters provide us with one basis for comparing and contrasting ecosystemic and solution-focused brief therapy discourses and practices. They show how solution-focused brief therapy emerged out of the practical and intellectual circumstances of ecosystemic brief therapy. Still, solution-focused therapy is more than a mere extension or refinement of ecosystemic therapy. It is a distinctive approach to understanding and remedying human troubles. We further consider the similarities and differences between aspects of ecosystemic and solution-focused brief therapy in the next chapter. The chapter deals with some of the general implications of brief therapy for clients and public issues.

PART III

IMPLICATIONS OF BRIEF THERAPY

CHAPTER **10**

FINAL MESSAGES

This is a good time to tell you how impressed I am that you have gotten this far in the book. We have come a long way together, and you have shown great patience in working through the details of the analysis. There is a colloquial saying in the United States that "the devil resides in the details" of social policies and practices. I agree. But I also believe that the complexities and, frequently, the most important positive contributions of policies and practices reside in their details. This is particularly true of brief and other therapy-based approaches to personal troubles. Understanding how therapy works requires that we pay close attention to the details of therapists' interactions with clients and each other. It is within these interactions that therapeutic meanings are constructed by therapists and clients, and applied to the concrete circumstances of clients' lives.

All therapists are conversationalists who use their social interactions with clients to create conditions for changing clients' lives. This is not to say that ideas are irrelevant in therapy. Clearly, brief therapists orient to different ideas than do many contemporary psychotherapists and family therapists, and, as we have seen, there are some important differences in the ideas advocated by ecosystemic and solution-focused brief therapists. However, it also bears emphasizing that therapists' and clients' ideas about personal troubles do not implement themselves. These ideas are given practical meaning by therapists and clients as they formulate the salient issues of each therapy session, construct contexts for understanding the issues, and discuss how clients' troubles might be remedied.

Becoming a brief therapist, then, involves both learning the ideas, assumptions, strategies, and vocabulary of this approach to therapy, and becoming adept at playing the distinctive language games through which ecosystemic and solution-focused brief therapy are actually done. Further, while it is possible to teach others the general "rules" and "moves" of these language games, there is always a point at which every therapist is on his or her own in interacting with clients—just as clients are on their own in dealing with their therapists. Every therapist-client interaction is distinctive because each of them includes opportunities and contingencies that cannot be anticipated prior to the interactions. Recognizing and dealing with these features of therapist-client relationships are major components of the art of doing therapy. They are skills that therapists largely acquire by doing therapy.

A major purpose of my analysis of ecosystemic and solution-focused brief therapy has been to analyze the interactional skills and moves that organize these language games. I have also displayed the artfulness of Northland Clinic therapists and clients in collaborating with one another, a necessary condition for doing brief therapy. Indeed, one postmodern implication that might be drawn from this study is to raise questions about the Western cultural distinction between radicalism and conventionality. They are usually treated as mutually exclusive and opposed kinds of knowledge, attitudes, and/or actions. Clearly, solution-focused brief therapy fits the radicalism category because it challenges and subverts many of the most basic assumptions and strategies of conventional psychotherapies and family therapies. But this radical development is also inextricably related to the Northland Clinic therapists' interest in understanding how ordinary—conventional—social interactions operate. Their interest was both revolutionary and practical, being focused on identifying the opportunities available in typical therapist-client interactions for creating changes in clients' lives.

However, the fact that you have read this far into the book is clear evidence to me that you already understand these points, so I won't dwell on them any further. Nor will I review how ecosystemic and solution-focused brief therapists would have responded to my youthful difficulties with others. I am certain that you figured out that issue long ago. I will, instead, use the rest of this chapter to discuss some general issues about language and meaning in brief therapy. While I use the discussion to note some continuities and differences between ecosystemic and solution-focused brief therapy, this is not my major concern. Rather, I focus on some of the social and cultural implications of brief therapy, particularly how ecosystemic and solution-focused brief therapy encourage clients to adopt constructivist and postmodern orientations to their lives and troubles.

Not only have brief therapists developed techniques for applying many of the ideas and claims of constructivist and postmodern philosophies, they have experimented with diverse reality-creating techniques and strategies. Constructivist social scientists—including myself—can learn a great deal from their experiments. Thus, one way of interpreting what follows is to treat it as a summary of some of the lessons that I have learned from my many years of reading, watching, and listening to brief therapists. We begin with some of the ways in which brief therapy may be analyzed as constructivist socialization. That is, how brief therapists introduce their clients to postmodern logic and orientations as they collaboratively construct solutions to the clients' troubles.

Brief Therapy as Constructivist Socialization

Brief therapy is a complex social invention. While remedying clients' troubles is brief therapists' primary concern in their interactions with clients, brief therapy is also organized to achieve several other ends. One of the most important of these alternative ends is the introduction of clients to the assumptions, logic, and skills involved in the constructivist interpretation of troubles and everyday life. This aspect of brief therapy was perhaps most obvious at Northland Clinic in the early years when the therapists practiced ecosystemic brief therapy. The therapists sometimes devoted part or all of their final sessions with clients to discussing how the clients might think about and deal with future troubles. The discussions provided clients and therapists with opportunities to review and to draw general lessons from their shared experiences in therapy.

But these occasions of therapists' explicit instruction of clients are only the most obvious examples of how brief therapy is organized as constructionist socialization. Other examples are more subtle, but just as significant. Indeed, nearly every aspect of brief therapist–client interactions is a potential occasion for the socialization of clients into constructivist perspectives. In ecosystemic brief therapy, for example, the process of constructing problems out of complaints is designed both to facilitate the remedying of clients' troubles and to provide clients with knowledge and practical skills in constructing solvable trouble definitions. Similar constructivist socialization is embedded in ecosystemic therapists' questions designed to map clients' problems and social systems, as well as questions that encourage clients to talk about positive changes in their lives. And, finally, the intervention messages and tasks given to clients by ecosystemic brief therapists may be viewed as instructions on how clients might use resources already available in their lives to construct new understandings of their lives and patterns of social relationship.

Solution-focused brief therapy pushes the constructivist themes in ecosystemic therapy much further by treating troubles and solutions as narratives. Both change and the resources needed to restory our lives, solution-focused brief therapists point out, are readily available to all of us. The important initial steps in using them are first to recognize that they already exist in our lives and then to learn how to identify them. Questions about how clients are already "getting by" despite their troubles, scaling questions, and inquiries about exceptions to clients' troubles are major strategies used by solution-focused therapists to display these features of life to their clients. The most explicit constructivist socialization of clients in solution-focused therapy, however, is centered on the therapists' use of the miracle question. One lesson that clients might draw from it is, "If I can imagine a new life, then it is possible to have one." Once this lesson is learned, clients can use other solution-focused strategies to begin "talking themselves into" new lives.

The miracle and related solution-focused questions also undermine the diachronic orientation to time that most clients bring to their first meetings with their brief therapists. That is, most clients assume that their lives can be neatly divided into clear-cut past, present, and future time periods. They also assume that the past always precedes the present which always precedes the future. These assumptions about time clearly run counter to the assumptions of solution-focused brief therapy, which stress how signs that clients' miracles—presumably future developments—may be seen in clients' past and present lives. They are evident, for example, as exceptions to clients' troubled lives. The future is now in solution-focused brief therapy, although clients cannot see it because they are absorbed in their trouble-focused stories.

Diachronic distinctions are more clear-cut in ecosystemic brief therapy, in which clients' problems are treated as aspects of their present lives and social systems. While they ask questions about clients' past and future lives, ecosystemic therapists assume that changes initiated in the present will continue into the future, and potentially create far-reaching changes in clients' social systems. The future is something to which ecosystemic therapists and clients look forward. It is a place that lies down the road, not in the present. The future is also a somewhat mysterious place for ecosystemic brief therapists and their clients, because they can never fully describe or predict how changes introduced in the present will affect clients' social systems in the future.

A significant difference in ecosystemic and solution-focused orientations to the relationship between the present and future is revealed in what the miracle question does not ask. Unlike the crystal ball technique, the miracle question does not ask clients to project themselves several weeks or months forward in time and then to describe how their lives have changed. Ecosystemic brief therapists use the crystal ball technique to justify asking their clients to observe when, and whether, these changes become evident in their lives. Solution-focused therapists, on the other hand, ask their clients to imagine that a miracle will happen when clients are asleep tonight or sometime soon. This phrasing of the question casts the change as something that just happens, and suggests that clients must work at recognizing that it has happened.

None of this is to say, of course, that all clients draw these lessons from their experiences in brief therapy. Clients are no different than brief therapists, who also vary in their insights into the language games that they play. Still, clients' participation in brief therapy provides them with opportunities to enter into—if only for a short time—the logic of constructivist interpretation. It is a logic that Steve de Shazer (personal communication) describes as a *culture of difference*, meaning that clients are shown that life does not have to remain as it presently seems to be. There are alternatives to troubled realities, and the steps involved in achieving them are simple and straightforward. Constructing new lives does require, however, that clients take some initiative, a prerequisite that clients sometimes describe as daunting and scary.

Life as a Narrative Project

But the constructivist socialization of brief therapy extends beyond the matter of personal troubles. Brief therapist–client interactions are opportunities for the development and expression of a general postmodern orientation to life and social reality. These opportunities are pervasive in solution-focused brief therapy, where clients are encouraged to orient to their lives as stories. Solution-focused life stories are largely constructed by clients by imagining signs of positive change in their everyday lives and then looking for concrete signs of change in their day-to-day activities and relationships. Ecosystemic brief therapists may encourage a similar perspective in asking their clients to describe how their lives are improving, and by routinely using the "first session task" with new clients. This task asks clients to pay attention to those aspects of their lives that they find satisfying and wish to leave unchanged.

These themes in ecosystemic and solution-focused brief therapy may be generalized as a postmodern maxim: life is an ongoing narrative project. It is something that we routinely do all of the time, although we are often unaware that we are doing it. Story construction is so pervasive in our lives, and familiar to us, that we take it for granted. We construct our social worlds, selves, and others by attending to and interpreting our life experiences in particular ways. Further, our ongoing story construction is not so much about describing the "objective facts" that shape our lives as it is about testing—and usually confirming—our assumptions about social reality. The facts of life change when we construct new life stories that recast what once was taken as immutable truth and objective reality. Put differently, the stories we tell about our lives, and the meanings that we draw from the stories, often operate as self-fulfilling prophecies. We use our stories to teach our-selves lessons that we already know. Brief therapists use their clients' skills in and proclivity for developing self-fulfilling prophecies by encouraging the clients to construct new stories about themselves and their lives. A notable example is the miracle question. It encourages clients to assume that their lives will get better and provides them with interpretive "lenses" for seeing how their lives are already better than clients had previously assumed. In this and other ways, brief therapists subvert the conventional Western dis-tinction between fact and fiction.

Further, the progressive stories that solution-focused brief therapists en-courage are not fantasies, at least not in the conventional sense of this word. They are, instead, "realist" stories made up of concrete, observable "facts," which confirm and extend solution-focused plots or story lines. These facts include the times when clients' troubles are not so bad (or even absent from their lives), the numbers that clients use to "measure" how their lives are changing, and the details of clients' miracles. The details define the concrete goals toward which clients' new stories and lives will move and/or have moved. Thus, the process of talking clients out of their troubles in solution-focused brief therapy cannot be described as wishful thinking. The therapy is designed to literally show clients that their lives are not so troubled and hopeless as they initially assumed.

Clients' central role in constructing their life stories is also a distinguish-ing aspect of brief therapy. This is particularly true for solution-focused therapists, who are much less inclined than ecosystemic therapists to use intervention strategies designed to disrupt clients' perspectives and relation-ships. Rather, solution-focused therapists usually accept and emphasize the goals defined by clients in responding to the miracle question. They also depend on their clients to provide virtually all of the information that they use in renaming clients' troubles, in pointing out how clients are getting by, and in drawing lessons from the exceptions to troubles reported by clients. The major contribution that solution-focused therapists usually make to the restorying of their clients' lives, then, involves using the potential story lines and "facts" provided by clients to initiate and extend progressive stories. Indeed, solution-focused brief therapists might be described as narrative opportunists, scavengers in search of the resources needed to construct preferred stories about their clients' lives.

Finally, I must stress that, while brief therapists treat life as an ongoing narrative project, they are uninterested in using therapy to develop compre-hensive stories about clients' lives. They especially avoid constructing stories that emphasize clients' past lives. Usually, the further in the past the issue, the less interest solution-focused therapists' show in it. Solution-focused brief therapists' focus is, instead, on providing clients with opportunities and resources for constructing new stories. It is enough, solution-focused therapists state, to get their clients started on new narrative projects. Clients can continue the process on their own. It is not as though there is only one "right" story for anyone's life, or that all clients want to construct comprehensive life stories that integrate all aspects of their past, present, and future lives.

Aspects of Storytelling in Brief Therapy

In their interactions with brief therapists, clients are introduced to and encouraged to adopt a postmodern orientation of serious play toward their lives and troubles. One part of the orientation might be summarized as another maxim: Don't sweat the small stuff, and everything is small stuff. Brief therapists encourage this approach to life and troubles through their questions about and responses to clients' troubles, as, for example, when they respond to clients who state that they hear voices by asking, "So, what's the problem?" Serious play is also an aspect of brief therapists' responses to clients complaining of depression. They sometimes reply by saying that the clients' depression is actually a sign of mental health, since the world is such a depressing place. This is another way of asking, "So, what's the problem?"

Brief therapists use such "playful" responses to encourage their clients to be serious about the ways in which they define social realities. This is a major lesson of constructivist therapy and philosophy. If, in other words, life is an ongoing narrative project and we are all storytellers, then we are responsible for the stories that we tell about ourselves and others. This is not to say that others are irrelevant to our narrative projects. Many of the stories that we tell are collaborative—multiauthored—constructions. But this situation only spreads the responsibility for our stories; it does not eliminate it. Thus, brief therapy—particularly solution-focused therapy—might be described as a collaborative process designed to show clients how to take responsibility for their narrative projects. It is also organized to persuade clients to accept this responsibility by developing new life stories. One part of taking responsibility for one's life story may involve developing a less serious orientation to the typical troubles of everyday life, treating them as "small stuff."

Brief therapists also convey their distinctive professional orientation to clients by providing clients with narrative resources that clients might use to construct postmodern life stories. We have already considered how these stories involve playful uses of language and subvert conventional Western assumptions and distinctions. Brief therapists sometimes provide these resources by undermining the formal categories and linear logic that clients use to make sense of and remedy their troubles. We have seen, for example, how clients sometimes define their troubles as instances of the formal trouble categories of paranoid schizophrenia, alcoholism, and nymphomania. Clients usually adopt linear logic by assuming that human behavior and relationships operate as causes and effects, such as when parents assume that the most effective way to change their children's undesired behavior is to punish it, or when they assume that solving their problems requires that they identify *the* cause of the problems.

Brief therapists do not reject formal categories or linear logic out of hand; rather they state that these approaches to personal troubles are useful only some of the time. Thus, one way that brief therapists undermine formal categories and linear logic is by pointing out to clients that, while clients' theories may make sense in the abstract, they aren't working to solve clients' problems. All cultural categories, logics, and definitions of reality are ultimately assessed by brief therapists by asking, "Are they useful in solving problems?"

Brief therapists also encourage their clients to use new rhetorical devices or tropes in orienting to and describing their lives. The word *trope* is often treated as a synonym for such figures of speech as metaphor, synecdoche, and metonymy. We use these rhetorical devices to assert indirect associations between concepts, events, and/or objects. We speak metaphorically, for example, when we refer to the "face" of a clock, since clocks do not have faces like human beings or other animals. Where are the lips or eyelashes on a clock's face? It is also true, however, that our sense of this claim as metaphor has been lost over the years as we have come to routinely use it in referring to clocks. We use it without asking about such facial characteristics as eyes, noses, and chins, or about how a face could have hands attached to it. This shift in orientation to clocks suggests one way in which new social realities are created. They start as new symbolic associations and eventually become standardized cultural categories and connections that are expected and taken for granted.

Other figures of speech may evolve in similar ways. Metonymy, for example, involves substituting one name for another, such as when reporters say, "The White House is concerned about taxes" (a most unlikely prospect if you think about it) instead of saying, "The president of the United States is concerned about taxes." Synecdoche involves substituting a part for the whole, or the whole for a part. One way in which we use synecdoche is when we say that one school, city, or country "defeated" another in a sports competition. A more literal description would emphasize that the competition was between teams associated with different schools, cities, or countries. Of course, the literal interpretation of such competitions is often glossed over by devoted sports fans, who take personal pride in their teams' accomplishments, or feel depressed about their teams' failures. Both responses treat the status of a part—the team—as the status of the whole.

I use the word *trope* in the more general way suggested by White (1978), who defines it as "style." This definition includes figures of speech as well as the orientations to reality conveyed through people's use of particular language devices. Tropes are interpretive resources that we use to construct realities and convey preferred orientations toward those realities. When we describe a person's behavior as evidence of mental illness, for example, we assert a connection between that behavior and the biomedical concept of disease. This terminology also suggests and justifies an appropriate orientation toward the behavior in question. Like physical illnesses, mental illness is a serious matter involving symptoms of disease, is a departure from health, and thus warrants some form of treatment.

It should be emphasized, however, that while tropes are important resources used by speakers and writers, they do not speak or write for themselves. Tropes are used by embodied people in concrete social contexts. Indeed, people's use of tropes might be thought of as an interpretive activity: troping. A focus on troping also reminds us that the practical meanings associated with a trope vary across situations as speakers and writers use them to achieve different ends. It is especially important to take account of situational factors in analyzing how tropes are used in social interactions, such as those between brief therapists and their clients. These contexts are distinctive because they involve more than one speaker, and the meaning of a trope within any ongoing interaction is always potentially subject to disagreement and negotiation by the interactants.

Brief Therapy as Troping

One way in which speakers and writers create new—even revolutionary—realities is by using familiar figures of speech to construct unconventional relationships and orientations. Tropes are tools in the hands of people interested in social and cultural change, because they can be used simultaneously to assert new realities and to counter old realities. Our own and others' unconventional uses of tropes may also remind us that the realities to which we regularly subscribe are social constructions. White explains:

> Tropes generate figures of speech or thought by their variation from what is "normally" expected, and by the associations they establish between concepts

normally felt not to be related or to be related in ways different from that
suggested in the trope used. . . . [I]t is always not only a deviation *from* one
possible, proper meaning, but also a deviation *towards* another meaning, con-
ception, or ideal that is right and proper *and true* "in reality." Thus considered,
troping is both a movement from one notion of the way things are related *to*
another notion, and a connection between things so that they can be expressed
in language that takes account of the possibility of their being expressed otherwise. (1978:2)

Much of brief therapy—particularly solution-focused therapy—is concerned with providing clients with new tropes and logics for constructing
untroubled life stories. Troping is a central aspect of both the practical
workings of and the constructivist socialization taking place in brief therapy.
Indeed, brief therapists' encouragement of their clients to use new tropes
and logics in constructing new life stories is central to the therapists' and
clients' achievement of binocular vision (Bateson 1979). That is, they use new
tropes to construct spaces in which two different—but complementary—
perspectives are focused on an issue. Change emerges, Bateson states, through
therapists' and clients' management of the differences before them.

Reframing, for example, is a strategy that sometimes involves constructing
new metaphors for describing clients' lives, and other times involves renaming
aspects of clients' lives (metonymy). We have considered several examples
of ecosystemic brief therapists' use of these rhetorical devices, including the
recasting of a client's penchant for seeing prostitutes as an addiction and
renaming a client's troublesome granddaughter from paranoid schizophrenic
to spoiled brat. Also, solution-focused brief therapists' questions—which
focus on positive changes in clients' lives, exceptions to clients' problems,
and how parts of clients' miracles are already happening—are designed to
treat untroubled aspects of clients' lives as representative of their whole lives.
This use of synecdoche by solution-focused therapists counters clients' tendencies to define their lives by emphasizing their troubles, another use of
synecdoche.

These examples illustrate how de Shazer's concept of the culture of difference is rhetorically constructed in brief therapist–client interactions as therapists, clients, and team members propose and negotiate new orientations to
and depictions of clients' lives and troubles. A related aspect of this process
is brief therapists' assumption—one might even say faith—that their clients
will eventually come to treat the new, symbolic connections constructed in
therapy as literal truths. They assume that the new connections will become
taken for granted aspects of clients' ordinary orientations to everyday life,
much as we uncritically talk about the faces of clocks and how the White
House gets upset about political issues. When and if this happens, clients
will have sufficiently changed their modes of living so that, through the very

process of living, they will confirm the brief therapy assumption that clients are competent managers of their own lives.

Further, many of the new tropes and much of the new logic provided to clients in brief therapy treat irony and paradox as expected aspects of life. We use the trope of irony to construct contradictory realities involving incongruities between what is expected and what is presented as the actual case. We sometimes use irony to construct stories that cast ourselves as knowing the truth about an issue or event, and others' understandings of it as false. We also use irony—as I have done in the above discussions of metaphor, metonymy, and synecdoche—to undermine literal orientations to everyday concepts and claims. Ironic stories sometimes involve a sarcastic or satirical orientation to conventional understandings of social reality. But these stories may be associated with other orientations, including the orientation of serious play, which is neither sarcastic nor satirical. Paradox involves constructing what appears to be a contradiction between two ideas or events, and then showing how they are both true and/or compatible with one another. While different, both of these tropes are useful for telling stories asserting that reality isn't what it seems to be, or that the world does not have to be the way it now seems to be.

Postmodern theorists treat these tropes as central to life in postmodern societies where, they state, people have learned to live with uncertainty, paradox, and contradiction (Best and Kellner 1991; Connor 1989; Rosenau 1992). These theorists analyze postmodern culture as oxymoronic, meaning that it is filled with claims and relationships that often appear as irreconcilable contradictions. While some people treat these "contradictions" as problems to be resolved through some sort of intellectual exercise, many postmodernists are just as likely to react by asking, "So what?" Living with uncertainty, paradox, and irony is, from this perspective, an expected aspect of life. They are conditions that we must learn to live with, and sometimes they actually serve our self-interests. This is one of the paradoxes of postmodern life, and one reason why many postmodernists—including brief therapists—do not take life too literally or seriously.

Constructing Postmodern Stories in Brief Therapy

The idea that life is a narrative project is perhaps the most ironic aspect of brief therapy. It contradicts, challenges, and subverts the conventional Western assumption that we live in social worlds that are filled with facts that we must take into account because we have limited control over them. Solution-focused brief therapists state, on the other hand, that if you don't like the facts of your life, then change your story. Their argument is not that we can simply wish difficult circumstances out of existence; at least we can't do this all of the time. Rather, like other constructivists, brief therapists assert that our orientations to and experiences with difficult circumstances change when we define them in new ways. The circumstances may, for example, be transformed from major roadblocks in our lives into manageable annoyances. Roadblocks keep us from moving ahead by doing what we want and need to do in life; annoyances do not.

One way in which brief therapists encourage their clients to adopt their ironic orientation to life and troubles is by questioning clients' assumption that developing solutions to their problems requires that they also find the causes of the problems. Brief therapists sometimes tell these clients that they are not certain whether they can ever identify the causes to the clients' problems, and ask if it would be acceptable to the clients if they were *only* successful in collaboratively solving the clients' problems. Brief therapists use this ironic response to challenge and subvert clients' linear orientation to troubles and their solutions. The response also suggests to clients that they do not need to reconcile the contradictions, or eliminate the uncertainties, in their present lives in order to have better future lives. Indeed, the response might be interpreted as suggesting that one part of constructing better lives involves accepting contradiction and uncertainty as expected aspects of "normal" life.

While irony is an important aspect of ecosystemic brief therapy, it is pervasive in solution-focused brief therapy. Solution-focused therapists convey an ironic orientation when they ask their clients to describe the times when clients' troubles are less severe, and when they express amazement at how well their clients are getting by, despite the severity of the clients' troubles. Irony also sometimes emerges as an aspect of clients' answers to scaling questions. An example is when clients, during their first therapy sessions, rate their lives as having improved since making the appointments for the sessions. We usually don't think of making an appointment for therapy as a therapeutic act. Finally, brief therapists often use the miracle question to achieve ironic ends, particularly by asking related questions designed to reveal to clients that their trouble-focused descriptions of their lives are contradicted by contrary—and previously overlooked—evidence in their lives.

Paradox is also a major rhetorical device used by brief therapists, although it is more emphasized in ecosystemic than solution-focused brief therapy. Indeed, ecosystemic therapists categorize one of their intervention techniques as paradoxical. It involves advising clients to continue doing whatever it is that is troublesome in their lives or to slow the rate of positive change in their lives. The logic of this intervention message is that clients will resolve the contradiction between the message and their desire to change their lives by recognizing that they are making choices to maintain their troubles or to keep the changes in their lives going. Ecosystemic therapists also assume that, upon making this realization, most clients will choose to reduce their troubles or to increase the desired changes present in their lives. But this is only one way in which the logic of paradox is evident in ecosystemic brief therapy. It pervades ecosystemic therapist–client and therapist–team interactions.

Paradox is central to ecosystemic brief therapists' interest in solving clients' problems by using indirect and circular means. They use ecosystemic questions and intervention techniques to suggest to clients that sometimes the most effective solution to their problems involves using indirect methods that—at first glance—seem unlikely to be effective. The "Dick's Jane" intervention, for example, involves the following logic: A good way to get the attention of an inattentive spouse is to suggest that you have replaced the spouse with a new romantic interest. This intervention strategy assumes that the most effective solution to some problems is for clients to become problems for the troublesome others in their lives. It is, in other words, sometimes better to let others solve your problems for you.

Another paradoxical response used by ecosystemic therapists involves asking family members to consider how the "troublesome" behavior of a family members might be understood as an indirect signal that there is another—more serious—problem in the family. That is, while the behavior in question is troublesome, it is not so serious a problem as some other aspect of current family life. The contradiction is resolved when family members construct new problems that do not involve scapegoating the original "troublemaker," or when they decide that they were mistaken in the first place and that they actually have no problems worthy of therapists' attention. Paradox is also central to the pattern interruption techniques used by ecosystemic therapists. These techniques involve responding to others' behavior in new and unexpected ways. Clients might, for example, hug a misbehaving child, ignore the child when he or she is misbehaving, or shoot the child with a water pistol during his or her tantrums. This response puts the onus on the other person, who must figure out the meaning of these unexpected and seemingly contradictory responses.

While they do not stress paradox so much as ecosystemic brief therapists, the strategies employed by solution-focused brief therapists may also be used to paradoxical effect. Questions about exceptions, for example, might be taken by clients as evidence that the distinction between typical and exceptional events is neither clear-cut nor always useful. It is also difficult to argue that you are totally controlled by your problems when your therapist keeps pointing out how well you are managing, while also agreeing that you a victim of your problems. And the miracle question might be interpreted as suggesting that dreams and reality are not mutually exclusive categories.

Taken together, these potential lessons of solution-focused therapy emphasize that clients' choices are not organized as either/or decisions. Rather, clients may choose both sides of the seeming contradictions in their lives. As we have seen in previous chapters, solution-focused brief therapists work to make these potential meanings real for clients by asking scaling questions. Solution-focused therapists use them to concretize the emerging—postmodern—realities that solution-focused therapy is designed to create.

The Politics of Brief Therapy

To this point, I have avoided distinguishing ecosystemic and solution-focused brief therapy from other aspects of the so-called postmodern movement. This was justified because I have largely focused on general themes that cut across diverse approaches to postmodernism. But there are also some important differences that distinguish various orientations to postmodern society and living. Appreciating these differences is helpful in understanding some of the general implications of ecosystemic and solution-focused brief therapy, particularly their political implications. I conclude by briefly discussing these issues.

Rosenau's distinction between skeptical and affirmative postmodernists is a start for getting at these differences and implications. She analyzes skeptical postmodernism as a pessimistic orientation to postmodern life, a view that stresses how "the post-modern age is one of fragmentation, disintegration, malaise, meaninglessness, a vagueness or even absence of moral parameters and societal chaos" (1992:15). One lesson that skeptical postmodernists draw from their assessments of the postmodern condition is that projects designed to change and improve the world are doomed to failure. These projects can, at best, produce temporary improvements, thus only putting off the inevitable crises and catastrophes that await us in the future. Serious play for these analysts, then, is a way of occupying our time—perhaps also entertaining ourselves—while we wait for future environmental, nuclear, and/or demographic devastation.

Rosenau portrays affirmative postmodernists as agreeing with much of the skeptics' analysis of postmodern life, but they draw different conclusions from the analysis. She explains that affirmative postmodernists

> have a more hopeful, optimistic view of the post-modern age. More indigenous to Anglo-North American culture than to the Continent, the generally optimistic affirmatives are oriented toward process. . . . Most affirmatives seek a philosophic and ontological intellectual practice that is nondogmatic, tentative, and nonideological. These post-modernists do not, however, shy away

from affirming an ethic, making normative choices, and striving to build issue-specific political coalitions. Many affirmatives argue that certain value choices are superior to others, a line of reasoning that would incur the disapproval of the skeptical post-modernists. (ibid., 15–16)

Given the choice between the affirmative and skeptical categories, both ecosystemic and solution-focused brief therapists must be classified as affirmatives. Both are process oriented and advocate an optimistic view of their clients' lives and troubles, including stressing the many reasons why clients should be hopeful about their future lives. Brief therapists are also willing to make value-based choices on their own, and in collaboration with their clients. These choices include Northland Clinic staff members' commitment to developing the more client-focused techniques of solution-focused brief therapy, and their rejection of therapy approaches that treat clients as sick and incapable of properly managing their lives.

Finally, ecosystemic and solution-focused brief therapists' practical focus reduces whatever tendencies they might have to turn their orientations and knowledge into dogmas. While brief therapists clearly prefer some therapy techniques and strategies over others, the test of any response to clients' problems is whether it works. Solving clients' problems as quickly and effectively as possible is a major ethical commitment of these affirmative postmodernists. As with other postmodern themes discussed in this chapter, the postmodern skepticism toward generalization and ideology is most developed in solution-focused brief therapy. It is central to solution-focused therapists' refusal to develop a general theory of troubles and solutions, as ecosystemic brief therapists do with their analyses of troubles as systemic problems. To be sure, solution-focused brief therapists draw from aspects of poststructuralist thought, but their major professional interest in poststructuralism is practical. They emphasize the ways in which poststructuralist insights might be used to develop briefer, more effective, and client-oriented therapy techniques.

There is a sense, however, in which Rosenau's skeptical-affirmative distinction is not useful in analyzing the postmodern orientation and politics of brief therapy, particularly solution-focused brief therapy. There are many ways of being hopeful about the future, being nondogmatic in one's pronouncements, and being willing to make value-based choices. Thus, it is important to distinguish solution-focused brief therapy from other intellectual and therapy approaches that might also be classified as types of affirmative postmodernism. Indeed, we have already considered one major distinguishing factor. It involves the extent to which solution-focused therapists avoid generalization. They are radically particularistic in their orientations to their clients' troubles, and to their own professional practices. Their focus is on the details and unique possibilities of each client's story.

Solution-focused therapists' particularistic orientation is multidimensional. It involves at least three major aspects that distinguish it from other perspectives that might also be classified as examples of affirmative postmodernism. First, solution-focused brief therapists are radical processualists. They treat the solution-focused therapy process as the solution to their clients' troubles. It is enough that therapists and clients are willing and able to play this language game. Once the process is started, solution-focused therapists believe, solutions literally emerge before therapists' and clients' eyes as they talk about how clients get by, the exceptions to clients' troubles, and the details of clients' miracles.

Solution-focused brief therapists' emphasis on process and faith that solutions will eventually emerge from it are central to the second important distinguishing aspect of their particularistic orientation. That is, solution-focused therapists avoid narrative closure. The stories constructed in solution-focused therapy are not designed to end: they are new beginnings for clients, which will continue into the future. Much of solution-focused brief therapy, then, is organized to provide clients with interpretive resources for pursuing their narrative projects, wherever the projects may take the clients. Suggesting that there is only one right story for clients, trying to integrate all aspects of clients' lives in one story, or restorying clients' lives and troubles within general political ideologies or metanarratives would be counterproductive to this process. It would close off a process that solution-focused brief therapy is designed to open up.

The final and related aspect of solution-focused therapists' particularistic orientation involves their approach to social problems and social change. Solution-focused therapists respond to social problems one session or client at a time, and stress that there are many ways of solving any problem. This focus is, of course, partly a product of their work environment, which involves meeting with one client (or group of clients) after another. But there is also a general, political issue at stake here. When Northland Clinic staff members consult with governmental and other organizational officials, they continue to recommend intervention techniques designed to focus on clients' unique life circumstances and stories.

This emphasis is one way in which solution-focused brief therapists resist pressures to "overgeneralize" about personal troubles and social problems. Examples of such overgeneralization include inflexible bureaucratic procedures and legislative mandates that treat everyone in the same ways. Overgeneralization is also central to social scientific theories that treat everyone who might be classified within a troubles category—such as juvenile delinquent, neglectful parent, anorexic, or alcoholic—as having similar life experiences and perspectives, and theories that analyze personal troubles as epiphenomena of larger and more important political and economic structures. This overgeneralizing tendency in the social sciences is complemented by therapy approaches that assume that everyone classified in the same trouble categories warrants the same kind of treatment.

Viewed from a solution-focused brief therapy perspective, social problems are better managed by listening to people's stories, providing them with resources for managing their lives in preferred ways, and then letting them use the resources as best they can. This view undermines commonplace debates about how to define and respond to poor, homeless, imprisoned, or other people sometimes defined as social problems and other times as suffering from social problems. The debates ask, Are these people victims of society or are they responsible for their plight? Solution-focused brief therapists avoid this debate by treating their clients as capable of solving their own problems if they are given a little help by therapists and others. Troubled individuals may or may not be part of the problem, but they are always part of the solution in solution-focused brief therapy. These therapists might also add the following rules:

- If your current efforts aren't working to solve your own or others' problems, try something different.
- When you see positive change, do more of it.

But there I go again, telling you about matters that you already understand. My story is becoming redundant. This must be a sign that it is time for us to stop meeting like this.

REFERENCES

American Psychiatric Association. 1994. *Diagnostic and Statistical Manual of Mental Disorders* (4th rev. ed.). Washington, DC: American Psychiatric Association.

Anderson, Walter Truett. 1990. *Reality Isn't What It Used to Be: Theatrical Politics, Ready-to-Wear Religion, Global Myths, Primitive Chic, and Other Wonders of the Postmodern World.* San Francisco: HarperCollins.

Bateson, Gregory. 1979. *Mind and Nature: A Necessary Unity.* New York: Dutton.

Bateson, Gregory, Don Jackson, Jay Haley, and John Weakland. 1956. "Toward a Theory of Schizophrenia." *Behavioral Science* 1:251–54.

Berg, Insoo Kim. 1994. *Family-Based Services: A Solution-Focused Approach.* New York: Norton.

Berg, Insoo Kim and Scott D. Miller. 1992. *Working with the Problem-Drinker: A Solution-Focused Approach.* New York: Norton.

Best, Steven and Douglas Kellner. 1991. *Postmodern Theory: Critical Interrogations.* New York: Guilford.

Billig, Michael. 1987. *Arguing and Thinking: A Rhetorical Approach to Social Psychology.* Cambridge: Cambridge University Press.

Burr, Vivien. 1995. *An Introduction to Social Constructionism.* New York: Routledge.

Cade, Brian and William Hudson O'Hanlon. 1993. *A Brief Guide to Brief Therapy.* New York: Norton.

Caws, Peter. 1988. *Structuralism: The Art of the Intelligible.* Atlantic Highlands, NJ: Humanities Press International.

Connor, Steven. 1989. *Postmodernist Culture: An Introduction to Theories of the Contemporary.* Oxford: Blackwell.

Corsini, Raymond and Danny Welding, with Judith W. McMahon (eds.). 1989. *Current Psychotherapies* (4th ed.). Itasca, IL: Peacock.

de Jong, Peter and Insoo Kim Berg. 1996. *How to Interview for Client Strengths and Solutions.* Pacific Grove, CA: Brooks/Cole.

de Shazer, Steve. 1978. "Brief Hypnotherapy of Two Sexual Dysfunctions: The Crystal Ball Technique." *American Journal of Clinical Hypnosis* 20(3):203–8.

———. 1982. *Patterns of Brief Family Therapy: An Ecosystemic Approach.* New York: Guilford.

———. 1984. "The Death of Resistance." *Family Process* 23:11–21.

———. 1985. *Keys to Solution in Brief Therapy.* New York: Norton.

———. 1988. *Clues: Investigating Solutions in Brief Therapy.* New York: Norton.

———. 1991. *Putting Difference to Work.* New York: Norton.

———. 1994. *Words Were Originally Magic.* New York: Norton.

de Shazer, Steve, Insoo Kim Berg, Eve Lipchik, Elum Nunnally, Alex Molnar, Wallace J. Gingerich, and Michele Weiner-Davis. 1986. "Brief Therapy: Focused Solution Development." *Family Process* 25:207–22.

de Shazer, Steve and Alex Molnar. 1984. "Four Useful Interventions in Brief Family Therapy." *Journal of Marital and Family Therapy* 10(3):297–304.

Derrida, Jacques. 1976. *Of Grammatology.* Baltimore, MD: Johns Hopkins University Press.

———. 1978. *Writing and Difference.* London: Routledge and Kegan Paul.

———. 1981. *Positions.* Chicago: University of Chicago Press.

Dingwall, Robert. 1980. "Orchestrated Encounters: An Essay in the Comparative Analysis of Speech-Exchange Systems." *Sociology of Health and Illness* 2(July):151–73.

Dolan, Yvonne. 1991. *Resolving Sexual Abuse: Solution-Focused Therapy and Ericksonian Hypnosis for Adult Survivors.* New York: Norton.

Eagleton, Terry. 1983. *Literary Theory: An Introduction.* Minneapolis: University of Minnesota Press.

Efran, Jay S., Robert J. Lukens, and Michael D. Lukens. 1988. "Constructivism." *Family Therapy Networker* 12:27–30, 32–35.

Emerson, Robert M. and Sheldon L. Messinger. 1977. "The Micro-Politics of Trouble." *Social Problems* 25(Dec.):121–35.

Erickson, Milton H. 1954. "Special Techniques of Brief Hypnotherapy." *Journal of Clinical and Experimental Hypnosis* 2:109–29.

———. 1967. "A Transcript of a Trance Induction with Commentary." Pp. 395–97 in *Advanced Techniques of Hypnosis and Therapy,* edited by Jay Haley. New York: Grune and Stratton.

Erickson, Milton H., Ernest L. Rossi, and Sheila I. Rossi. 1976. *Hypnotic Realities: The Induction of Clinical Hypnosis and Forms of Indirect Suggestion.* New York: Irvington.

Foucault, Michel. 1972. *The Archeology of Knowledge and the Discourse on Language,* translated by A. M. Sheridan Smith. New York: Harper & Row.

———. 1977. *Discipline and Punish,* translated by Alan Sheridan. New York: Pantheon.

———. 1988. "Technologies of the Self." Pp. 16–49 in *Technologies of the Self: A Seminar with Michel Foucault,* edited by Luther H. Martin, Huck Gutman, and Patrick Hutton. Amherst: University of Massachusetts Press.

Franklin, Cynthia. 1995. "Expanding the Vision of the Social Constructionist Debates: Creating Relevance for Practitioners." *Journal of Contemporary Human Services* (September):395–407.

Franklin, Cynthia and Paula S. Nurius. 1996. "Constructivist Therapy: New Directions in Social Work Practice." *Journal of Contemporary Human Services* (June):323–25.

Freedman, Jill and Gene Combs. 1996. *Narrative Therapy.* Norton.

Furman, Ben and Tapani Ahola. 1992. *Solution Talk: Hosting Therapeutic Conversations.* New York: Norton.

Garfinkel, Harold. 1967. *Studies in Ethnomethodology.* Englewood Cliffs, NJ: Prentice-Hall.

George, Evan, Chris Iveson, and Harvey Ratner. 1990. *Problem to Solution: Brief Therapy with Individuals and Families.* London: Brief Therapy.

Gergen, Kenneth J. 1991. *The Saturated Self: Dilemmas of Identity in Contemporary Life.* New York: Basic Books.

Gergen, Kenneth J. and Mary M. Gergen. 1983. "Narratives of the Self." Pp. 254–73 in *Studies in Social Identity,* edited by Theodore R. Sabin and Karl E. Schiebe. New York: Praeger.

———. 1986. "Narrative Form and the Construction of Psychological Science." Pp. 22–44 in *Narrative Psychology: The Storied Nature of Human Conduct,* edited by Theodore R. Sabin. New York: Praeger.

Goldenberg, Irene and Herbert Goldenberg. 1991. *Family Therapy: An Overview.* Pacific Grove, CA: Brooks/Cole.

Gubrium, Jaber F. 1992. *Out of Control: Family Therapy and Domestic Order.* Newbury Park: Sage.

Gubrium, Jaber F. and James A. Holstein. 1990. *What Is Family?* Mountain View, CA: Mayfield.

———. 1995a. "Qualitative Inquiry and the Deprivatization of Experience." *Qualitative Inquiry* 1(June):204–22.

———. 1995b. "Individual Agency, the Ordinary, and Postmodern Life." *Sociological Quarterly* 36(Summer):555–70.

Haley, Jay. 1963. *Strategies of Psychotherapy.* New York: Grune and Stratton.

——— (ed.). 1973. *Uncommon Therapy: The Psychiatric Techniques of Milton H. Erickson, M.D.* New York: Norton.

Haley, Jay and Lynn Hoffman. 1967. *Techniques of Family Therapy.* New York: Basic Books.

Hansen, James C. and Luciano L'Abate. 1982. *Approaches to Family Therapy.* New York: Macmillan.

Harland, Richard. 1989. *Superstructuralism: The Philosophy of Structuralism and Post-Structuralism.* London: Routledge.

Heritage, John. 1984. *Garfinkel and Ethnomethodology.* Cambridge: Polity.

Hoffman, Lynn. 1981. *Foundations of Family Therapy: A Conceptual Framework for Systems Change.* New York: Basic Books.

Holstein, James A. and Gale Miller. 1993. "Social Constructionism and Social Problems Work." Pp. 131–52 in *Constructionist Controversies: Issues in Social Problems Theory,* edited by Gale Miller and James A. Holstein. Hawthorne, NY: Aldine de Gruyter.

Hoyt, Michael F. (ed.) 1996. *Brief Therapy and Managed Care.* San Francisco: Jossey Bass.

Johnson, Lynn D. 1995. *Psychotherapy in the Age of Accountability.* New York: Norton.

Keeney, Bradford P. 1979. "Ecosystemic Epistemology: An Alternative Paradigm for Diagnosis." *Family Process* 18:117–29.

Lipchik, Eve. 1988. "Purposeful Sequences for Beginning the Solution-Focused Interview." Pp. 105–18 in *Interviewing,* edited by Eve Lipchik. Rockville, MD: Aspen.

Lipchik, Eve and Steve de Shazer. 1986. "The Purposeful Interview." *Journal of Strategic and Systemic Therapies* 5(Spring/Summer):88–99.

Lynn, Steven Jay and John P. Garske (eds.). 1985. *Contemporary Psychotherapies: Models and Methods.* Columbus, OH: Merrill.

Lyotard, Jean-François. 1984. *The Postmodern Condition: A Report on Knowledge,* translated by Geoff Bennington and Brian Massumi. Minneapolis: University of Minnesota Press.

Merry, Sally Engle. 1990. *Getting Justice and Getting Even: Legal Consciousness among Working-Class Americans.* Chicago: University of Chicago Press.

Miller, Gale. 1991a. *Enforcing the Work Ethic: Rhetoric and Everyday Life in a Work Incentive Program.* Albany: SUNY Press.

———. 1991b. "Family as Excuse and Extenuating Circumstance: Social Organization and Use of Family Rhetoric in a Work Incentive Program." *Journal of Marriage and the Family* 53(August):609–624.

———. 1992. "Human Service Practice as Social Problems Work." *Current Research on Occupations and Professions* 7:3–21.

———. 1994. "Toward Ethnographies of Institutional Discourse: Proposal and Suggestions." *Journal of Contemporary Ethnography* 23(October):280–306.

———. 1997a. "Building Bridges: The Possibility of Analytic Dialogue between Ethnography, Conversation Analysis, and Foucault." Pp. 24–44 in *Qualitative Analysis: Issues of Theory and Method,* edited by David Silverman. London: Sage.

———. 1997b. "Contextualizing Texts: Qualitative Strategies for Studying Organizational Texts." Pp. 77–91 in *Strategic Qualitative Research,* edited by Gale Miller and Robert Dingwall. London: Sage.

O'Hanlon, William Hudson and Angela L. Hexum. 1990. *An Uncommon Casebook: The Complete Clinical Work of Milton H. Erickson.* New York: Norton.

O'Hanlon, William Hudson and Michele Weiner-Davis. 1989. *In Search of Solutions: A New Direction in Psychotherapy.* New York: Norton.

Peräkyla, Anssi. 1995. *AIDS Counselling: Institutional Interaction and Clinical Practice.* Cambridge: Cambridge University Press.

Pollner, Melvin. 1987. *Mundane Reason: Reality in Everyday and Sociological Discourse.* Cambridge: Cambridge University Press.

Potter, Jonathan and Margaret Wetherell. 1987. *Discourse and Social Psychology: Beyond Attitudes and Behavior.* London: Sage.

Rosenau, Pauline Marie. 1992. *Post-Modernism and the Social Sciences: Insights, Inroads, and Intrusions.* Princeton, NJ: Princeton University Press.

Shotter, John. 1993. *Conversational Realities: Constructing Life through Language.* London: Sage.

Shumway, David R. 1989. *Michel Foucault.* Boston: Twayne.

Silverman, David. 1997. *Discourses of Counselling: HIV Counselling as Social Interaction.* London: Sage.

Spector, Malcolm and John I. Kitsuse. 1987. *Constructing Social Problems.* Hawthorne, NY: Aldine de Gruyter.

Stone, Elizabeth. 1988. *Black Sheep and Kissing Cousins: How Family Stories Shape Us.* New York: Penguin.

Walter, John L. and Jane E. Peller. 1992. *Becoming Solution-Focused in Brief Therapy.* New York: Brunner/Mazel.

Watzlawick, Paul P. 1983. *The Situation Is Hopeless, But Not Serious: The Pursuit of Unhappiness.* New York: Norton.

——— (ed.) 1984. *The Invented Reality: How Do We Know What We Believe We Know? Contributions to Constructivism.* New York: Norton.

Watzlawick, Paul P., John H. Weakland, and Richard Fisch. 1974. *Change: Principles of Problem Formation and Problem Resolution.* New York: Norton.

Weiner-Davis, Michele. 1993. *Divorce Busting: A Revolutionary and Rapid Program for Staying Together.* New York: Summit.

Weiner-Davis, Michele, Stever de Shazer, and Wallace J. Gingerich. 1987. "Constructing the Therapeutic Solution by Building a Pretreatment Change: An Exploratory Study." *Journal of Marital and Family Therapy* 13(4):359–63.

White, Hayden. 1978. *Tropics of Discourse: Essays in Cultural Criticism.* Baltimore: Johns Hopkins University Press.

White, Michael and David Epston. 1990. *Narrative Means to Therapeutic Ends.* New York: Norton.

Wittgenstein, Ludwig. 1958. *Philosophical Investigations,* translated by G. E. M. Anscombe. New York: Macmillan.

Index